Great Architects of International Finance

Who were the great thinkers on international finance in the mid-twentieth century? What did they propose should be done to create a stable international financial order for promoting world trade and economic growth?

This book studies the ideas of some of the most innovative economists in the mid-twentieth century including three Nobel Laureates. These great thinkers helped shape the international financial system and the role of the World Bank and the International Monetary Fund. This book covers the period from the late 1940s up to the collapse of the fixed US dollar–gold link in 1971.

The impact of Hansen, Williams, Graham, Triffin, Simons, Viner, Friedman, Johnson, Mises, Rueff, Rist, Hayek, Heilperin, Röpke, Harrod and Mundell is assessed.

This book will prove invaluable to students of international economics, international finance, economic history and the history of economic thought.

Anthony M. Endres is Associate Professor of Economics in the School of Business and Economics, University of Auckland, New Zealand.

Routledge international studies in money and banking

1 **Private Banking in Europe**
Lynn Bicker

2 **Bank Deregulation and Monetary Order**
George Selgin

3 **Money in Islam**
A study in Islamic political economy
Masudul Alam Choudhury

4 **The Future of European Financial Centres**
Kirsten Bindemann

5 **Payment Systems in Global Perspective**
Maxwell J. Fry, Isaak Kilato, Sandra Roger, Krzysztof Senderowicz, David Sheppard, Francisco Solis and John Trundle

6 **What is Money?**
John Smithin

7 **Finance**
A characteristics approach
Edited by David Blake

8 **Organisational Change and Retail Finance**
An ethnographic perspective
Richard Harper, Dave Randall and Mark Rouncefield

9 **The History of the Bundesbank**
Lessons for the European Central Bank
Jakob de Haan

10 **The Euro**
A challenge and opportunity for financial markets
Published on behalf of the *Société Universitaire Européenne de Recherches Financières (SUERF)*
Edited by Michael Artis, Axel Weber and Elizabeth Hennessy

11 **Central Banking in Eastern Europe**
Nigel Healey

12 **Money, Credit and Prices Stability**
Paul Dalziel

13 **Monetary Policy, Capital Flows and Exchange Rates**
Essays in memory of Maxwell Fry
Edited by William Allen and David Dickinson

14 **Adapting to Financial Globalisation**
Published on behalf of the *Société Universitaire Européenne de Recherches Financières (SUERF)*
Edited by Morten Balling, Eduard H. Hochreiter and Elizabeth Hennessy

15 **Monetary Macroeconomics**
A new approach
Alvaro Cencini

16 **Monetary Stability in Europe**
Stefan Collignon

17 **Technology and Finance**
Challenges for financial markets, business strategies and policy makers
Published on behalf of the *Société Universitaire Européenne de Recherches Financières (SUERF)*
Edited by Morten Balling, Frank Lierman and Andrew Mullineux

18 **Monetary Unions**
Theory, history, public choice
Edited by Forrest H. Capie and Geoffrey E. Wood

19 **HRM and Occupational Health and Safety**
Carol Boyd

20 **Central Banking Systems Compared**
The ECB, the pre-Euro Bundesbank and the Federal Reserve System
Emmanuel Apel

21 **A History of Monetary Unions**
John Chown

22 **Dollarization**
Lessons from Europe and the Americas
Edited by Louis-Philippe Rochon and Mario Seccareccia

23 **Islamic Economics and Finance**
A glossary, 2nd edition
Muhammad Akram Khan

24 **Financial Market Risk**
Measurement and analysis
Cornelis A. Los

25 **Financial Geography**
A banker's view
Risto Laulajainen

26 Money Doctors
The experience of international financial advising 1850–2000
Edited by Marc Flandreau

27 Exchange Rate Dynamics
A new open economy macroeconomics perspective
Edited by Jean-Oliver Hairault and Thepthida Sopraseuth

28 Fixing Financial Crises in the 21st Century
Edited by Andrew G. Haldane

29 Central Banking in Eastern Europe
Edited by Nigel Healey and Barry Harrison

30 Exchange Rates, Capital Flows and Policy
Edited by Rebecca Driver, Peter Sinclair and Christoph Thoenissen

31 Monetary Policy and Unemployment
The U.S., Euro-area and Japan
Edited by Willi Semmler

32 Great Architects of International Finance
The Bretton Woods era
Anthony M. Endres

Great Architects of International Finance

The Bretton Woods era

Anthony M. Endres

Routledge
Taylor & Francis Group
LONDON AND NEW YORK

First published 2005
by Routledge
2 Park Square, Milton Park, Abingdon, Oxon OX14 4RN

Simultaneously published in the USA and Canada
by Routledge
270 Madison Ave, New York, NY 10016

Routledge is an imprint of the Taylor & Francis Group

Transferred to Digital Printing 2006

Typeset in Times by Wearset Ltd, Boldon, Tyne and Wear

British Library Cataloguing in Publication Data
A catalogue record for this book is available from the British Library

Library of Congress Cataloging in Publication Data
A catalog record for this book has been requested

ISBN 0-415-32412-2

Contents

Tables

Preface

There have been no modern, systematic studies of proposals made for international financial reconstruction or reform by economists, bankers and international financial commentators from the 1940s to the present. This study examines the work of some of the world's most innovative international financial reformers in the fixed exchange rate era from the mid-1940s to the early 1970s. To understand the merits and limitations of recent international financial reform proposals as well as the functioning of the international financial system in the early twenty-first century, this book should be read first. A companion study continuing the story begun here to cover the period from the 1970s until the end of the twentieth century will follow in due course.

Currently, international finance as a subdiscipline of economics is a highly technical subject. A technical approach is not taken in this book. Instead, the following chapters offer a non-technical exposition of the continuing interplay between economic ideas and recommendations on policy matters for a period in which international economic relations were dominated by the blueprint set out in the Bretton Woods Agreement in 1944. While for economists interested in formal rigour the subject of international finance has become a technical one, it has at the same time become less accessible to a wider audience. One of the main purposes of writing this book was to make the debates and controversies on this subject more accessible to those with interests in the policy sciences, history, international relations, international law, political science and finance. Hopefully a balance has been struck between making the subject accessible to a wider audience than economists – emphasized by taking seriously the vital normative judgements and policy prescriptions embodied in the ideas presented – and rendering an accurate account of the substantive economic analysis contained in various proposals.

The following story takes a long-run view of the development of international financial doctrines; it does not contain a series of intellectual biographies, a financial history or an economic history. No serious attempt is made fully to outline actual international financial developments or the detailed history of international reforms during the Bretton Woods era.

There are already some excellent sources available on these events, especially Solomon (1977, 1999) and James (1996).

Earlier versions of some parts of this book have been presented at the 4th Australian Macroeconomics Workshop, Australian National University (1999), the 28th Annual Conference of Economists, La Trobe University (1999) and the 16th History of Economic Thought Society of Australia Conference, Australian Catholic University, Melbourne (2003). I am obliged to workshop and conference participants for their patience, interest and criticisms of these early drafts. On completing a book on economic thought in international organizations (Endres and Fleming 2002a), I identified an urgent need for more work of a doctrinal kind in the field of international financial relations. I am especially indebted to Grant Fleming who gave me the early impetus to undertake this study at a time when the history of economic ideas, even the history of quite modern ideas, was not a priority field for research in economics faculties and was not generally seen as necessary for the training of economists or those specializing in international finance. I am obliged to the Research and Study Leave Committee in the University of Auckland for sabbatical leave in 2000 and 2004 to complete this study. Sean Kimpton gave helpful advice on Chapter 8, and two Routledge readers offered encouragement and valuable criticisms.

Finally, no line gives me more satisfaction to write than this one in which I have the fortune to be able to express gratitude to A.R.T. for her unfailing support in completing this work.

Abbreviations

BIS	Bank for International Settlements
BW	Bretton Woods
CRS	commodity reserve standard
EPU	European Payments Union
FRBs	Federal Reserve Banks
FRC	Federal Recovery Corporation
IBRD	International Bank for Reconstruction and Development
IFI	international financial institution
IMF	International Monetary Fund
SCB	supranational central bank
SDR	special drawing right
UN	United Nations
WB	World Bank

1 Essential elements of a doctrinal approach

The primacy of ideas

From the mid-twentieth century the clash of ideas on the organization of the international financial system became more amplified than at any time in history. Controversies in international finance seem to reach a crescendo when evoked by war, impending or actual depressions and financial crises. Only then is the viability of existing international financial relationships called vigorously into question. The range and diversity of proposals on international financial reform offered by economists from about the mid-twentieth century were unprecedented.

The merits of particular forms of international financial arrangements have been debated on and off for centuries. Events such as the economic depression of the 1930s and economic reconstruction following the Second World War placed international financial reform squarely in front of politicians and policymakers concerned to increase or reduce, as they saw fit, international economic interactions such as free trade and cross-border investment. More recently these issues have resurfaced under the guise of 'international economic integration' or 'globalization'.

International economic events and associated monetary upheavals in the twentieth century have been accorded much analysis in some outstanding economic histories (e.g. Solomon 1977, 1999).[1] The genesis of international financial arrangements in the second half of the twentieth century in both their economic and political dimensions has also been given considerable research attention. For instance, retrospectives on the performance of the 1944 Bretton Woods Agreement and the international financial system established thereafter are widely available (Scammell 1975; Tew 1988; Bordo and Eichengreen 1993). Two magisterial studies covering events and policies from 1944 to the 1970s deserve special mention. First, there is J.K. Horsefield's (1969) three-volume study of the International Monetary Fund (IMF) which concentrated on the institutional evolution of that organization in the context of an international financial system governed by rules established at Bretton Woods. Second, there is Harold James's superb *International Monetary Cooperation Since*

Bretton Woods (1996) which highlights actual experience in financial arrangements between countries, ongoing amendments to the Bretton Woods (BW) system and the effects of events and institutional changes on the evolution of international finance up to the 1970s.

Notwithstanding the important contribution made by these studies, along with the vast array of monographs, journal articles and conference compendia which have improved understanding of international monetary events and reforms in practice, a crucial dimension of the subject remains blurred. No searching study has been conducted on the development of international financial ideas and doctrines since the Second World War.[2] Doubtless the neglect of doctrinal research may be ascribed to a decline in the popularity of intellectual history in the discipline of economics since the 1970s.[3]

This book will examine competing economic doctrines embodied in plans, blueprints and proposals offered by prominent economists for international financial reform following the Bretton Woods Agreement in 1944 and concluding at the point where the Bretton Woods arrangements were dissolved in the 1970s. The substantive ideational content of the Bretton Woods Agreement which established codes of conduct for participants in the international financial system has been widely discussed. Doctrinal studies on the 1940s concentrate almost exclusively on the Keynes and White plans which formed the initial basis for negotiation over the final Bretton Woods structure (Gardner 1969; Mikesell 1994; Eichengreen 1994). Key proposals and ideas contributed by luminaries in the economics profession in the 1944–74 period have been neglected; many of these vigorously opposed the Bretton Woods arrangements. It will be the purpose of this book to make these ideas accessible, give the reader an appreciation of their richness, subtlety and intellectual strength. The latter turns pre-eminently on the internal logical basis of each set of ideas and the originality or innovativeness of the principles, concepts and analytical frameworks made available by the authors concerned. To the extent that originality and innovativeness also related to specific policy implications for governments and international financial organizations charged with managing the international financial system, the empirical relevance and practicability of the ideas will also provoke discussion and comment in the following chapters. Intellectual rigour will constitute only one element in the exposition of each doctrine; consideration of feasibility, taking account of political constraints, will also have a place. In short, the propagation of a particular set of ideas cannot be fully understood without an appreciation of their practical policy implications.

We aim to describe how and why different ideas on international finance were formulated, who formulated them, and why certain doctrines enjoyed more commanding positions in the debate among economists and policymakers at particular times; why other ideas fell from favour, appeared too idealistic, obscure or radical, or were regarded as unfeasible or at worst downright cranky and idiosyncratic. This book's preoccupation with ideas will remedy the forementioned imbalance in the literature produced by economists and economic historians; it will treat ideas first and foremost as abstract considerations relating to issues in international finance without direct reference to events and immediate policy pressures. In this we shall be following the recommendations of some of the most celebrated thinkers in twentieth-century economics. John Maynard Keynes announced in his *General Theory of Employment, Interest and Money* (1936: 383) that there were two principal reasons for reflecting on economic ideas in their own right: first, because 'the ideas of economists . . . are more powerful than is commonly understood' and, second, because 'the power of vested interests is vastly exaggerated compared with the gradual encroachment of ideas'. And we also follow Friedrich Hayek who wrote in *Monetary Nationalism and International Stability* (1937: 94) that one is justified in confining attention at least provisionally to 'theoretical problems' in the monetary field because 'in the long run human affairs are guided by intellectual forces. It is this belief which . . . gives abstract considerations of this sort their importance, however slight may be their bearing on what is practicable in the immediate future'. In his monumental *History of Economic Analysis* (1954) Joseph Schumpeter also endorses the study of economic ideas in the purest sense. What all this means for the evolution of ideas on international financial problems is that the origin, motivation, scope and content of economic ideas should be understood first. In reflecting on the Bretton Woods international financial arrangements so widely accepted in principle in the 1960s, Herbert Grubel (1963: 11) recognized that

> the dreams and impractical plans of one generation are often the political and economic dogma of the next. The present international monetary system is itself the outcome of plans developed by men who analyzed what was wrong with the system of the 1930's. Resistance to change now makes us the slaves of ideas worked out twenty years ago.

On the intellectual architecture of the international financial order

The quest for national and international economic stability from the 1940s to the 1970s prompted many economists to act as 'architects' of international financial reform. Various blueprints, nostrums and pragmatic schemes for reconstructing or renovating the 'system' have recently been likened to architectural projects (Bank for International Settlements 1998; Eichengreen 1999; IMF 1999). Like architects, economists have drawn up plans – some with a clear conception of an extant structure in mind, others with a stated desire to modify key pillars of a current structure. Still other economists have designed structures beginning with a clean slate of possibilities, without appreciating the need to account for the merits of an existing structure, and with scarce respect for immediate practical contingencies such as national political imperatives and international financial diplomacy.

Certainly material presented in this book may usefully be considered as sets of intellectual constructs or designs with contrasting features, advantages and disadvantages. As purely intellectual creations they may be propounded and subsequently studied and appraised for their relative aesthetic appeal, just as the art of designing physical structures may be undertaken for aesthetic reasons rather than for immediate functional purposes. However, architecture as a discipline is also pursued with a view to rendering buildings comfortable and secure under special environmental conditions (Ballantyne 2002b: 2). Likewise, the architecture appropriate for particular observable international financial conditions may need to have more than purely aesthetic appeal. Therefore, many of the ideas examined below will make references to functions as well as logical form, that is to existing circumstances which make the design relevant and more appealing as a resolution to a problem with an existing structure.

Important clarifications must be made at the outset concerning the notions of 'doctrine', 'system' and 'order' used in the following chapters. Intellectual constructs proposing to change or remake international financial arrangements resemble what Schumpeter (1954: 38) called 'political economy'; they involve articulation of a *doctrine*: a 'comprehensive set of economic policies' advocated by their authors 'on the strength of certain unifying (normative) principles'. Now the doctrine may comprise ideas on the essential structure of an international financial '*order*' and the financial '*system*', to use Robert Mundell's (1972: 92) terminology. An order 'represents the framework and setting' in which international financial arrangements – the financial system – operate. Many of the Schumpeterian doctrines on international political economy surveyed in this book are concerned not with the system, that is with the *modus operandi* of the international financial order. Instead, they consider the

> framework of laws, conventions, regulations and mores that establish the setting of the system and the understanding of the environment by the participants in it. A monetary order is to a monetary system somewhat like a constitution is to a political or electoral system.
>
> (Mundell 1972: 92)[4]

When passing from the formulations of the architects about the international financial order to their advocacy of policies to be adopted within that order, the precision of highly technical economic analysis must usually be abandoned. For policy discussion invariably deals with a world resonant with imperfections and approximations.[5] At any one time, any *real* international financial *system* is a hybrid form of the architects' ideal construct; it possesses attributes of the ideal financial order in varying degrees. In other words the architects produce stylized 'schemes of interpretation' explaining many features of a real, evolving financial system, though ideal-typical examples of their construction can never be observed in reality (Machlup 1978: 251). The architects of international finance write down thought experiments or generalized abstractions and much of the discussion that follows in subsequent chapters will consider these abstractions. As abstractions, they constitute variegated types of economic theory constructed with reference to the broad contours of an existing economic epoch. The general rules of each international order so constructed may be fully outlined by each architect and interpreted with detailed provisions and contingencies relevant to contemporary circumstances or an imagined set of future circumstances. Often reference to concrete circumstances overshadows reference to general abstract principles governing an international financial order, to the extent that the architect will appear to offer an eclectic plan or proposal for financial reform.

Overall, the aim of the following chapters is to compare ideas on financial orders and associated systems. The orders constitute formal rules of the game guiding each nation's participation and operation in an observable, historically specific international financial system. In the discussion that follows it should be kept in mind that use of the term system will apply to the day-to-day 'mechanisms governing the interaction between trading nations, and in particular the money and credit instruments of national communities in foreign exchange, capital, and commodity markets' (Mundell 1972: 92).

Choice of great architects

In explaining the essence of each doctrine on international finance this book will use the following questions for guidance:

1 What are the expected objectives and requirements of a genuinely international financial order and its associated systems?
2 What key aspects of the existing system were targeted for reform (e.g. exchange rate regime; capital account liberalization, role of international financial institutions and so forth)?
3 In the immediate period after the Bretton Woods Agreement, did economists' interpretations of interwar experience influence their proposals and how did their expectations of the postwar world influence their ideas?
4 How well, if at all, did the economists' doctrines identify defects in the existing Bretton Woods financial order that would lead to serious problems later and how might their proposals have avoided these problems?
5 In different doctrinal traditions on international financial reform, what were the normative bases of reform proposals?

Not all doctrines expounded in the 1944–71 period will be considered in the light of the foregoing questions. The choice of doctrine and 'great' representative architect(s) of that doctrine rests on several considerations. First, the doctrine must be significantly differentiated from others, differentiation implying either major framework changes incommensurable with another architectural form or major changes in the existing system which were controversial and extensively debated at the time. Second, the leading architect or group of architects must be associated with a tradition or school of economic thought and policy which has long standing in the discipline of economics and may have received a distinctive title (e.g. Austrian, Chicagoan, Keynesian). Third, the doctrine must have had a dominant intellectual influence in the sense that it has been widely recognized and cited by contemporaries and subsequent commentators. Fourth, the cosmopolitan nature of international political economy demands that the coverage of 'great' doctrines must go beyond Anglo-American economic thought in the period under review; thinkers of continental European origin (and perhaps resident in Europe) will be chosen where appropriate.

This book will present a procession of leading ideas – a historical array of doctrines – mostly in chronological order and classified where possible by school of thought on the subject. As for possible omissions from the 'great architect' category, it should be realized that major contributors to the pure economics of international money may not have reflected extensively on order or system reform issues. In that case they will not be given special attention here. Account must be taken of M. June Flanders's *International Monetary Economics 1870–1960* (1989), which treats pure economic analysis and does not study the relationship between relevant ideas and policy questions connected to the international monetary order or system. Thus James Meade, an influential contributor to the economics of the balance of payments in the 1950s and 1960s, figures in Flanders's work as an economist who made notable analytical advances, but that does not in itself qualify him for 'great architect' status.[6] By contrast, Roy Harrod's contributions, while not given much space by Flanders, will be given careful treatment here because he wrote extensively on system reform and international financial policy.

Crucial to the doctrinal orientation adopted here is the need to preserve ideas about international financial orders and systems that appeared irrelevant or unfeasible at the time they were articulated. Mundell's valuable distinction between financial orders and systems permits consideration of alternative orders even if they were constructed to house a hypothetical international financial system. Our story will begin with the Bretton Woods international order already in place. The plans of J.M. Keynes and H.D. White – great architects of the Bretton Woods order – will not be considered in detail. Instead, the fundamental ideational features of Bretton Woods will be outlined in the next chapter. The Bretton Woods outline will function as a benchmark for subsequent architectural projects beginning in Chapters 3 and 4 with two Harvard University-based contributions: Alvin Hansen's American Keynesian reinterpretation of Bretton Woods and John H. Williams's key currency approach which proposes an alternative financial order to that constructed at Bretton Woods. In Chapter 5 we shall see how Frank Graham at Princeton offered a wholesale rejection of Bretton Woods, and his broad commodity reserve currency proposal later drew support in Europe from Nicholas Kaldor and Jan Tinbergen. The plans and arguments of Robert Triffin produced at Yale University in the 1950s and 1960s also attract full consideration in Chapter 6. Triffin salvaged what he thought were the best elements of the Bretton Woods order and reworked some of its central principles. Well-known economists at the University of Chicago – notably Henry Simons, Milton Friedman and Harry Johnson – railed against the Bretton Woods order for over two decades; their Chicagoan alternative is discussed in Chapter 7. Perhaps a more radical approach than that of the Chicagoans was taken by the Austrians – Ludwig von Mises and Friedrich Hayek together with some prominent continental European economists – Charles Rist, Jacques Rueff, Michael Heilperin and Wilhelm Röpke. These Austrian and other European writers wished to design the international financial architecture around the automatic gold standard, and their views are explored in Chapter 8. When the 'Bellagio Group' of leading thinkers on international financial reform reported in 1964 (after several conferences in Princeton University and in Bellagio, Italy), a general consensus was forming around reworking the BW architecture though the fixed exchange rate pillar remained a preferred feature (Machlup and Malkiel 1964). Two proponents of both fixed exchange rates and the role of gold in the international order are considered in Chapter 9: the ideas of Oxford economist, Roy Harrod and Canadian (later Nobel laureate) Robert Mundell. Harrod's doctrine exemplified a distinctive British Keynesian approach laced with sentimentality towards gold while Mundell, in producing a critique of the BW order, also offered innovative options for policymakers wishing to preserve the basic Bretton Woods structure.

Chapter organization will conform broadly to the following pattern: (i) introducing the leading architect or group of architects; (ii) explaining their interpretation of the evolution of the Bretton Woods financial system up to the point in time when they made their key contributions; (iii) analysing the principles forming the basis of their alternative doctrine; (iv) outlining institutional arrangements constituting the proposed system; (v) stating their views on alternative proposals and plans (if any); (vi) assessing the normative basis of their proposal; (vii) appraising its feasibility; and (viii) setting out assignment rules or guidelines for the main instruments of economic policy in the context of the proposed international financial architecture.

Economic ideas and international financial policy: normative issues

Referring again to Schumpeter's conception of political economy, the intended approach to international political economy in this book openly accepts normative elements. Our great architects of international finance were active advocates of an order and associated system; they often made specific policy recommendations. Furthermore, their plans and proposals exhibit some common features: they embody alternative visions of the nature, scope and consequences of inter-country monetary interactions and interdependencies; they favour a specific set of rules or loose guidelines for the international financial order; take different positions on the necessity for joint responses to perceived negative spillover effects arising from international financial interactions; and consider different roles (if any) for international financial institutions in this connection.

All intellectual constructs in international political economy are inherently prescriptive; they proceed, sometimes implicitly, to state how policy-makers ought to behave, given deeply held presuppositions about the nature and consequences of international financial interdependencies. Generally, such presuppositions may embrace the entire spectrum of relations among national governments designed to react to cross-border financial spillovers. As a result, for instance, some ideas discussed below envisage limited scope for monetary policy coordination between nations.[7] Other doctrines are far more sanguine about strong forms of policy coordination compatible with an overarching financial order while still others propose much weaker policy cooperation, thereby preserving a greater degree of domestic policy autonomy.[8]

The main task in this book is not to study the impact of key economic and financial events on ideas. Nor is the task to assess the way in which events and policies have been influenced in practice by certain ideas or changes in economic knowledge. The deficiencies of the Bretton Woods financial order were gradually revealed by events and failed policies associated with the rules and guidelines applying to that order. Flaws in Bretton Woods were often perceived by economists' doctrines independently of events and usually before the full implications of that order had been revealed in practice. The policy implications of leading doctrines will carefully be appraised in the first place as part of the contemporary intellectual scene. The coherence and theoretical robustness of a doctrine may be considered against the backgrounds of critiques made of it at the time and later. Here analytical validity is a prime consideration. However, separating analytical issues in international political economy from those which might be resolved by observation and formal empirical investigation is not straightforward. While during the period under review economists placed great faith in the methods of positive economic science, especially empirical falsifiability, events, data and institutions could not easily be marshalled in a widely agreeable manner conclusively to test a particular doctrine. The problem was exacerbated by the fact that disagreements among economists over the organization of the international financial system were sometimes due to semantics such that different meanings were attached to different terms commonly used in international finance.[9] As well, the future-oriented character of international financial reform proposals prevented real experimentation to test crucial propositions. When particular experiments were undertaken, for example in the design and scripting of the roles of the World Bank and IMF in the Bretton Woods financial order, controversy continued unabated on whether or not these roles were successful. While many questions about the impact of international financial interactions and about the effectiveness of certain policies have been tentatively answered by positive economic analysis and empirical work, key normative issues remain unresolved. All that matters for the purposes of this book is that different value judgements need to be exposed because they are responsible for divergent policy recommendations.

The propagation of a doctrine in international finance cannot be understood without an appreciation of the policy implications arising from it. For it is undoubtedly these matters which provoke controversy among economists and policymakers. The normative issues, including political and ideological factors are inextricable aspects of each doctrine: they take for granted how the international financial order should work, or what aspect of the order or system should be modified. Some political scientists have attributed a pivotal role to 'embedded liberal' ideas in the construction of the global financial order from the mid-1940s (Ruggie 1983; Helleiner 2001). Another has interpreted the evolution of the Bretton Woods system as the playing out of certain power relations manifested in financial imperialism (Cohen 1970). It therefore behoves any serious doctrinal study in economics to elucidate the normative elements contained in each doctrine. Economic arguments developed by each great financial architect discussed in the following chapters are often concerned to facilitate a more efficient allocation of the world's resources; some are also concerned to generate greater equity in the sense of allowing opportunities for less developed nations to participate more freely in any proposed financial order, trade openly with more developed industrialized nations and raise their economic growth rates. Additionally, some proposals wish to promote a specific type of 'fairness' in the distribution of burdens when economic adjustments to the balance of international payments difficulties are required. Finally, a widely held presumption embodied in the doctrines surveyed below is that each doctrine on financial arrangements is intended to be consistent with a companion parallel position on international trade, trade policy and associated institutional arrangements.[10]

Main purposes of a doctrinal perspective

On 18 December 1963 a conference organized by Fritz Machlup and Burton Malkiel was held in Princeton to discuss 'International Monetary Arrangements'. Thirty-two selected economists with expertise in the field were sent an invitation which read:

> The purpose of this conference is ... to find out whether we can identify the differences in factual and normative assumptions that can explain the differences in prescription for solving the problems of the international monetary system. Presumably we all use logic. Hence, if we arrive at different recommendations, we must differ in the assumption of fact or in the hierarchy of values. To identify and formulate these assumptions would ... be a major step toward a better understanding of the conflict of ideas.
>
> (Machlup and Malkiel 1964: 7)

This passage expresses in capsule summary the purpose of this book, at least in terms of executing doctrinal study. There is one difference: expositions, commentaries and assessments in this book have benefited from events, ideas and controversies since the 1960s. Doctrinal study enables us to understand the strengths and weaknesses of present international financial arrangements and provides insight into the wide range of alternatives available to policymakers.

Reviewing the development of doctrines on international finance can render a sense of proportion to current debate on the subject. Revisiting past contributions also serves to demonstrate the influence of fads in economic writing and indicates what might have been fashionable in the generally accepted mainstream of economics from time to time (Bronfenbrenner 1966). For modern practitioners, contemplating doctrinal studies may also result in an unpleasant realization: the progress of research in the field of international financial reform and international policy coordination does not appear to exhibit a linear movement away from darkness (past error) towards light (present truth). While many questions about specific arrangements in the international financial system and their effectiveness have been satisfactorily answered since the 1940s, still others – especially important normative issues – have not by their very nature been settled once and for all, though they have been, and still can be, openly debated. This doctrinal study will present many normative questions on international finance which still pose challenges to the present generation of economists and policymakers.

Doctrinal discussion of sets of ideas on the international financial architecture can illuminate some fundamental, enduring and quite modern principles commonly used in the field (e.g. scheme feasibility, credibility, rule commitment and enforceability).[11] There is no suggestion, however, that the following study will resolve long-running disputes over normative issues, many of which are still alive today. Doctrinal discussion cannot decide for the reader which approach or architectural scheme is correct for a particular period or is supremely compelling in current circumstances. An array of schemes will be presented for readers to judge. I follow Schumpeter (1954: 40) once again in likening these schemes to a form of political economy in which, for example:

> There would be no sense in speaking of a superiority of Charlemagne's ideas on economic policy as revealed by his legislative and administrative actions over the economic ideas of, say, King Hammurabi; or of the general principles of policy revealed by the proclamations of the Stuart kings over those of Charlemagne; or of the declarations of policy that sometimes preface acts of Congress over those Stuart proclamations. We may of course sympathize with some of the interests favored in any of those cases rather than with the interests favored in others, and in this sense array such documents also in a scale of preference. But a place of any body of economic thought in any such array would differ according to the judge's value judgments, and for the rest we shall be left with our emotional or aesthetic preference for the various schemata of life that find expression in those documents. We should be very much in the same position if we were asked whether Gauguin or Titian was the greater painter.... And the same thing applies of course to all systems of political economy.

Retrospectives only permit reasoned reflection on alternative architectural frameworks articulated in a particular time and context. They explain, for instance, why contemporaries viewed a doctrine either as having maverick qualities that made it anathema to supporters of a received doctrine on the international financial order, or as possessing qualities that rendered it able to modify the current international financial arrangements.

The following doctrinal study will identify schemes that have a modern flavour – doctrines that have perennial character and appeal. Ideas from the leading architects of international finance laid out below may be conferred the title of 'fertile' constructs in international political economy, though only in historical perspective. These ideas were already in the air when more persuasive proponents of arrangements such as flexible exchange rates, monetary unions and free world capital markets came on the scene in the late twentieth century. As one modern commentator in the history of economic thought has argued, the practices of past generations of economists still shape our current thinking, whether we are aware of it or not (Blaug 1996: 7). This comment is especially relevant in the debate among economists on international financial reform. Doctrinal research therefore has a modest function. It can identify key features of older ideas that have not become obsolete. Given our conception of the ebb and flow of architectural forms in international finance, it would have been extraordinarily short-sighted to place these ideas on the scrap-heap.

While modern terminologies and expressions on the issues might differ, doctrinal disputes in the 1944–71 period were then, as now, concerned with fundamental questions: (i) does the configuration of the international financial order matter? (ii) does that configuration expose participating nations to so-called violent fluctuations in international financial markets which reduce long-run growth prospects at the national level? To use modern idioms, these fluctuations, mostly caused by an international financial architecture (promoted in the doctrines of one or more leading architects), could weaken the case for increasing global economic integration predominantly based on market forces; they could threaten the otherwise laudable cases for freer world trade, the transnational integration of supply chains in product and services markets and freer world capital markets. That is why many (but not all) the architectural schemes constructed by economists whose work is surveyed in the following chapters seem so preoccupied with the questions of international financial order and stability.

Each chapter below relies on primary sources to provide direct access to the content and style of reasoning in the work of selected, leading architects. Informed readers working outside the formal discipline of economics should remember that each architect's first points of reference were the intricacies of the existing international financial system and the proposals and plans of other 'experts'. As one great architect ruefully affirmed:

> These . . . are formidably technical topics. To deal with them in simple, commonsense terms, would inevitably classify the author as a crackpot whose views deserve no more than a raising of eyebrows and a shrugging of shoulders on the part of serious-minded people. I felt compelled, therefore, to meet the experts . . . on their arguments, and to anticipate their objections. This makes unnecessarily forbidding reading for the layman.
>
> (Triffin 1960: vii)

Nonetheless, an attempt will be made below to make the material accessible to a wide audience extending beyond the narrow confines of specialist economists and those interested in international finance. The latter now seem disproportionately concentrated on topics in the positive economics of international money; accordingly they are obsessed with measurement and empirical issues.[12] Readers with interests in international finance, political science, international organizations and international relations should keep the following point in mind throughout: in all instances where a leading architectural scheme is presented below, the international financial order was perceived by the architect(s) as an *instrument* for facilitating the transfer of goods, services, labour and capital among nations. And it has been almost axiomatic in economics since Adam Smith that such transfers are generally wealth-creating. This is essentially why the great architects identified in each chapter took a strong interest in designing and constructing the instrument.

Finally, to anticipate one of my conclusions, the appearance of an international financial order and the associated system at the time of writing (in early 2004) will disabuse economists of a belief in their supreme architectonic power. Economists have often taken the view that the international financial system must be designed and managed in some determinate way and that they have *the* analytical tools to do the job. In fact, economists' ideas may not clinch an argument or act as a perfect predictor of observed outcomes in international finance; those outcomes evolve organically as the undesigned results of events, politicians' policy choices and the decisions of a multitude of market participants. None of these factors need necessarily conform to the dictates issuing from the minds of economists. Furthermore, like most economic policy analysis, the architecture of international finance appreciated as doctrine is an art more than a science like engineering or chemistry. As with architectural work itself, work on the international financial architecture incorporates a style (or genre) which only later becomes clearly visible to historians. Ideas on international financial arrangements can only be fully appreciated in historical perspective and by way of comparative analysis.

We turn in the following chapter to examine a founding attempt to design the international financial order. The Bretton Woods Conference held in New Hampshire in July 1944 created a governing blueprint for international finance. Not without good cause, the blueprint has been described as 'one of the great social inventions of the twentieth century' (Gordon 1971: vii) and 'a notable landmark in human affairs' (Harrod 1972: 5).[13]

2 The Bretton Woods financial order

A distinctive economic doctrine

Some intellectual background

When Ragnar Nurkse's study for the League of Nations entitled *International Currency Experience* (1944) was distributed to delegates at the United Nations Monetary and Financial Conference at Bretton Woods in July 1944, his conclusions would have been scarcely surprising and indeed widely accepted. As the last major economic research contribution of the League, Nurkse's study contained all the fundamental tenets of the BW Agreement. The interwar years from 1919 illustrated how, without a sound legal and institutional framework for the international financial order in which all major industrialized nations sought to cooperate, the result would be generalized economic disorder. Financial disorder brought deleterious economic, social and political consequences. Commentators have since discussed these consequences at length: trade wars, severe economic depression, rampant economic nationalism, competitive currency devaluations and even, to stretch the point, military conflict. Nurkse's major conclusions should briefly be outlined here, for they give open entry to the factors uppermost in the thinking of economists at BW.[1]

Exchange rates

In the first place, the twenty years between the wars had furnished much evidence against freely flexible exchange rates between currencies; that is, flexibility in the price of a nation's money expressed in terms of others. On Nurkse's reading of the evidence, flexible rates had overwhelming disadvantages: (i) trade in goods and services is hampered by the uncertainty engendered by fluctuating rates while hedging facilities merely add to the costs of trading currencies over time; (ii) movements in exchange rates much larger than justified by changes in relationships among nations' internal price and cost levels result in disruptive shifts of resources in and out of industries producing exports; and (iii) exchange rate movements in a particular direction promote anticipation of further movements in that direction, leading to speculative capital transfers between currencies, aggravating and in some cases thwarting orderly adjustment of a nation's balance of payments (if the current account on the balance of payments is in deficit or surplus).[2] In short, the world needed 'stable exchanges' since these have 'proved essential not only for international economic intercourse but for domestic stability as well' (Nurkse 1944: 211). Exchange rate stability is a matter of degree; certainly Nurkse rules out 'absolute rigidity' in the face of major, long-term structural changes in economic conditions when rates may need to change. Ensuring exchange rate stability is considered a prerequisite for the stabilization and management of domestic economies.

Foreign reserves

Second, according to Nurkse, the functions, form and distribution of international financial reserves need to be clearly understood by all nations participating in an international monetary order sanctioning fixed exchange rates. Presuming stable, relatively fixed exchange rates – meaning that residents of a country may convert their domestic money into foreign money at a fixed rate – international, foreign money essentially becomes an extension of national money.[3] Thus gaps in a nation's international payments, due for instance to a deficit in receipts over payments for trade in goods and services, must somehow be settled. A nation's cash reserves of foreign currencies (held at the central bank and/or at commercial banks) would be used to settle a deficit. Alternatively a surplus would increase these reserves. In any event, institutional arrangements of this sort permit convertibility of one nation's currency into another; they are essential when residents of different nations make payments to each other yet hold a high proportion of their money in the form of domestic currency. In brief, the function of a nation's foreign reserves is to facilitate convertibility in a fixed exchange rate environment. Discrepancies between foreign receipts and payments may arise due to normal trading activities and will usually be larger when affected by non-synchronized cyclical movements in economic activity among nations, crop failures, long-running labour disputes, natural disasters and so forth. Thus a store of international moneys will soften the domestic impact of such shocks. These moneys may take the form of foreign currencies supplemented by foreign borrowing facilities, trade credits and gold holdings. Instead of acting as a purveyor of changing economic conditions from abroad, increasingly during the interwar period international reserves came to act as a buffer stock absorbing international economic shocks. The new-found macroeconomic policy aim later in the 1930s turned on 'a growing desire for economic stability; there was a growing realization of the need to maintain national income and outlay so as to secure an adequate level of employment'. As part of this trend, the policy practice of 'sterilizing' the effects of foreign reserve movements on the domestic credit base was widely observed (Nurkse 1944: 213, 215).[4] This practice – offsetting or stabilizing, for instance, adverse movements of foreign export demand on domestic output and employment – implied greater tolerance of government external account management through a central banking authority. As for the broad economic rationale underlying this move, Keynes's *General Theory of Employment, Interest and Money* (1936) had already provided the *locus classicus* but resort to this practice was widespread before 1936.

In the post-1944 international financial order, Nurkse recommended that liquid reserves be established and constituted by foreign currencies and gold, with the mix of currencies being determined by the diverse trade patterns of individual nation-states. Crucially, reserves should be used as a buffer *only* for 'temporary discrepancies' between international payments and receipts. It was believed that signals transmitted by long-run market forces (produced by changes in tastes and by technological and productivity advances) could be garbled especially in the short term and no damage could therefore be done by intervening during that period (Nurske 1944: 214).

The emerging buffer function of international reserves in the 1930s implied an inverse relationship between a country's national income and its international liquidity (as measured by the reserve position). Previously, 'legal stipulation requir[ed] countries to hold a certain minimum "cover" of gold or foreign exchange reserves against their notes in circulation or the notes and sight deposits combined'. Increasingly, this stipulation lost its prestige and acceptability. As for the distribution of foreign exchange reserves among countries, Nurkse concluded that the interwar period exhibited a chronic maldistribution caused by the unequal distribution of wealth, economic devastation from wars or natural catastrophes, speculative capital movements and possibly inadequate reserves relative to trade-financing requirements. In any of these events, without an adequate buffer against balance of payments shocks, countries were forced to use trade restrictions, myopic beggar-thy-neighbour currency devaluations to maintain export competitiveness, or allow foreign exchange fluctuations fully to impact on the domestic economy (Nurkse 1944: 215, 217–20). It is suggested that reserve maldistribution problems may be resolved by: (i) better management of international capital movements, especially 'disequilibrating' speculative capital flows; (ii) officially subordinating the gold stock and changes in it to the growth of money income, which entails legally augmenting the supply of gold by revaluing gold in terms of its exchange rate with national currencies; and (iii) securing international agreements that somehow engineered acceptability of a wider range of foreign currencies perceived as genuine international finance held in central bank reserves.

Capital movements

The third lesson from interwar currency experience drawn from Nurkse's study is that exchange rate stability required government intervention to impose controls on capital movements ('exchange control'). Controls were particularly necessary when capital movements disrupted balance of payments adjustment (away from either a deficit or surplus on current account towards balance). Here the 'mass psychology' connected with 'hot money' and 'flight capital' required rational management. And such management must be symmetrical. In fact, countries accruing large, persistent surpluses on their balance of payments current account 'may constitute the real source of trouble'; they may be 'the centre' of an international financial disturbance. By contrast, it was commonly assumed that only small, open economies suffering deficits must manage capital flows more carefully. In the surplus nations' case, their currencies would be rendered 'scarce' by insufficient domestic demand for foreign imports or inadequate foreign lending. An 'international stabilization fund' or 'exchange union' ought then to be established to receive short-term loans from the surplus countries which would then be recycled by international agreement to deficit countries.

The Nurksian penchant for exchange controls is set against a clear warning: 'exchange control is plainly a harmful and obnoxious means' of dealing with chronic or persistently recurring deficits (or surpluses) on the current account of the balance of payments. In the deficit case for example, exchange controls could be used to protect a national currency which was seriously overvalued. To block capital movements which have responded to a persistent deficit is tantamount to destroying the price signals so essential to efficient allocation of the world's resources.[5]

Nurkse's League of Nations doctrine in 1944

The core proposals from economic work completed at the League of Nations in 1944 may be stated as follows: the international monetary problem was one of determining a configuration of currency relations compatible with the requirement of domestic economic stability understood in loose Keynesian terms as sustaining a high level of output and employment. Concerted international action was required to resolve the problem. The first task was to secure a set of workable currency exchange ratios ('parities') at least for the major industrialized nations. Given gold's role as an important token in international reserve holdings, gold should continue to have an official place in the international financial system. Furthermore, international cooperation was required to mitigate the effects of erratic, 'abnormal transfers' of private capital across national borders and accordingly to defend established exchange rate parities. Additional cooperation was needed between large industrialized nations to effect some degree of monetary and fiscal policy coordination so as to combat 'violent fluctuations' in their incomes. As a consequence, small export-dependent open economies would find secure markets for their products (Nurkse 1944: 230).

Certainly, it is acknowledged by the League of Nations' economist that the nineteenth-century gold standard did not emerge from a formal international agreement or constitution. However, merely to wait for spontaneous adoption of a new international financial order could invite a postwar economic depression.[6] It was inconceivable in 1944 that governments would stand by idly, given the consensus building around Keynes's *General Theory* (1936). On Nurkse's recommendation, only two aspects of the gold standard pre-1914 and the occasionally operative gold exchange standard in the interwar period should be retained. First, international prosperity will be furthered by a *fixed* exchange rate system. Second, no postwar system should deny contemporary conventions in international finance. Therefore gold had an undeniable role though it should emphatically not act as a limit on the production of money in any national monetary system, or as a brake on the expansion of international trade by restricting international liquidity.

Bretton Woods: first principles

The Bretton Woods International Monetary Agreement in 1945 has been discussed, dissected and analysed by countless historians, economic historians and economists.[7] This chapter does not intend to offer thorough retrospective accounts of the origins of the BW Agreement, of its workings in practice or of its actual performance and effectiveness. We wish to outline the Agreement as a distinctive doctrine, that is as a unified Schumpeterian political economy bound by normative principles. It is vital to view the Agreement creating what was later dubbed the BW 'international monetary order' (McKinnon 1996: 41–3) as a blueprint – a set of constitutional rules and guidelines for the world economy. It must not be seen as a precise guide to the actual conduct of participating nations within that order over the period from its promulgation in 1945 to its widely acknowledged demise in the early 1970s. By comparison, the actual operation of the nineteenth-century gold standard corresponded very imperfectly with the rules which academic economists formulated as a model or representation of that international financial order. As Bordo (1993: 36) maintains, the BW order's 'architects never spelled out exactly how the system was supposed to work'. Indeed, the workings of the BW principles established in the 1944 Articles of Agreement were somewhat flexible and open-ended; they were interpreted over time in a manner not obviously consistent with the intentions of the architects.[8] All this would not have surprised major contemporary observers, including George Halm (1944: 174) who reported that the BW Agreement 'will be flexible enough to fit the post-war world, whatever its success ... in a world wide scheme of economic stabilization'. Be this as it may, clear guidelines were set, forming a framework within which an international financial system could be constructed, much as architects can set out the main pillars of a construction within which detailed characteristics of a building may eventually evolve.

The formal BW Agreement follows all the elements of Nurkse's study, *International Currency Experience.* The Agreement dealt with exchange rate stabilization, foreign reserve creation and distribution, foreign reserves conceived as a 'buffer', exchange controls, scarce currency problems and the creation of international institutions aimed at policy cooperation and coordination. Furthermore, BW promoted a rule amounting to a full-blown case against readily flexible (and floating) exchange rates; it granted governments discretion to manage (rather than passively accept) immediate impacts of price and income changes brought about by temporary international trade and payments disturbances. The policy background was one in which a broad consensus had already formed around the desirability of governments managing and fine-tuning national aggregate expenditure (consumption, investment and government outlays) to maintain high levels of domestic employment. Lastly the BW Agreement indirectly acted as a facilitator of multilateral trade even though trade policy issues were not part of the BW conference agenda. BW set in train international financial arrangements which would contribute to exchange rate stabilization and multilateral currency convertibility, both of which potentially enhanced trade in goods and services. Protectionist, restrictive trade policy practices no longer needed to be the first resort in responding to international payments imbalances.

Specific principles relating to financial questions are reconstructed and paraphrased below, in keeping with the original BW Articles of Agreement. The core principles are outlined without the minutiae being laboured. Important in effecting our reconstruction is the recognition that capturing what was intended by the BW architects is not a straightforward matter. Many previous interpretations have been made using hindsight and have been coloured by events and developments in economic terminology and understanding since 1944. Therefore we shall make the following reconstruction using original documents and as much *contemporary* interpretative literature as possible.[9] The objective is to express the core ideas around which an architectural consensus was formed at BW.

1 International Monetary Fund (IMF)

A permanent, impartial international financial institution – an International Monetary Fund – is to be created to:

a promote financial cooperation and function as a centre for consultation and collaboration on financial problems;

b facilitate expansion and growth of international trade, thereby supporting the policy priority of maintaining high income and employment;
c assist in establishing exchange rate stability, orderly exchange rate adjustment and avoidance of competitive currency devaluations;
d assist in establishing multilateral payments in respect of transactions on the current accounts of member nations' balance of payments;
e eliminate foreign exchange convertibility restrictions which hamper multilateral trade;
f monitor (and generally tolerate) restrictions on capital transactions;
g provide confidence to member nations by giving access to the IMF's resources to assist in correcting balance of payments imbalances;
h provide guidelines to correct maladjustments in members' balance of payments without resorting to measures ultimately destructive of output and employment; and
i shorten the duration and lessen the extent of imbalances in international payments among member nations.

2 *The IMF's resources*

Structure

Member countries subscribe to the IMF in gold and national currencies. Each member is assigned a quota, the gold component of the subscription being a minimum of 25 per cent of quota or 10 per cent of its net official gold reserves and US dollars, whichever is the smaller. IMF holdings provide a reserve on which members may draw to meet foreign payments obligations during periods of deficit imbalances on the current account of the balance of payments. This facility is linked to the BW intention to reduce exchange restrictions and exchange discrimination on current account transactions (for trade in goods and services), and promote currency convertibility.[10]

Financial assistance

The IMF does not lend its resources. A member remits to the IMF an amount of its own currency equivalent (at an agreed par value) to the amount of foreign currency it wishes to purchase for current account transactions. In due course the member must repurchase its own currency from the IMF within three to five years. Repurchase may take the form of a payment in gold or US dollars or a convertible currency acceptable to the IMF. Certain charges are levied in proportion to the amounts transacted and the duration of the arrangement. In total, no member country can purchase foreign currencies with its own in an amount which would leave the IMF holding its currency to the extent of more than 200 per cent of its quota.

Technical assistance

Officials are employed by the IMF and are despatched to member countries deemed needy of economic and financial advice. Often the officials will be involved in advising on and monitoring IMF programmes designed to assist balance of payments adjustment.

3 Exchange rate rule

Each member must maintain an agreed par value for its currency. Gold convertibility (into one or other currency) is mandatory. Thus gold or a currency tied to gold is to be used as a common denominator setting initial par values.[11] IMF consultation is required for any change in excess of 10 per cent from the initial parity.

All currencies are to be treated equally or symmetrically insofar as no special reserve currencies are sanctioned, though liquid reserves are needed to defend the fixed exchange rates (par values). Each country is therefore obliged to intervene in foreign exchange markets and buy (sell foreign reserves) their own currency when it is in excess supply and sell (buy foreign reserves) when it is in excess demand. Daily exchange transactions on the market must be conducted at rates not varying by more than 1 per cent from the par value. Clearly reserve assets, possibly IMF resources, are needed for intervention purposes.

In circumstances of long-term 'fundamental disequilibrium' in the current account of the balance of payments, the IMF offers extensive consultation and may permit a proposed exchange rate change to assist in payments adjustment. Objections by the IMF to the national social and political policies of member countries proposing an exchange rate change is forbidden. In the case of a fundamental 'scarcity' (as officially declared by the IMF) of a country's currency due to persistent surpluses on current account, other members may be permitted to impose restrictions against transactions with that country, thereby implying some degree of trade policy discrimination against the 'scarce currency' country.[12]

4 Reserves and their use

Countries should restrict deficits to that which can be financed by official reserves and IMF drawing rights. Reserves are to be used as a buffer, allowing time for a nation to adjust to a short-term external payments imbalance. IMF drawing rights for additional reserves allow, under specified constraints, access to a pool of currencies. Provision is made for four-yearly reviews of the size of a member's drawing facility so that it may be adjusted to reflect inflation and the growth of international trade in goods and services.

5 Exchange controls

Capital controls may be used to counter currency speculation which might otherwise force inadvertent parity changes. The IMF is empowered to determine whether specific transactions in foreign exchange markets are capital or current account transactions. Current transactions, that is those needed to finance trade in goods and services, should generally be free from controls.

6 International investment

A coordinating institution concerned with long-run economic reconstruction and economic development projects is to be created. The International Bank for Reconstruction and Development (IBRD) is to be established for these purposes.[13] Its main function is to act as a financial intermediary, a conduit for world capital intended for long-term investment projects (not short-term balance of payments financing). The IBRD is to have two major powers: (i) to borrow from private capital markets, then lend on commercial or near-commercial terms to worthy projects; and (ii) to guarantee loans made directly by private creditors.

Commentary

While an elaborate code of conduct for international financial cooperation was drawn up in the original BW Agreement, the degree of ambiguity and openness in many of its founding principles provide considerable room for contention and reinterpretation. No matter how much detail is provided in each 'Article' (or clause) of the Agreement, not only could observers quibble over fine technical points but major principles as outlined above were open to a wide range of interpretations. Through all the noise of interpretation, however, and there was much of that in the debates that followed the Agreement, the signal – viewed here as the style of policy analysis and core substantive content of the BW doctrine – is abundantly clear.

The contrast between patent disorder in international financial affairs in the interwar period and the BW Agreement could not be sharper. BW satisfied the Nurksian, League of Nations' plea for cooperation around key principles: exchange rate stability; orderly exchange rate adjustment when required by long-term current account conditions; international liquidity (or reserve) arrangements with a buffer role; encouraging free multilateral currency convertibility and payments practices; retention of gold as a stabilizing anchor; use of exchange controls to support a fixed exchange rate rule; and the inviolability of national macroeconomic policy which could still, in principle, employ a variety of economic and social policies as befitted national circumstances. Overlaying the whole Agreement was an abiding consensus formed around a policy goal structure which gave full employment top priority – a goal that must be engineered by government management in the international sphere. Full employment was not regarded as something achievable automatically by relying exclusively on the long-run outcome of the free play of markets in the international financial arena.[14] The ultimate point of BW was to design a system of international payments central to which were intergovernmental cooperation and government intervention in international finance. The BW order was intended to allow any system which evolved within its bounds to encourage trade expansion as opposed to supporting bilateral trade, rampant protectionism and pernicious, competitive currency devaluations.[15]

As is well known – and this occurs with most policy packages and agreements – the BW Agreement was the outcome of compromise between mostly British and United States officials whose separate plans (the Keynes and White plans respectively) were submitted for conferees' deliberation (Kahn 1976; Eichengreen 1989). The Agreement envisaged that all the principles established in the separate parts (or 'Articles') would be mutually reinforcing. Superficially understood, the Agreement appears to satisfy this requirement. For instance, the principles which established the IMF as recounted earlier in this chapter were stated at a very high level of generality. These almost appeared as leitmotifs or, at worst, slogans around which member countries could rally. The principles were also a counsel of perfection.

On the exchange rate principle it was thought that the BW rule would not suffer either the rigidities of the fixed rate system under a gold standard or the wild fluctuations believed to characterize a flexible rate system. Moreover, the use of capital controls to stem the tide of speculative capital flows would engender greater stability in exchange rates. And after all, it was stability that mattered most, for stability, according to BW reasoning, promotes trade. But in which direction should stability be reached when a change is called for? The meaning of 'fundamental disequilibrium' allowing a major exchange rate change appeared *prima facie* to apply to all countries whether experiencing persistent deficits or surpluses on current account. However, this expectation is not made explicit in the Agreement. Bemused by fine distinctions made in the scarce currency clauses of the Agreement, a contemporary observer immediately suspected that the BW architects 'lay practically the whole burden of correcting any disequilibrium on those countries which find themselves on the deficit side of the disequilibrium' (Crowther 1948: 334). Which country or countries should in fact adjust? Surplus or creditor countries are arguably in a state of disequilibrium, along with deficit countries. Did the architects intend that the burdens of adjustment in the move towards 'stability' would involve 'joint responsibility', as a commentator later suggested (Scammell 1975: 116)? Contemporaries were more sceptical: 'Unfortunately the Agreement is entirely vague concerning the policies of the creditor countries which would help restore equilibrium' (Halm 1944: 172). On this matter Halm proceeds to fill lacunae remaining in the Agreement. Both creditor (surplus) and debtor (deficit) countries in a state of long-run 'fundamental disequilibrium' ought to have been given clear policy direction. In the creditor case, policy should support expansion of foreign investment, rising domestic credit, increases in money wages, tariff reductions which boost imports and currency appreciation. As for the latter, in the view of Halm and other prominent contemporary observers, 'appreciation can scarcely be read into the plan. Yet it may be pointed out that the case for appreciation of a scarce currency is, theoretically, just as strong as the case for depreciation of a deficit currency' (Halm 1944: 174). Finally, on the exchange rate adjustment rule, there was confusion over the precise operational meaning of a 'fundamental disequilibrium'. The term was not formally defined. How would such a state be identified in practice? The concept was meant to be taken seriously; its architects seemed to presume that this disequilibrium state would easily be recognized by policymakers (assisted by IMF officials) when it was confronted.[16]

On the reserves question, liquidity used to finance world trade would *not* be increased by the Agreement. Currencies and gold would only be recycled through the IMF in a manner that would make them readily available. As formally constituted, the IMF had no power to *create* money, produce a new unit of account, or loan its resources. Members must buy the foreign currencies they required under strict conditions and only when there were relatively small, short-term payments disturbances on current account transactions. An alternative doctrinal position on all this would have followed Keynes (1943a: 27), who had wished for an IMF with credit-creating power:

> Just as the development of national banking systems served to offset a deflationary pressure which would have prevented otherwise the development of modern industry, so by extending the same principle into the international field we may hope to offset the contractionist pressure which might otherwise overwhelm in social disorder and disappointment the good hopes of our modern world. The substitution of a credit mechanism in place of hoarding would have repeated in the international field the same miracle, already performed in the domestic field, of turning a stone into bread.

The undeniably persuasive power of Keynes's rhetoric, while appealing to many audiences, did not carry conviction with officials in the United States who feared the potential inflationary impact of the credit creation mechanism advocated by Keynes. Keynes's expansionist doctrine, increasingly popular among many prominent economists at the time, did not hold sway in 1944; this confirms our view that the BW Agreement was not as Keynesian as it might have been.

On exchange controls, Keynes (1943a: 31) railed against capital flight undertaken for political reasons or to evade taxation. In addition, capital moving into a country not employed for long-term investment purposes was deemed suspect; it should be permanently regulated. Central control of capital flows must in Keynes's view be an abiding feature of the postwar international financial system (Crotty 1983: 623). Similarly, Nurkse questioned short-term capital movements which sought 'safety rather than employment' and he condemned the use of capital for currency speculation because it caused balance of payments disturbances rather than just acting as an aggravating factor threatening exchange rate stability (Nurkse 1944: 103).[17] The BW Articles of Agreement on capital controls were not so strident in criticizing short-term capital flows and speculative capital. Article IV Section 3 calmly provides that 'members may exercise such controls as are necessary to regulate international capital movements'. No prior approval from the IMF is required. As Margaret De Vries (1969: 224), an official historian of the IMF, revealed:

> As the Fund's . . . Articles were drafted against the background of the disturbing capital movements that had taken place during the 1930s, there was an understandable desire to prevent movements of 'hot' money and to minimize the risk that inadequate foreign exchange reserves could be depleted by more or less panic-inspired capital transfers.

That the BW capital controls were driven by a particular reading of the international financial upheavals in the 1930s is one thing; clear guidance proffered to BW member countries in respect of capital movements is not forthcoming. The BW principle on capital controls fails to distinguish between 'hot', presumably speculative, capital and other types of capital beneficial to trade and economic development. While the guidelines on controls are rather hazy, a clear normative position emerged. Foreign capital which is not directly allocated to new fixed investments of an income-generating type or with potential income-generating power should be studiously monitored, regulated and prohibited. The entry of such capital into the domestic economy was based on allegedly 'irrational', panic-driven motives, speculative motives and illegal tax evasion, none of which had a place in the BW financial order.

The BW architects offered a heavy-handed approach to world capital supplies. That approach was matched by the extraordinary (by late twentieth-century standards) breadth and depth of governmental controls on domestic financial markets during the postwar years. For example, interest rate ceilings as well as government restrictions and directions on bank lending were the rule rather than the exception in most western industrialized economies. The regulation of domestic and international capital supplies went hand in hand with the popularity of national economic planning: economic development paths need to be mapped out by governments with a view to maximizing output and maintaining high levels of employment. Finally, on the exchange controls question, free international capital flows could not be openly endorsed by BW architects, given their commitment to the principle of non-interference in domestic policy. The corollary of this principle of autonomy is that foreign capital movements must obviously be restricted since they may easily disrupt domestic capital markets, which invariably lacked depth and sophistication in the 1940s.

The most unclear aspects of the BW Agreement relate to the policies which might be adopted, consistently with its exchange rate rule, to create and maintain full employment and high output at the national level. There is no denying that the Agreement was founded on pursuing high growth and full employment, using the international economy as a springboard. The creation and maintenance of free, multilateral international payments and freer trade goes with the BW principles. However, can the pursuit of domestic full employment be reconciled so easily with these objectives? For example, could countries live without exchange controls on current transactions (upon which they had relied heavily during wartime), assuming that they could be distinguished from disturbing, speculative capital transactions? What was the desired mix of domestic monetary and fiscal policies consistent with the BW obligations? Granted, increased trade protectionism and competitive currency devaluations are ruled out. Domestic monetary policy may have to be calibrated in a manner which supports the fixed exchange rate; if monetary policy is too expansionist it could create pressure on international reserves which would rapidly diminish. The conduct of monetary policy is not spelt out in the BW Agreement. Yet monetary policy required careful design, given the spirit of the times in favour of active, discretionary monetary actions with a bias towards expansion and in particular towards accommodating fiscal policy. The matter becomes more complex once it is acknowledged that fully satisfying BW principles depends crucially on adopting consistent domestic policies harmonized across BW member countries. Just as the BW international financial order takes on the appearance of a system (in practice) of managed flexibility (with a set of loose rules and guidelines), domestic macroeconomic policy would need to have the same general orientation from country to country.[18]

Protecting member nations' policy autonomy is an outstanding feature of the BW Agreement. The idea is given clear expression though it resembles window dressing. For while the domestic monetary and fiscal policy mix is not normally subject to the jurisdiction of the IMF, exchange rate stability and the state of a nation's foreign reserves are governed by the BW Agreement. Since the latter are not independent of the choice and operation of domestic macroeconomic policies, it may be inferred that the BW international financial order merely tolerates different styles or shades of government macroeconomic stabilization policy which, driven by contemporary political necessity and dominant economic doctrine, would be charged with achieving and maintaining high levels of employment, come what may. The BW principles were idealizations. It cannot be claimed that the BW architects uncritically generalized from the principles to actual policy practice in diverse contexts. The potential conflict between the principle of non-interference in domestic policies and the exchange rate stability requirement was surely understood though the tradeoffs were not made clear probably because member-country circumstances were quite different.[19]

Undoubtedly, the BW principles were a compromise. As impatient commentators ever since have complained, the balance of payments adjustment process consistent with these principles is left up in the air. Presumably domestic macroeconomic policy action is required as soon as reserve losses (for example) are indicated and initial IMF drawing facilities are utilized. Precisely what policy action? The BW Agreement offers no direct advice. In the long run the whole burden of adjustment must fall on the exchange rate if no other policies are enacted.[20] Consider the following scenario: a balance of payments current account deficit, indicative of a 'fundamental disequilibrium', should lead to an exchange rate devaluation. Domestic financial conditions would at that point be in a parlous state, yet only then would the IMF agree to currency devaluation and only then would market forces lead to adjustment of domestic expenditure, costs, wages and possibly government outlays. And, only at that point would the costs of domestic policy objectives forgone by *not* adjusting macroeconomic policies earlier be realized. The BW Agreement takes for granted that member nations would make necessary monetary and fiscal policy changes (to switch and/or reduce domestic expenditure in the appropriate direction) in the short term when initially using their IMF drawing facilities. Needless to say, there are no enforcement measures in the Agreement guaranteeing that policymakers will act appropriately.

Underlying the non-interference principle is a belief in policymakers' power actively to use monetary and fiscal policy, depending on domestic political constraints and on a presumption that such policies can have a potent impact on output and employment in the short term. Reading between the lines of the Agreement, it is assumed that when entering international obligations under BW national political decisionmakers, under pressure to maximize public popularity in short electoral cycles, will overcome their own interests in a cooperative spirit of responsibility in international finance. Perhaps this position is justified on the strength of a fundamental causal relation in BW doctrine: exchange rate stabilization precedes and is at least a first step towards domestic economic stabilization rather than the other way around.[21] Therefore the domestic macropolicy mix is a secondary consideration. According to Paul De Grauwe (1989: 22), the whole cooperative intent of BW was inspired by the very same idea. Further raking over the historical record of interwar international financial experience or further learned empirical work would not have moved BW architects on the direction of this causal relation. High in their collective memories was the searing experience of exchange rate volatility in the interwar years. It is therefore little wonder that scant attention was paid at the BW Conference to what BW architects considered as second-order issues. Reconciling BW international financial principles and guidelines with the design and operation of disciplined national monetary and fiscal policies would follow naturally on the achievement of exchange rate stability.

Policy assignment guidelines at Bretton Woods: a reconstruction

In obtaining membership of the BW international financial order and complying with the Articles of Agreement, members needed to submit to the admittedly broad, implicit policy guidelines embodied in the system. The international BW rules were straightforward enough since they are outlined (if rather loosely) in respect of exchange rate management, membership subscriptions, drawing rights and scarce currency arrangements. Other matters in the Agreement (such as exchange controls) amounted to guidelines rather than formal rules. The principle of non-interference or domestic policy autonomy seems vacuous because it is inextricably linked to the exchange rate commitment, specifically the BW fixed rate (but adjustable in the long run under special conditions).

Whither a completely autonomous monetary policy in all this? If a country adopted a very expansionary monetary policy, thereby producing more national money to the point where its international acceptability (against gold or the US dollar) declined, a foreign reserve drain and eventual exchange rate crisis would supervene. The BW international rules and guidelines do not prevent inconsistent policies developing at the national level – policies that could impact negatively on an originally stable exchange rate. IMF consultation and advice or even cajoling did not carry strong, credible enforcement. The spectre of national insolvency in an economic crisis might be the only effective antidote for domestic macroeconomic policy indiscipline.

It is too simplistic to propose that the BW architects blithely accepted the achievement of exchange rate stability as a *guarantor* of policy discipline at the national level. Equally, it is inconceivable that the architects would not have had clearly in mind a linking of their international rules and guidelines to specific types of national policy actions implementable when divergences appeared in a country's international accounts. Two types of divergence are possible: first, in the temporary, short-term situation, and second at the point where a 'fundamental disequilibrium' is experienced. In the first case a country with a deficit and exercising IMF drawing rights would responsibly implement macroeconomic stabilization policies designed to minimize the risk of exhausting IMF entitlements. In practice it is known in retrospect that certain types of policies using specific monetary policy instruments were favoured by the IMF in the period up to the 1970s (Spitzer 1969). Actual practice notwithstanding, the original BW architecture did not formally recommend rules for the operation of national monetary and fiscal policies in the face of balance of payments disturbances. Certainly, as Eichengreen (1994: 50–1) has emphasized in respect of monetary policy, the BW Agreement excluded 'robust monetary rules'.

We are led therefore to reconstruct what BW architects must have thought about the assignment of a range of economic policy instruments to the policy objectives in hand.[22] The question of 'assignment' concerns the procedures that should be followed to relate available policy instruments to economic and social objectives (Williamson and Miller 1987: 13). The first objective was usually considered to be high employment, then high output growth, balance of international payments, price stability and a reasonable income distribution. Strictly speaking, BW architects dealt with the international payments objective, though because the various objectives often overlap and conflict, attempts to achieve the international stabilization (external balance) objective would inevitably impact on the other objectives.

In correcting balance of payments disturbances in the short term the exchange rate instrument could not be used; par values were only adjustable when long-run disequilibrium emerged. This is why reserve positions were developed both domestically and at the IMF to avoid the need for continuous balance of international receipts and payments. And the *implicit* rule for reserves is that employing them in exchange market interventions must not be allowed to impact on the domestic monetary base; monetary policy must therefore be conducted actively to sterilize the use of foreign reserves.[23] The domestic money stock must decline to restrict the demand for foreign currencies, all the more so when excess demand is persistent. The sale of foreign currency by a central banking authority in this situation comes in return for local currency which is automatically removed from circulation. An obvious danger is that governments might not permit this automatic rule to apply immediately – they may alter monetary and fiscal policies to reduce the short-run negative impact on output and employment. When should monetary and fiscal policy become restrictive? The BW Agreement is not clear on this matter because its architects probably regarded timing issues as having to be considered on a case-by-case basis. It is clear, however, that policies should 'reduce aggregate spending and therefore also spending for imports', and ensure that the exchange rate returns to the bounds established under the BW par value system (De Grauwe 1989: 18).

The BW-managed exchange rate policy could retain credibility so long as reserves were sufficient. Domestic policies were vital in ensuring reserve sufficiency, as Williamson plausibly supposed:

> By the absence of alternative provisions to deal with modest non-self-reversing imbalances, one infers that the architects of Bretton Woods accepted that *it would be necessary to shade fiscal-monetary policy* with a view to the balance of payments position.
>
> (1985: 74, emphasis added)

If Williamson (along with other modern commentators, McKinnon and De Grauwe) is right, then domestic monetary and fiscal policy must be conducted responsibly in the short term so as not to put pressure on aggregate domestic expenditure to the point where a nation's international liquidity is seriously depleted. Yet at the same time, domestic macroeconomic policy must be operated in order to attain a high level of output and employment. The 'shading' act referred to in the above passage should not be underestimated, for some tradeoff among policy objectives must be chosen. The BW architects were no doubt alive to the tradeoff problem and, within the bounds of available foreign reserves, insisted that national policymakers should have autonomy to choose their preferred tradeoff between policy objectives in the short term. With an eye to meeting their obligations under the exchange rate rule, macroeconomic policymakers could use discretion in fine-tuning monetary and fiscal policy; they must be policy activists. In the medium to long run, the fixed exchange rate rule had an escape clause if the short-term policy 'shading' process was unsuccessful in restoring stability. In the case of deficit countries, a 'fundamental', persistent deficit warranted currency devaluation. While 'fundamental disequilibrium' is not formally defined by BW architects, 'there was never much doubt' in their minds (according to Williamson) what the term meant in practice; it was a 'situation in which a country could not expect to achieve basic balance over the [business] cycle as a whole without deflating output from full capacity or restricting trade or payments for balance of payments reasons' (Williamson 1985: 74).

Now this reconstruction makes perfect sense for a time when experiments were starting to take root in applying the basic ideas of Keynesian economics to policy problems. Exchange rates should not, in this approach, be used as an instrument of anticyclical policy to stabilize or balance the internal economy. Instead, monetary and especially active fiscal policy should be used for that purpose.

Altogether, the intellectual framework stated and implied by the BW architects amounted to much more than a commitment to the binding exchange rate rule. The set of assignment guidelines for broad categories of economic policy instruments are presented below in Table 2.1. This is a 'best guess' tabulation, in keeping with the foregoing reconstruction. It represents a contrived consensus position: that is, what the BW architects were generally disposed to believe on the subject of using certain policy instruments. The aims of policy, both domestic and international, are not specified in detail in the BW Agreement and it is not made clear how domestic policy in particular might be conducted. We have broadly stated and defined these aims as 'internal balance' and 'external balance', even though these terms were not used in the BW Agreement. The BW architects preferred to use the term 'stabilization' (see the definitions accompanying Table 2.1). Applying the term 'guidelines' to the BW Agreement is controversial for the word is not used extensively by BW architects. The Agreement specifies some formal international policy rules, as already noted, and these act as codes of conduct for member countries. That some rules were rather open-ended and might not have been rigorously enforceable is beside the point. While the term 'rules' is widely applied in the literature on BW, we prefer to use the softer 'guidelines' because it has connotations entirely consistent with the BW architects' stated principle of domestic policy autonomy.[24]

Conclusion

Why did policymakers from 1945 need guidelines for the operation of domestic anticyclical policies and full employment policies? If they joined with policymakers from other nations and accepted the international codes of the BW Agreement, they would have an obligation not to adopt short-sighted domestic policy assignments that would undermine exchange rate commitments. As well as offering international policy guidelines, the BW discussion was underwritten by an agenda to provide an international framework for national economic policies. The fundamental normative judgement of BW architects was that member nations should be protected from themselves; that is, from the wealth-destructive consequences of individual nations engaging in competitive exchange rate devaluations and protectionist trade policies. In modern language, economic interdependencies and macroeconomic interactions among countries require some degree of mutual recognition, followed by cooperation over economic policy. More formal policy coordination is likely to be successful in countries entering a BW-type agreement *if* there is a transnational consensus on at least some major policy goals (Bryant 1995). The emerging doctrinal consensus *circa* 1944 was well signalled in Nurkse's work and a consensus on policy was indeed discovered at BW soon after.

The place of international financial institutions in the agreed BW order is clear: the IMF and IBRD were necessary, first because many elements of the BW Agreement required formal monitoring in practice. Second, member nations needed advice and direction. Third, institutional leadership was required to effect ongoing collaboration and consultation, especially on the subject of integrating domestic macroeconomic policies with BW obligations. Fourth, member nations desired a neutral arbiter in

Table 2.1 Summary: BW Agreement: guidelines for policy instruments

Policy instrument	*Time horizon*	*Primary assignment**	*Secondary assignment*	*Guidelines*
Exchange rate	Short term	External balance	–	• Binding fixed rate rule
	Medium–long term	External balance		• Adjustable rate subject to 'fundamental disequilibrium'
Exchange controls	Short term	External balance	–	• Restrict short-term capital flows
	Medium–long term	Internal balance		• Regulate and direct capital for growth
Official reserves and IMF facilities	Short term	External balance	–	• Draw on (or augment) as buffer for financing current transactions • Use as indicator of 'fundamental disequilibrium'
Monetary policy	Short term	Internal balance	External balance	• Use anticyclically though support sterilization of exchange market interventions
	Medium–long term	Internal balance	–	• Accommodate fiscal policy
Fiscal policy	Short term	Internal balance	External balance	• Support sterilization of exchange market interventions
	Medium–long term	Internal balance	–	• Maintain aggregate domestic expenditure to achieve full employment
Trade policy	Short term	External balance	Internal balance	• Discriminate against scarce currency countries
	Medium–long term	Internal balance	–	• Liberalize
Investment policy	All	Internal balance	–	• Use IBRD support if necessary; intervene in capital markets to direct growth path

Notes

* In using the shorthand expressions (1) external balance and (2) internal balance we mean respectively:

1 sustainable balance over a defined time period, usually several years, in the external accounts (whereas perfect external balance occurs when a country spends and invests internationally no more than other countries spend and invest in it); and

2 a high, sustainable level of domestic employment and price level stability over a defined time period, usually several years (whereas perfect internal balance occurs at full employment and changes in the general price level are low and constant).

The terms external and internal balance were not used in the 1940s. Instead of balance the BW architects preferred the term stabilization. The terms

disputations over interpreting BW principles and in the disbursement of finance from the IMF. These four functions are all necessary dimensions of any system of international cooperation whether or not concrete policy actions and formal policy coordination are undertaken within that system. In the case of the IBRD the presumption was that world capital markets were in a parlous state in 1944. In addition, capital markets exhibited significant imperfections – for instance they lacked depth and were bedevilled by poor information flows. Therefore the supply of private and government capital needed direction by a central authority. Economic analysis and technical expertise not readily available in private markets at the time were also provided by the IBRD to reduce information problems and supposedly, therefore, to increase the rationality and efficiency with which capital was allocated.

The BW Agreement undoubtedly takes as empirically confirmed the trade-reducing impact of exchange rate *in*stability. Exchange rate stabilization is *the* route to domestic economic stabilization (internal balance). Adjustment to imbalances in the external accounts should take place slowly to minimize effects on output and employment. Some semblance of internal balance is to take precedence over external balance in the short term.

The focal point of the BW Conference was to find a means of central control for the international financial order in place of what the architects possibly perceived as the other extreme – a market-based, automatic mechanism which would somehow spontaneously bring together the mutual interests of various countries. BW denied two related propositions on international finance: first, that deliberately designed blueprints were not feasible and, second, that if a country chose to use domestic policy instruments responsibly according to the dictates of macroeconomic fundamentals, it could then freely join a loose, cooperative international financial arrangement.[25] As Keynes (1943a: 21) so eloquently stated, any international financial plan must:

> reduce to practical shape certain general ideas belonging to the contemporary climate of opinion.... It is difficult to see how any plan can be successful which does not use these general ideas, which are born of the spirit of the age.

The overarching *Zeitgeist* embodied in the BW Agreement endorsed technocratic, scientific management of the international financial order.[26] BW represented supreme faith in conscious, rational design for international finance – precisely what Keynes had been working towards from the early 1920s.[27]

For all the legalese in the BW Articles of Agreement it is striking how much of their original content reads as being open-ended and flexible. For example, moral suasion as much as paternalism seemed to inform the creation and operation of the IMF (Scammell 1975: 122). The 'rules' for balance of payments adjustment and guidelines for domestic economic policy relied heavily on eschewing 'indiscipline' and 'bad-neighbourliness' (to use Keynes's 1943a: 36 felicitous terms). It was as if the BW architects trusted member nations to collaborate and abide by loose rules, suspend short-term political interests, harmonize policies to achieve high growth and full employment and conduct orderly financial behaviour in the international economic realm. In 1944, the impending peace process resonated beyond the contemporary military hostilities into international financial affairs; it carried with it a reservoir of goodwill and optimism.[28] An agreed, fruitful framework for international financial order had been established. It was a new architectural genre compared to the frame of the automatic gold standard pre-1914, the disordered gold exchange standard system and floating exchange rate arrangements in the interwar period. Last, BW produced a variety of hybrid arrangements in the international financial system from 1944 to the 1970s as particular events required adaptations and as interpretations of the original Agreement changed. We turn next to consider a full-blown American Keynesian interpretation.

3 Alvin Hansen's Keynesian interpretation of Bretton Woods

An American Keynesian at Bretton Woods

Much has been written about the arrival of Keynesian economics and its impact on national economic policy in the United States in the 1940s and 1950s (Stein 1969; Jones 1972). By contrast, it is difficult to locate any retrospective assessments on the impact of Keynesian ideas in the United States specifically in connection with American attitudes to *international financial problems* from BW onwards. This chapter considers the work of Alvin Hansen, a Harvard economics professor from 1937 to 1956, well known among contemporaries as the doyen of Keynesianism in the United States in the period under review.[1]

As Paul Samuelson (1976a: 25) concluded, there is 'much that is just' in bestowing on Hansen the title 'the American Keynes'. Hansen's more prominent contributions, hailed by historians of twentieth-century economic thought, turned on the development of domestic compensatory fiscal and monetary policies to ensure internal economic balance. As we shall see below, the latter for Hansen meant reaching and then sustaining full employment and 'reasonable' price stability. In the 1940s and 1950s the original model of the economy introduced by Keynes (1936) seemed quite applicable to the United States with its largely closed economy.[2] However, Hansen was well aware of international economic problems. He appreciated the ongoing forces making for international financial collaboration and integration from the mid-1940s. Hansen strove to use economics as an instrument for achieving international economic stability (Samuelson 1976b: 986).

In 1942 when Keynes was busy drafting parts of a financial plan to be submitted at BW, Hansen made a State Department-sponsored visit to London. One tangible outcome was a memorandum proposing, among other things, establishment of an international economic board to advise on domestic policies to promote full employment, economic stability and trade, and to create an international development corporation with special responsibility for less developed countries (Horsefield 1969a: 13). Reflecting on this material, Roy Harrod (1972: 14) believed that Hansen's

London visit 'helped matters along' in the sense that it indicated American thinking on international financial problems. In the event, continued Harrod, Hansen's memorandum 'was very much in line with [Keynes's ideas] in the *Means to Prosperity*' written some years earlier. Hansen later attended the BW Conference. It is to be regretted, therefore, that his post-BW work on international financial problems has been overlooked; it is, in fact, substantial. Hansen provided a distinctive doctrine for reforming the international financial order as it evolved from 1945 to the late 1960s. His ideas on specific aspects of the international financial system as constituted by the BW Agreement changed on matters of detail as the system altered with events. Nonetheless, his fundamental outlook always remained 'Keynesian' in spirit insofar as international policy proposals were seamlessly interweaved into his favoured policy mix for national macroeconomic management. Before proceeding to outline specific elements in Hansen's 'Keynesian' doctrine, it is important to identify persistent themes in typical Keynesian perspectives on international economic stability (or instability) in the 1940s and 1950s.

In the *General Theory* Keynes exhorted nations 'to provide themselves with full employment by their *domestic* policy' (1936: 382–3, emphasis added). In this view, the policy sequence is critical: once full employment is achieved, then external policy could be designed less in an isolationist manner as a 'desperate expedient' to shore up advantage at home, and more as a long-term strategy to create an environment which encouraged multilateral trade where considerations of 'mutual advantage' are paramount. As Keynes (1946: 186) remarked in an article published posthumously, the 'great virtue' of the BW Agreement is that it allows the use of 'necessary expedients', yet promotes a 'wholesome long-run doctrine' based on formal rules. The route Keynes envisaged to achieve international financial stability was paved by a vision of strong Anglo-American cooperation supported by a formal architecture such as the BW Agreement. The automatic play of free market forces in the international realm was subsequently rejected by all Keynesians because, along with Keynes, they held that the world market was subjected to 'violent and seemingly uncontrollable fluctuations' (Hansen 1953: 226). Keynesians believed that while employment depended on the level of aggregate demand, there was no automatic mechanism to keep aggregate domestic expenditure near its full employment level – deliberate government action was therefore required. Equally, they believed, the international economy did not possess an automatic mechanism which would achieve and sustain full employment – deliberate intergovernmental action and cooperation were required.

Following Keynes, Hansen and other Keynesians wished to reconstruct international financial arrangements so that they did not unduly rely on the impersonal, automatic forces of an international gold standard. Uppermost in Hansen's mind were the perceived failings of gold standards which relied on inflation in surplus countries and deflation in deficit countries to secure international payments adjustment. This adjustment mechanism jeopardized the maintenance of employment. Matters were made worse when nominal domestic prices including wages were slow to adjust or extensively administered (as indeed they were in the 1940s). Under a gold standard the adjustment process could therefore be very long drawn out (Hansen 1944c: 29). A rigid exchange rate under a gold standard was also rejected since it entailed the 'absurd procedure of compelling a country to adjust the entire price and income structure to that rate' (Hansen 1945a: 50). In addition, Hansen's attitude to a gold standard of any kind is clearly indicated pre-BW in his book *Full Recovery or Stagnation?* (1938: 216):

> It will not do for nations simply to reach an agreement on gold parities and then retire, each to its separate national domain, leaving the international monetary system to run its course. The automatic gold standard may be likened to a loose federation of nations in which each country agrees unconditionally to remain pacifist at all costs, regardless of acts of monetary aggression perpetrated by other countries. But monetary pacifism is perhaps almost as unrealistic in the current financial world as sentimental pacifism is in the current political world.

The alternative Keynesian course lies along a path involving extensive international cooperation with exchange rate stabilization deliberately managed by policymakers. Indeed, a genuinely international financial system which operates as a counterpart to national managed paper currencies must presuppose 'the existence of well-established international regulations' and these were definitely not in evidence in 1938 (Hansen 1938: 218–19, 234).

Another hallmark of typical Keynesian approaches attempting to include considerations of international economic stability related to the manner in which reforms of the international financial environment should be managed. At the level of national economic policy, Keynesians insisted on discretionary policy activism without too many constraints on policymakers save that full employment ought to have top ranking in the list of policy objectives. The only salient constraint on activist policymakers would therefore be the minimization of the employment effects of any policy choice or policy change. In the international realm not only would international cooperation among national governments aimed at elevating the full employment objective be desirable, prescriptive rules or guidelines should also be agreed upon and formally established. At the very least, 'the essential foundation upon which the international security of the future must be built is an economic order *so managed and controlled* that it will be capable of sustaining full employment ... as world productivity will permit' (Hansen and Kindleberger 1942: 409, emphasis added). In the 1940s and 1950s one could speculate that a more rabid Keynesian would happily sign up to a system of strong activist economic policy coordination between nations dedicated to mutually expansionary policies which achieved a sustained, high level of employment internationally.

Clarifying the BW exchange rate principle

As we saw in Chapter 2, the BW exchange rate principle was ambiguous because it relied on the non-operationalized criterion of a 'fundamental disequilibrium' in the current account of a nation's balance of payments. While Hansen endorsed the general BW principle as the best means of establishing exchange rate stability it all seemed too simplistic: the 'BW charter employs the phrase fundamental disequilibrium. This was the easy way out. Any effort to define the term clearly and unequivocally would have led to endless controversy' (Hansen 1965: 170). In 1944 he produced a modestly titled note seeking to clarify the conditions under which the BW fixed, adjustable exchange rate rule should operate in practice.[3] Concentrating on the deficit country case he raised a vital issue: what if the deficit, no matter how persistent, is not a reflection of an incorrectly set exchange rate? Historical evidence is brought to account, illustrating that deflationary conditions – falling prices, wages, incomes and employment – could produce an ongoing deficit. Moreover, the benefits of currency devaluation may be questionable in such conditions if the price elasticity of both demand for a nation's exports and demand for foreign imports are not favourable.[4] In Hansen's estimation, if a country is experiencing 'continuous and strong price deflationary influences from the outside world ... the country's exchange rate is out of line and should be adjusted. This is a case of fundamental disequilibrium'. However, strong deflation may not necessarily be associated with a current account deficit simply because domestic incomes have been deflated to the point where the demand for imports has declined considerably. Contrariwise, a persistent current account deficit may not be a sufficient condition for exchange rate adjustment. Market losses owing to depression among a country's trading partners may be responsible. And major trading partners may be experiencing severe economic readjustments due to secular factors such as changes in demand patterns or technological change. In those countries, various long-run 'developmental processes' including structural adjustment policies should be implemented rather than relying on the 'weak reed' of exchange rate changes (Hansen 1944a: 183).

Hansen's central point is that however interpreted in practice, the BW exchange rate rule carried a clear set of implications:

> No nation will be required to correct an international imbalance by means of deflation of income, employment, and prices, and no nation will be denied a readjustment of the foreign exchange value of its currency, even though the fundamental disequilibrium to be corrected

> has been caused by domestic policies. No country will be required to force its domestic price, wage, and income structure into line with the existing exchange rate.
>
> (1949: 210)

As we argued in Chapter 2, the BW Agreement did not say much about the domestic policy mix consistent with its exchange rate rule. Hansen's exoneration of the domestic policy mix adopted in the past, even though it may have been the primary cause of a 'fundamental disequilibrium', is, on the face of the matter, rather peculiar. He needed to offer a new policy mix which would avoid revisiting a fundamental disequilibrium *after* an exchange rate adjustment. In fact, this is precisely what Hansen attempted to articulate in extensive work on monetary and fiscal policy up to the mid-1960s. He was aware that attributing the *cause* of fundamental imbalances in a nation's external accounts to national monetary and fiscal policies, instead of external shocks, was a quite different matter. Yet the magnitude of any exchange rate change may have to be greater in the latter. As we shall see below, changes in monetary and fiscal policies in collaboration with other countries, perhaps through the IMF, may contribute to reducing the size of an exchange rate adjustment. Exchange rate realignments must not, according to Hansen, be the prime instrument of an expansionary policy aimed at generating output growth sufficient to sustain full employment.

Hansen's scepticism towards exchange rate changes in the BW financial order continued through to the 1960s. It is notable that his attitude accorded with actual country practice. Exchange rate adjustments or their absence following the BW rule left much to be desired, not least because none of the BW architects anticipated the enormous amount of time IMF officials would spend persuading reluctant member countries to devalue. In practice, the BW financial order 'became a virtual fixed exchange-rate system' (Krueger 1998: 1985). The general tenor of the BW exchange rate rule amounted in practice to placing a rigid barrier against exchange rate changes except in special circumstances. Reluctance to alter exchange rates, and especially to devalue when experiencing persistent current account deficits, was understandable in Hansen's mind because the accumulated evidence in favour of such a major operation was usually insufficient. In particular, doubts may emerge over:

1 programmes of economic policy pursued in some countries which made policymakers uncertain as to the status of current account deficits (e.g. fundamental, temporary or cyclical?);
2 a country's wage structure, especially the 'productivity–wage ratio' which may have become misaligned, though this problem could have direct remedies other than exchange rate changes;
3 monetary and fiscal policies which may not be finely tuned to enable

an economy to produce at full capacity so that national average costs of production may be higher than necessary (that is, higher than would be the case if industries were producing at a level consistent with minimum efficient scale given existing technology); and
4 industry-specific technological developments and trends in product differentiation which may be lagging in the country in question.[5]

Hansen agreed with critics of the BW Agreement who had questioned the lack of symmetry in the balance of payments adjustment process in which surplus countries seemed to avoid sharing some of the burden. For Hansen (1965: 177–8) the 'Bretton Woods Agreement ... might advisedly have chosen to resist devaluation in the case of advanced industrial countries'. Instead it could have explicitly set down various methods of adjustment including active foreign investment of surpluses, encouragement to open the surplus nations' markets to imports, some degree of reflation through more expansionary policies and exchange rate appreciation. Hansen agreed with Keynes (even though Keynes's position probably reflected weaknesses in the balance of payments of the United Kingdom in the 1940s): surplus countries should always lead by generating full employment at home, invest actively in countries requiring resources for expansion and higher employment and, if necessary, grant deficit countries greater competitiveness by revaluing the exchange rate. He held trenchantly that 'no firm foundation for international stability can be laid upon any basis except that of *internal* stability in the various countries' cooperating in the BW financial order (Hansen 1945a: 82, ephasis added). In this view, full employment in major industrial nations will lead to exchange rate stability. Mutual determination of full employment and exchange rate stability does not seem to have been entertained. It was essential to promote a 'direct attack upon the problem of full employment and parallel programs of economic stability in the leading countries, and not [a policy] of juggling the foreign exchange rate' (Hansen 1944a: 183).[6]

Hansen never gave up on the idea that exchange rates 'must be adjusted so as to promote and sustain ... domestic ends', namely internal balance, though initially he insisted on irregular, last-resort, orderly and significant exchange rate changes in an agreed international framework. This attitude accorded with the managed exchange rate policy agreed at BW (Hansen 1945a: 52).[7] By the 1960s the pressure increased on countries to demand additional foreign exchange reserves and borrowing facilities to finance temporary international payments imbalances. The BW fixed exchange rate regime created what were then termed 'liquidity' pressures. Countries experiencing deficits became less able to finance them; on the margin this trend thwarted gradual implementation of domestic policies required to correct deficits. In the conditions described above, Hansen prescribed greater exchange rate flexibility than the early BW principle permitted. Such flexibility would, he thought, ease pressure on domestic policies in the short term. Discontinuous exchange rate changes sanctioned by original BW principles 'should be replaced by something better' (Hansen 1964b: 686, 1965: 181). Along with twenty-six other prominent economists he signed a statement in 1965 advocating two proposals to increase exchange rate flexibility.[8] The bounds specified for 'flexibility' were quite narrow. The proposal was agreed to by economists of varying persuasion; indeed it would have been difficult to imagine Hansen concurring in any other scheme which also included Milton Friedman as a signatory. Two modifications to the BW exchange rate rule were urged:

1. a 'minimum band': widen the limits within which countries were required to keep the gold value (or US dollar value) of their currencies so that they might freely vary the range by up to 4 or 5 per cent either side of parity; and
2. 'shiftable parity': allow countries unilaterally to change the par value of their currencies by no more than 1 or 2 per cent of the previous year's par value.[9]

Notwithstanding this concern to increase exchange rate flexibility, the institutional machinery required for a Hansen-style managed international financial system still had to be comprehensive. Permitting free market processes to 'stabilize' exchange rates was, in this view, a contradiction in terms. Detailed international agreements and large pools of international finance were needed to hold exchange rates within specified bounds. Careful planning was essential. This made room for international financial experts and officials of international financial institutions. Spontaneous or organic developments in international finance were to be neither trusted nor permitted.

In time, Hansen predicted that reserve holdings in all countries would 'dispense altogether with gold' (1964b: 686). In a period during the early 1960s when an array of new schemes for international financial reform were being propounded, Hansen weighed in with his own 'modest' suggestions for modifying BW liquidity arrangements. First there is his conviction that there 'is no need to dismantle existing structures' (Hansen 1965: 109). However, joint international action, preferably through the Group of Ten leading western industrial nations, should be prosecuted to deal with emerging liquidity shortages. IMF member countries needed sufficient liquidity to deal with payments imbalances. Hansen formulated a simple rule: countries must agree to hold no more than 60 per cent of their aggregate official reserves in gold. Furthermore, they should hold the balance in reserve currencies of various kinds as their situation (e.g. trading needs) determined.[10] Countries exceeding the 60 per cent ratio must agree to reduce their gold holdings over time in return for currency reserves. Reserves would be accumulated on a country's own account. Lack of confidence in currency reserve media could be allayed by the creation of an international currency unit or 'international dollar', measured as an official composite and 'based on the financial security of the ten leading industrial countries' (Hansen 1965: 112). The IMF would have officially to anoint such a unit or dollar. In creating a new 'International Reserve System' the IMF would allow holders of reserve currencies to deposit their foreign currency balances in exchange for the new international unit or dollar. The international unit would need to carry a 'gold-value guarantee', earn interest (unlike gold), be freed from the risk of devaluation and be usable for trade and foreign investment. The IMF would be able to invest the foreign currency balances in interest-bearing government securities in the United States or United Kingdom. In other words, the IMF would monetize the long-term government securities it purchased into new international financial units but it would not, strictly stated, have a credit-creating function.[11] Overall, in Hansen's reasoning, national monetary systems were able to dispense with dependence on gold and in the United States the 'creation of Federal Reserve credit' had become the 'modern alchemy'. In time the international financial order might create a managed international currency unit which could free the world from dependence on gold; that unit could augment and channel the supply of liquidity in a rational manner. Once such a process had begun Hansen was open-minded about the possibility of these developments ultimately leading to managed, more flexible exchange rates still within the BW architecture and perhaps to a full-fledged credit-creating function for the IMF.

In his last substantive remarks on the subject at a conference on the economics of international adjustment in 1969, Hansen continued to adapt his architectural suggestions to the environment as then prevailing. That environment was characterized by heavy accumulation of US dollars in the reserves of foreign monetary authorities; it gave birth to a new suggestion for a US dollar standard, perhaps, though not necessarily, as a transitional step towards creating a genuine international currency unit. He urged the US Treasury to invite foreign monetary authorities to present, as required, US dollars in return for gold. This policy, if pursued to its limit, would exhaust the United States' gold reserve after which it could introduce an officially managed, 'flexible' exchange rate – with US monetary authorities buying and selling foreign exchange to stabilize the US dollar over the medium to long term (Hansen 1971). Whether or not foreign monetary authorities would covet all the world's monetary gold – a non-income-bearing asset after all – was debatable. Hansen was asking the United States to call the gold bluff on the rest of the world while holding out a clear, come-what-may defensible alternative for managing the US dollar.

What place did exchange controls have in Hansen's doctrine? Ordered exchange rate management on a global basis had the task of establishing 'currencies [which] represent *true* values in goods, services and assets' between countries (Hansen 1964b: 687, his emphasis). Given his original preference for large, exceptional exchange rate realignments and accepting a slight shift in his views during the 1960s, exchange controls played a central role in maintaining 'true' international currency values. The latter were disturbed by speculative capital movements. Like Keynes, Hansen possessed a favourable view of exchange controls, depending on country circumstances. As a separate instrument of economic policy, exchange controls did not figure in Hansen's survey of the full range of policies available to US policymakers wanting to achieve 'stability and expansion' from 1945 (Hansen 1945b). What this apparent omission means, however, is that exchange controls were in fact an integral part of Hansen's idea of 'an exchange rate policy' and the rule for using that instrument as set out in the BW Agreement.

The controls Hansen had in mind consisted in government regulations placing quantitative limits on external asset and liability transactions of domestic residents. Controls on capital outflows from residents protected the level of investment in the domestic economy. The IMF's Articles of Agreement risked taking a minimalist view of exchange controls; it did not account for country-specific contextual problems.[12] It was all very well in theory to permit controls over capital movements provided they did not mask the long-term trend in current account transactions, or unduly delay the settlement of international payments and contracts. As well, Hansen illustrated why full, free convertibility for current transactions needed to be controlled, despite idealistic strictures embedded in BW principles (and IMF Articles). For instance, countries with a high propensity to import consumer goods needed to bring this under control with carefully structured controls on current account transactions. Less developed countries with scarce savings and severe foreign exchange constraints were also candidates for the use of exchange controls; they had limited scope for conducting international exchange. Hansen understood the potential downside for implementing exchange controls in these cases but the benefits outweighed the costs. The costs were small in the 1940s and 1950s because these countries were not easily able to attract foreign capital; they had underdeveloped capital markets and relied on World Bank finance, other international financial institutions and intergovernmental finance for their economic development needs. Exchange controls at certain stages of a country's development should be regarded as not only legitimate; they were virtually necessary in Hansen's view 'in order to promote world prosperity and international equilibrium'. Furthermore, primary-producing countries at more advanced stages of economic development and needing to advance towards a more industrialized stage might make good use of exchange controls. Capital was scarce and world capital markets were very imperfect. Before being fully absorbed into the circle of fully industrialized nations involved in freer multilateral exchange, the primary producers could use exchange control 'as a useful incubator in the process of growth and development' (Hansen 1945a: 185, 186). Major supply-side shocks, such as drought and crop failure, and demand-side depression caused sudden changes in markets for primary produce and agricultural raw materials. Such shocks did not justify drastic exchange rate adjustments. Exchange controls were, however, useful in these instances. In Hansen's doctrine, exchange rate changes were emphatically not an instrument either for dealing with a short-lived economic shock or for actively promoting economic development. Yet exchange rate management could not usually do without the support in practice (or as a potential threat) of exchange controls in some form.

Promoting international economic stability through monetary and fiscal policies

Hansen's *Monetary Theory and Fiscal Policy* (1949) contains all the necessary tools for those working as practitioners in the Keynesian tradition and wishing to create internal economic balance in the international financial order established by the BW Agreement. Discretionary, activist monetary and fiscal policy at the national level is combined with a presumption of strong activist policy coordination internationally. Accordingly, countries could adopt parallel policies designed to ensure full employment, growth and exchange rate stability.[13] The necessary scope of international collaboration, consultation and eventual policy coordination is significant in Hansen's doctrine even though he appears to understate difficulties in implementation (practical, administrative and political).

Hansen pressed for monetary and fiscal action vigorously led by the United States. Such American-led action would not only effect the immediate task of postwar reconstruction, it would thereafter provide sound foundations for the international financial order. A 'desirable' order was one in which full employment was sustained.[14] Indeed, 'world prosperity and world stability depend in no small measure upon . . . the achievement of full employment in the United States' (Hansen 1945a: 8). The United States must support the formation and ongoing operation of the IMF and IBRD.

Typically, vulgarized versions of Keynesianism turned on equating fiscal policy with deficit financing and defining an expansionist programme as one which involves long-run deficit financing. By contrast, Hansen held that an increase in government expenditure will tend to increase national income over time whatever the method of financing, though the degree of impact on national income would differ depending on the method used (1945c, 1949: 167). According to Hansen's four scenarios, (i) when government expenditure is financed by borrowing from the banking system the money supply increases; (ii) if borrowing from the public is used exclusively, deposits in the banking system will be spent, drawing on what might otherwise have remained as idle hoards of liquidity; (iii) if a progressive tax system is used to finance the increase in government expenditure, savings of the higher income groups are reduced, and private consumption may fall; and (iv) if financing uses a more regressive tax option (such as consumption tax), national income may expand from the effects of an increase in government expenditure though not by a very significant amount. At the national level Hansen appreciated complexities in the application of the basic Keynesian idea that an increase in government expenditure can increase national income. He inquired into the conditions under which such an increase financed by (ii), (iii) and (iv) above does *not* raise aggregate demand and thence national income and employment.

As far as monetary policy is concerned, Hansen was interested in the effectiveness of monetary management in the pure case where the independent use of monetary policy (not directly linked to government or private expenditure on goods and services) could raise national income. He delineates three stylized cases, all utilizing the pivotal Keynesian idea of 'liquidity preference'.[15]

Case A

In a less developed country, rich in unexploited natural resources and therefore with many investment opportunities, residents' existing liquidity preference is completely unresponsive to interest rates so that as the money supply increases and interest rates fall, the demand for active investment finance increases in a very responsive manner. The final outcome (which also includes an increase in consumption) is fully effective in raising national income. In such a case fiscal policy in the form of additional government expenditure or income-generating government investment outlays is not required.

Case B

Residents of a more developed industrialized economy possess a liquidity preference that is partially responsive to interest rates. Here, if an easier monetary policy is operated independently of fiscal policy, it will be partially effective in raising private demand for investment finance as interest rates fall, so that there is a positive effect on national income (but not as strong as in Case A).

Case C

In this highly developed industrialized economy there is a 'temporary saturation of investment opportunities following a pronounced upsurge in investment'. Residents' liquidity preference is completely interest responsive and the demand for private investment finance is completely insensitive to the money rate of interest. Here monetary policy is ineffective in raising national income.

Overall, monetary policy alone, unsupported by fiscal policy, would only be fully effective in Case A. In the other two cases, monetary and fiscal policy 'are both needed to reinforce each other'. In particular, monetary policy will at least need to accommodate fiscal policy changes in Cases B and C.

In the more normally observed Cases B and C, cyclical movements in national income should activate a 'managed compensatory' programme of fiscal policy supported by monetary policy; otherwise national economies could fall into periodic depressions and perhaps even long-run economic stagnation. Built into such a programme must be an allowance for government activity though not merely as an ad hoc anticyclical force. Long-term government investment projects having the capacity to be 'highly flexible and subject to quick adjustment and change' must be implemented in such areas as housing, health care, education and infrastructural works (Hansen 1945d: 410, 1949: 180–1). A really effective, managed compensatory programme should rely on a flexible tax system to permit timely financing of government expenditure initiatives.[16] All this by the late 1940s was still a counsel of perfection. In Hansen's mind the principles were laudable. In practice, however, the implementation of Keynesian activist policies had been found wanting. As he admitted, 'we have not learned how to make government an effective, flexible and responsive instrument in a fluctuating and highly complex society' (Hansen 1949: 183).

Monetary policy has limited effectiveness in most situations and is in fact usually subordinated to fiscal policy or recruited into the role of supporter of fiscal activism. An adequate money supply is regarded as 'a *necessary*, but *not a sufficient* condition, for economic expansion' in most cases (Hansen 1949: 198, his emphasis). Full employment is the ultimate objective and is assumed to be a condition arising 'at a substantially stable price level'; it is an objective which can be achieved by activist fiscal policy appropriately financed. Hansen's *obiter dicta* on the means of achieving price level objectives are always framed in terms of preventing 'both inflation and deflation' and ensuring 'substantial stability in the cost of living price index' (Hansen 1946: 72–4). Furthermore, it is the prime responsibility of fiscal policy to pursue full employment with the price level objective in mind. Monetary discipline is not considered in isolation as a means of tackling a single price level objective. In the stylized cases presented earlier, any given fiscal policy setting implies a definite monetary policy stance and the analytical objective is to determine the impact on national income and employment, *not* the price level.

How would Hansen's monetary and fiscal policy activism be carried over to the international realm? The difficulties of implementing his programme at the national level had already seemed almost insurmountable in the late 1940s. Hansen's later work, drawing on successful experience with Keynesian policies during the 1950s and early 1960s, became more optimistic. International stability and full employment run into potential incompatibilities when they are expected to coexist with 'uncontrolled gaps ... in the international accounts' (Hansen 1949: 202).[17] 'Gaps' cannot be sustained over the long term, though over a business cycle use of foreign exchange reserves can support the national full employment objective (assuming the exchange rate remained fixed).

The preferred Hansen mix of monetary and fiscal policy promoting both full employment and external balance (in international payments) runs as follows. Assign monetary policy to the balance of payments and fiscal policy to full employment at the national level. Monetary policy has a secondary assignment – to accommodate fiscal policy. Potential conflicts in the use of monetary policy in this dual role are ignored. Deficit countries experiencing high unemployment should push up interest rates through monetary policy to prevent capital outflows and, if necessary, use exchange controls to reduce the pressure on monetary policy. Fiscal policy ought to be expansionary to achieve the full employment objective, provided it is not financed in a manner that defeats the monetary policy stance. Surplus countries must expand their monetary policy, thereby reducing interest rates and encouraging capital outflows (attracted by relatively higher interest rates elsewhere). In addition, exchange controls should be eased (where they have been applied previously) and fiscal policy should become more restrictive to damp unsustainably high levels of economic activity. Finally there is a place for trade policy. Hansen favoured a liberal trade policy precisely in the set of circumstances presented by surplus countries. Trade policy changes can correct surpluses. Liberalization of commercial or tariff policy regimes should proceed apace in countries experiencing persistent surpluses in their international accounts. Trade policy liberalization in other circumstances is not normally feasible because the employment objective is negatively affected.[18]

The assignment of policies described in the foregoing paragraph sounds 'so easy', in fact 'too easy'. Other policy instruments should be considered. For example, an interest equalization tax on domestic residents' purchases of foreign assets may be designed to reduce the upward pressure on interest rates used to prevent capital outflows. Another subsidiary instrument of monetary policy might be one that drives a wedge between short- and long-term interest rates – official selling of short-dated government bonds and buying back long-term bonds. Then, raising 'the short-term rates help[s] to keep short-term money at home, which helps the payments balance; lowering the long-term rate helps employment' (Hansen 1965: 161, 162).

Broadly characterized, Hansen's doctrine maintains that international payments imbalances should not damage the national goal of full employment; the problem of price level stability must be kept in mind. An identifiable trend to inflate at a faster rate than other countries must eventually destabilize the exchange rate. Therefore:

> Reasonable price stability is a goal that any responsible modern society must seek quite apart from any balance-of-payments problem.

> The international restraint is not a necessary condition. The external roadblock to full employment is an evil that must be removed. *Once* it is removed there will still remain plenty of good reasons why the goal of reasonable price stability should be pursued.
>
> (Hansen 1965: 166)

In short, the immediate threat of inflation is minimized. Note that Hansen's doctrine depends crucially on the nature of exchange rate arrangements (fixed-adjustable rate in BW style); it also relies on ad hoc exchange controls on international capital flows. Monetary and fiscal policy on their own would not generally be effective in preserving full employment and external balance. For international harmonization of the long-term, sustainable full employment outcome there is no escaping the need for international economic agreements or treaties. The key industrial countries are expected to agree on the same broad economic policy objectives – achieving internal balance, reducing cyclical fluctuations in national income and reaching full employment (Hansen 1949: 210–11).

Hansen proposed an International Economic Board to coordinate fiscal policy between countries; it would act as an inter-country advisory and monitoring agency and 'seek to induce . . . coordination of internal policies of the various governments designed to maintain high levels of employment' (Hansen 1944b: 254). The Board would advise on the timing of simultaneous expansionist policies among countries while monitoring 'inflationary tendencies'. Countries would be urged to 'keep in step' and avoid precipitate action leading to sharp fluctuations in national income and employment. The idea of an internationally coordinated fiscal policy is something Hansen was optimistic about, given the successful coordination of tax and expenditure policy in the United States' federal system (Hansen and Perloff 1944). In the international realm there seemed to be no enforcement mechanism to encourage fiscal policy coordination except the fear of deflation. Hansen recognized some tacit pressure to conform emanated from World Bank and IMF lending policies. In the case of monetary policy, *independent* monetary management designed to support the Hansen programme for economic stability and full employment 'offers no assurance that equilibrium will be achieved in the balance of payments'. Again countries are urged to keep their monetary policies 'in step' with one another, since independent action threatens to 'greatly intensify' balance of payments problems (Hansen 1949: 210). Once more, enforcement procedures do not appear to have been seriously considered, perhaps because Hansen's perspective on the existing international financial order was that the mere act of signing the BW Agreement was sufficient. Finally, and this factor should not be underestimated, goal congruence between nations, especially commitment to full employment, is a crucial element ensuring policy 'self discipline' (Hansen 1944c: 28–9, 1964a: 79).

International action to combat secular stagnation and underdevelopment

Output and employment depend on the national level of expenditure – this was one of the starting propositions of any Keynesian approach from 1944 to 1971, including Hansen's. Viewed by taking a global panorama, the sources of expenditure for growth, including capital supplies, were exceedingly scarce in some countries; in others financial capital remained misdirected or unallocated (in idle hoards) while economies spiralled into depression and sometimes into secular stagnation.

Full Recovery or Stagnation? (Hansen 1938) emphasizes structural change inherent in the development of mature capitalist economies. This work identifies three key trends.

1 The rate of population growth is slowing in advanced, mature capitalist economies.
2 Investment outlets will be exhausted in these capitalist economies while the savings rate will increase.
3 Underlying trends 1 and 2 above is technological change, the rate of which is declining in mature economies.

Now technological change poses a threat: when its rate diverges in different national economies at different stages of development, it 'becomes a highly important [factor] from the standpoint of international stability'. For example, if 'one important country makes more rapid technological progress than is made in competing countries, the international cost structure may be thrown out of balance' (Hansen 1938: 216).[19] The three trends identified could create persistent policy difficulties; they imply deficient aggregate demand irrespective of the stage of a normal business cycle. Hansen believed that there was another and greater 'swing' underlying normal business cycles. Some sectors of mature economies did not experience recovery from the depression of the early 1930s. Indeed, capital formation collapsed in some industries and did not recover.[20]

Expansionary fiscal policies must be designed to counter secular changes which threaten to entrench a trend towards long-run economic stagnation. Accordingly, certain government expenditures must be undertaken for their own sake to revive and maintain particular industries and not just provide an employment stimulus to counter temporary cyclical recessions. This aspect of Hansen's fiscal programme was growth promoting and developmental rather than compensatory. Minimum rates of economic development must be assured by ongoing government expenditure initiatives. Some contemporary commentators were concerned that Hansen's fiscal programme did not fully consider the limits of public debt which could be reached when fiscal policies went beyond the compensatory function and tried to counter secular stagnation (Chamberlain

1945). Hansen was supremely optimistic that fiscal policy could be designed to guarantee a rising national income. There would always be *some* continuing technological change and productivity improvements along the way. As one editorial comment on the Hansen debate with Chamberlain summarized the outcome:

> Hansen assumes that savings at full employment will always be a constant proportion of income because of upward shifts in the consumption schedule. At worst, therefore, if private investment opportunities were zero, government deficits would have to grow in geometric ratio along with the compound interest rate of growth of income. And it turns out that the debt would also grow at the same compound rate of interest – leaving the ratio of debt to income unchanged. This is precisely what Hansen has always meant.
>
> (In Chamberlain 1945: 406)

What does the secular stagnation idea mean for policy in the international economic order? First, the wise use of fiscal policy and allocation of scarce capital to achieve economic growth in the mature industrialized economies is predicated on recognizing secular trends and not being blinded by short-run aggregate demand problems. Nevertheless, neglect of the latter can result in 'continual maintenance of semistagnation' (Hansen 1964b: 675). Long-term economic stagnation is then invited. Contrary to his view expressed in 1938, it was no longer enough to rely on exchange rate changes to correct 'fundamental disparate [secular] trends in national economies too deep-seated to be removed by internal adjustments' (Hansen 1938: 219). For the exchange rate instrument was too weak and unreliable; it depended solely on relative price changes to effect adjustment when the real causes of stagnation and underdevelopment required enlightened government expenditure responses. And for reasons already stated, Hansen was opposed to using the exchange rate to promote economic development.

The managed allocation of capital in a world of imperfect capital markets was an essential purpose of international collaborative arrangements. Foundational international agreements creating special capital management institutions of the type which established the IBRD (later the World Bank, WB) were preferred. Such institutions promised active response to underdevelopment and the threat of stagnation arising from structural changes rather than ordinary cyclical phenomena. Before the BW Agreement Hansen proposed the creation of an 'International Development and Investment Bank' (along similar lines to the IBRD). Hansen's bank would offer comprehensive loans or partial loans in partnership with participants in world capital markets or guarantee loans made through those markets. Capital for the bank would be raised by bond issues and capital provided by member governments.[21]

Stagnation in the more mature industrial economies is prevented by providing an easy conduit for the transference of capital to less developed economies where investment opportunities are significant and where planned industrialization is under way. Creating an international institution such as the IBRD was a perfect foil for stagnation; it would, for example, promote a 'high sense of international responsibility and international goodwill ... Americans looking for outlets for their savings will find here a high-grade gold-edge security. American exporters will benefit through enlarged exports ... to the borrowing countries' (Hansen 1945b: 264).

For Hansen, the IBRD was satisfactorily constituted on economic grounds; it would be an underwriting institution. Private capital markets and member governments would provide capital through bond issues, and members would underwrite risk up to the extent of their founding subscriptions.[22] The rationale for an international development bank such as the IBRD arose from the fact that capital markets have insufficient depth and are liquidity constrained, particularly when it comes to funding large development projects with long-term horizons from inception to completion. As well, many public infrastructural projects have indirect benefits to society that are difficult to price in private capital markets (or alternatively, in modern language, it is difficult for the projects' financiers to completely internalize all the benefits). Moreover, the large, positive, indirect spillover effects of these projects in the economy as a whole mean that governments through international governmental cooperation, and development banks, must support directly the allocation of capital (Hansen 1944b: 252–3, 1945a: 46–7). Uncertainties in imperfect capital markets which create high transaction costs and moral hazard can be reduced by international financial institutions such as the IBRD.[23] The IBRD created rules to encourage high standards of conduct and contract adherence. The impression of international financial imperialism was also reduced by the creation of the IBRD which from its inception enjoyed wide international membership. Hansen concluded that it was therefore not so easy to charge 'that the United States is playing Uncle Shylock' (1945b: 264).

A summary is now in order. The creation of international financial institutions is an essential prerequisite for setting an international lending policy, given existing capital market imperfections. Such institutions embody a principle of active cooperation between member countries to:

1 fund contracyclical projects supportive of the existing exchange rate structure, the long-term state of the current account of the balance of payments, and economic expansion;
2 augment the supply of capital for economic development per se; and
3 provide outlets for capital to thwart stagnationist tendencies in the industrially mature economies and countries experiencing persistent bouts of economic depression without signs of long-term recovery.

Finally, in a world with extensive controls on capital movements, formal intergovernmental collaboration to allocate capital acts as a positive counterbalancing force in permitting a managed, presumably more rational allocation on an international basis.[24]

Conclusion

Hansen's doctrine on the international financial order evolved with events over the twenty-year period from 1945 to 1965. Notwithstanding preferred changes in institutional detail, the core architectural framework he constructed in the mid-1960s did not change fundamentally. His minor proposals for reforming the international order did not constitute a sharp break from the BW tradition. He always hankered after 'a truly managed international currency' which ultimately jettisoned dependence on gold and relied on a centralized approach to international monetary management (Hansen 1965: 60). By contrast with BW, he favoured more regulation of international payments rather than less; was more sympathetic to the idea of a full-fledged, credit-creating international bank of the type originally contained in Keynes (1943a) and he adopted a less liberal position on trade policy issues, believing that the stage of a nation's economic development often justified greater protectionism. Table 3.1 outlines Hansen's assignment rules for the main policy instruments.

Underlying all Hansen's work on the international financial order is strong faith in the international coordination of policies in which full employment enjoyed first importance. While he did not use the words 'policy coordination', the idea is clearly implied by the plea for national policies to 'keep in step'. Complete coordination on policies designed to achieve full employment does not imply a conviction favouring a high level of policy coordination around achieving price stability. Yet when price level changes, for whatever reason, persistently diverge between countries, exchange rate adjustment may be required, though Hansen was wary of recommending exchange rate realignments of any great magnitude. His initial support for BW principles gave way to the realization that the BW exchange rate system did not function smoothly: adjustment to 'fundamental' payments imbalances depended more on sudden, potentially destabilizing changes of mind on the part of policymakers intent on making a major exchange rate adjustment. Inherent difficulties in making exchange rate adjustments were often in fact destructive of international stability.

In the meantime, while policymakers were contemplating exchange rate adjustments, monetary policy could not remain idle. Monetary policy had the task of not permitting large imbalances (e.g. deficits) in international payments to develop and then impact on the money supply and adversely affect output and employment. In Hansen's doctrine, monetary policy had to be assigned primarily to supporting the exchange rate (e.g. by limiting

Policy instrument	Time horizon	Primary assignment	Secondary assignment	Rules
Exchange rate	All	External balance	–	• Originally fixed rate • Later marginal flexibility subject to minimum band and shiftable parity rules
Exchange controls	Short term Medium–long term	External balance Internal balance	– –	• Control speculative capital • Actively adjust: tighten in deficit countries, ease in surplus countries • Preserve capital in less developed countries
Official reserves	Short term Medium–long term	Internal balance External balance	External balance –	• Support full employment policies • Draw on (or augment) for current transactions • Managed, 'flexible' US dollar • Create new international currency unit • Dispense with gold
Monetary policy	All	External balance	Internal balance	• Active interest rate policies to support official exchange reserves/ exchange market interventions • Accommodate fiscal policy with subsidiary monetary instruments
Fiscal policy	All	Internal balance	–	• Maintain aggregate domestic expenditure to achieve full employment • Activist policy adjustment depending on stage of cycle • Activist policy to avoid secular stagnation
Trade policy	Short term Medium–long term	Internal balance External balance	– –	• Maintain to preserve employment • Use as instrument to save foreign exchange in developing countries • Liberalize to reduce surpluses elsewhere
Investment policy	All	Internal balance	–	• Promote IBRD to manage capital allocation and growth • Use to avoid secular stagnation

excess drains on foreign currency reserves in the case of a deficit country). The obvious policy dilemma in Hansen's allocation of assignment rules is not squarely faced: monetary policy has two potentially conflicting assignments, especially if a payments imbalance is allowed to grow out of control perhaps partly because monetary policy must also to some extent accommodate fiscal policy. The latter must be consistent with the monetary policy stance, otherwise conflicts of policy objectives will inevitably arise. The matter is made worse given the prevalence of fixed, administered prices and wages, so that domestic economic adjustment to lingering payments imbalances in a fixed exchange rate regime could be painfully slow. Hansen realized most clearly in the 1960s that sole reliance on monetary and fiscal policy would not normally allow countries to achieve internal and external balance simultaneously or even over a reasonable period of time. Significant foreign reserve movements encouraged speculators. That is why Hansen supported the use of exchange controls to supplement other policy instruments. That is also why the international financial order must have an additional source of control. Far-sighted, active international collaboration is vital to protect employment levels during balance of payments adjustment processes. Collaboration is best formed around a resolve to avoid sudden, major exchange rate changes by designing agreed schemes for supplying the necessary liquidity to boost a particular nation's foreign exchange reserves. Other possible collaborative projects include designing schemes for more exchange rate flexibility than is permitted by the BW principles; for encouraging surplus nations to make policy changes consistent with sharing the burden of payments adjustment and for constructing institutional arrangements which would allow the efficient flow of capital to counter problems of underdevelopment and economic stagnation.

Hansen's optimism seemed boundless even though he understood that the BW Agreement was incomplete and on some matters quite ambiguous. The lack of symmetry in the adjustment process between deficit and surplus countries was for Hansen only apparent. For surplus countries would have built-in incentives to share adjustment burdens; otherwise they ran the real risk of declining into secular stagnation. In allowing countries sovereignty to conduct 'independent' monetary, fiscal and trade policies, the BW Agreement ignored the strong likelihood that industrially mature, surplus countries would find it increasingly difficult, if not impossible, to maintain positive economic growth rates. In the long term these surplus countries must modify their policies in the light of impacts on both deficit countries and less developed countries.

The Hansen doctrine had many contemporary followers and created what was regarded as a distinctive school of thought. It was a school driven by strong faith in extending the notion of national macroeconomic stabilization to the international financial order. Hansen advocated Keynesian macroeconomic management though he understood that Keynesian ideas applied originally in a relatively closed economy context (such as the United States in the 1940s and 1950s) required supplementation in the international realm. No retreat was possible from the view that the international financial order had to be deliberately designed – and not just the key architectural outlines. Institutional details and day-to-day policy adjustment rules demanded conscious planning. That deliberate planning might fail never seemed to occur to Hansen. It is scarcely surprising that his summary judgement of the 'new crusade against planning' epitomized by Hayek's new book – the *Road to Serfdom* (1944) – was so damning: 'Hayek's book will not be long lived. There is no substance in it to make it live' (Hansen 1945f: 12).

4 John Williams's 'key currency' alternative for the international financial order

> [T]he largest question, in my mind, has been whether it was best to approach the problem in terms of a global international monetary organization ... or to begin with the major countries whose currencies are the chief means of international payment and whose policies and circumstances will have a predominant effect upon the character of postwar international trade and currency relations.
>
> (Williams 1945c: 390)

International monetary problems in the interwar years: a view from Harvard

John H. Williams was a long-time colleague and friend of Alvin Hansen. Williams held the position of Professor of Political Economy at Harvard and was in fact responsible for bringing Hansen to Harvard in 1937 (Williams 1976). In his career as an economist Williams specialized in international finance, writing a doctoral thesis at Harvard before accepting an academic position in 1933. Later he was concurrently vice-president of the Federal Reserve Bank of New York.[1] Fundamental differences in economic doctrine between Williams and Hansen, and between Williams and Keynes for that matter, arose from Williams's respect for at least some of the economic principles enunciated by the classical economists. Williams was especially respectful of the classicalists' emphasis on the economic role of relative prices and costs. He focused on changes in the structure of relative prices as critical forces in economic adjustment – a factor also explaining the classicalists' support for gold in international finance. Admittedly, by the late 1940s the world had become more complex, so much so that there were widespread doubts about the classical system of free multilateral trade and free international payments based on a gold standard regime. Yet for Williams classical doctrine contained some enduring truths. His scepticism of Keynes's and Keynesian theories and policies carried over into the field of international finance. Accordingly, the form of international financial order envisaged by Williams diverged quite sharply from that favoured by the architects of BW, Keynes and the Keynesians (including Hansen).

Along with most other prominent architects of the international financial order in the 1940s and 1950s, Williams's view of desirable financial arrangements was strongly influenced by his assessment of international monetary experience in the 1930s. He lamented that much of the literature on the subject was nationalistic and 'acrimonious' (Williams 1944c: 171). On the face of it, the classical gold standard failed spectacularly in the economic depression of the late 1920s and early 1930s. However, this conventional view exaggerated the role of gold. Williams (1932a, 1932b) observed of the so-called 'crisis of the gold standard', as he titled one of his articles at the time: the world financial system was in fact founded 'upon the sterling standard' pre-1914 even though it was widely thought that universally acceptable and enforceable classical gold standard rules prevailed. From the 1840s up to about 1914 Great Britain enjoyed an unequalled world creditor position; it was a leading capital (gold) exporter, the centre of the free international market for gold, and an international banker facilitating payments and receipts for trade on behalf of many other countries. The 'sterling standard' was so pervasive that by the end of the nineteenth century London had become *the* centre for international financial transactions, and the Bank of England the chief administrator of the gold standard. In effect, Great Britain was on the gold standard and its currency issue strictly linked to official gold reserves. Much of the rest of the world conducted its international transactions and monetary policy on the sterling standard and was thus only indirectly governed by the rules of the gold standard. The supposed 'automatic' gold standard in fact operated on the basis of a common international financial centre which facilitated trade by offering all the necessary services. Substantial changes in the pattern of international trade were 'corrected' by the interaction of gold movements directed through London and by price adjustments (Williams 1937: 166, 1944c: 173).

From the 1920s, Williams observed the practice of managing and 'sterilizing' gold flows by central banks in a manner violating the simple gold standard rules. For example, central banks might conduct open market sales of government securities when gold flowed into a country, thereby decreasing the reserves of the banking system and damping the credit creation process. The United States' Federal Reserve system is singled out as a major culprit in the 1920s; the Reserve purportedly attempted to sterilize gold inflows to keep the domestic price level stable, thereby shifting some of the burden of adjustment to trade imbalances on to foreign countries and their price levels (Williams 1932a: 274–5). By the mid-1920s Great Britain's creditor status had dissolved, its role as administrator of the gold standard diminished. Two other leading industrial nations – the United States and France – began to assume dominance in their claims on gold. The subsequent maldistribution of gold supplies and the pressing need to economize on gold as a means of payment for the growing volume and value of international transactions in the 1920s both contributed to international monetary disturbances in the interwar period. The 'insistent pull on British gold' towards the United States and France appeared especially pernicious. In Great Britain prices and wages did not respond in a flexible manner to this situation, labour was not fully mobile in responding to structural changes in the British economy, and some industries did not willingly adopt new and more efficient techniques of production. All this contributed to further pressure on the outward movement of British gold. In addition, foreign investment was preferred to home investment. The cumulative effects of all these forces on output and employment were deleterious. By the 1930s, the sterling standard, founded indirectly on gold, lost its credibility in consequence.

What happened to the other gold standard administrators? The United States achieved its international creditor position during the 1914–18 export boom.[2] And on Williams's reading of economic history, despite the Federal Reserve's practice of gold sterilization – against which there was sound evidence of significant credit expansion in the United States through the 1920s – the US role as leading world creditor persisted because of German war reparations:

> The Allies bought our goods with the promises of future payment which they could not honour except as Germany supplies the means of reparation payments. Germany, lacking present capacity to pay, turned to the Allies' creditor. Insofar as this system works at all we substitute one debtor for another.
>
> (Williams 1932a: 280)

France, on the other hand, accumulated surpluses which it could not, and would not, easily run down. What follows is a damning indictment of French policy:

> France has long pursued the ideal of the self-sufficing nation and has neither the financial machinery, the business flexibility, nor the economic motivation which fits a nation for such a role. It is not possible to conceive a nation less fitted than France to hold the world's gold or administer the gold standard.
>
> (Williams 1932a: 280)[3]

A combined result of these events in the United States and France was upward pressure on the French franc and US dollar and downward pressure on sterling.

In the United States and France a damaging conflict emerged between the principles of central banking and the process of balance of payments adjustment. Central bankers in surplus countries built up reserves above normal requirements as protection against either unplanned capital flows internally (for hoarding purposes) or externally for foreign investment or imports. Accordingly, credit expansion in these surplus countries did not run its full course; gold flows were to some extent offset in their impact on economic conditions within those countries. In other words, the banking system was not fully 'loaned up' so that internal price adjustments were not synchronized with changes in the balance of payments on nations' current, trading accounts. Altogether, the effect was 'to throw a double burden of adjustment upon countries not similarly equipped with free reserves' (1932b: 294). The gold standard, as managed by central bankers in the 1920s, tended to work asymmetrically; it favoured economic contraction in deficit countries rather than expansion in surplus countries. Later, when discussing the international financial architecture post-BW, Williams attributed this asymmetry not so much to the practice of sterilization as to the markedly unequal dependence of nations on their balance of payments constraint, that is on international trade. A large export surplus for the United States attracted gold inflow but tended to have a less expansive impact in the United States by comparison with contractionary effects in deficit countries, many of which possessed small, open economies. The classical gold standard was based, in theory, on the 'interaction between homogenous countries of approximately equal economic size' (Williams 1944c: 173). The lesson from interwar experience is that economic size matters for the operation of the international financial order: any architectural scheme must take economic dominance into account.

What stands out in Williams's commentaries on interwar experience in the international economy is early recognition of the place of major industrial powers in international finance. If one or another country holds large quantities of the major means of international payment for trade in goods and services, it always has the potential (and sometimes the incentive) to misuse that responsibility, depending on national priorities and political circumstances. While Williams was inclined to absolve the United States of wilful neglect of international financial responsibility for the misuse of the gold standard in the 1920s, policies in France and to a lesser extent in Great Britain were represented as, respectively, perverse and unhelpful to adjustment. Williams acknowledged that the classical gold standard took for granted, in theory, continuous full employment, yet it was commonplace in the interwar years to complain of the cumulative, mostly deflationary effects of gold *in practice*. It was therefore scarcely surprising that policymakers wished to rely less on gold as a determinant of exchange rates. Williams concurred. The events of the interwar years had resolved in his mind how gold (that is, capital) movements were a potential *cause* of income changes and not, as in classical doctrine, an *effect* of income changes. In support, Williams singled out experience with 'panicky flights of capital' in the 1930s (Williams 1944: 172).[4] Much earlier, he predicted that the world 'will undoubtedly return' to a gold standard of some description, 'even though eventually it may be outgrown'. For all its recognized defects as perceived in Williams's mind, by the time of the BW debates he still favoured moulding and improving on the gold standard mechanism rather than abandoning it completely for another system (Williams 1932b: 298–9, 1944c: 173). That BW retained a role for gold therefore gave some cause for satisfaction but it was not enough for his unqualified approval.

The major international financial events of the 1930s saw the world turn away from full-scale reconstitution of the pre-1914 gold standard. Williams (1937) was in the vanguard of economists responsible for the idea of forming a new, loose international agreement to stabilize key currencies in the late 1930s. The United States, Great Britain and France established a Tripartite Agreement in September 1936, coordinating their foreign exchange market interventions to stabilize the franc and sterling exchange rate with the US dollar. A system of managed, flexible exchange rates between these currencies had prevailed since 1933.[5] In 1936, 'a gentlemen's agreement' establishing a 'compromise system' had been formed; it was built around the principle of stabilizing exchange rates between key currencies, and required (implicitly) national monetary management to maintain stability.

Williams was convinced in the late 1930s that different countries required different kinds of exchange rate management. Major countries required efficient monetary control though precise, binding rules for a coordinated international monetary policy were obviously difficult to establish and enforce. The operational characteristic of the Tripartite Agreement did not guarantee consistent, coordinated monetary policies. It created official stabilization funds in each country holding foreign currency and converting it into gold on demand at a price based on the agreed exchange rate. The three leading industrial countries would hold part of their official funds in each others' currency. If a currency was not in great demand it would be supported by selling other currency holdings in return or by being purchased directly by the stabilization funds. Persistent excess supplies of a weak currency could be relieved by adjusting the exchange rate – that is, varying the price of gold to which all three major currencies were ultimately anchored. More orderly exchange rate adjustment was thereby assured. The Tripartite Agreement's exchange rate mechanism involved a fixed buying and selling price for gold in terms of US dollars. This anchor was fundamental. Williams (1937: 164–6) made two portentous remarks on all this in the light of the later BW Agreement. First, there 'is no evidence thus far that this kind of exchange stabilization can operate without being anchored to a fixed price of gold in one or more markets'. Second, the international financial order emerging from collaborative agreements, whether of the 'Tripartite' form or more expansive international agreements, must rely heavily on a 'large measure of trust in the integrity and freedom from nationalistic motives' prevailing in the country or countries whose currencies act as the anchor. Moreover, having a multipolar group of stabilizing agencies might prove problematic, for they may not be able to reach consensus on when a major exchange rate realignment is desirable or on the magnitude of the required realignment (Williams 1937: 165–6).

The importance of the currency 'anchoring' country should not be underestimated. In the case of the sterling area pre-1914, monetary control exerted by the Bank of England – linked directly to the state of the internal gold reserve – had a powerful influence on the growth rates of economies associated with that currency area. Many countries (e.g. the British dominions) held sterling balances in London for later use and these fluctuated in concert with economic conditions in Great Britain. Upon the abandonment of the gold standard by Great Britain in the early 1930s, its importance as a key currency-anchoring centre did not diminish. The rise of monetary nationalism in the 1930s did not, in other words, deny a place for sound domestic monetary policy. The Bank of England could still control member bank reserves and thus credit creation without gold by using well-established monetary policy techniques (interest rate manipulation and open market buying and selling of official securities) as circumstances demanded. Williams was quite willing to take a leap of faith despite the lack of supporting historical evidence. Effective control of the major instruments of economic policy in key countries – implying 'some community of action in monetary and general economic policy' – might well stabilize currencies internationally *without* gold (Williams 1937: 168).

The case of the United States in 1937 was very special indeed. The economy was relatively closed. Therefore policymakers in the United States should be 'less concerned about exchange variation' as a means of correcting business cycles, and could rely more on policies aimed at achieving internal balance. The total value of economic activity in the United States and Great Britain in 1937 represented more than half the world's output. Economic fluctuations originating in these two countries naturally transmitted outwards to smaller countries. That is precisely why stable exchange rates among the larger industrial countries should be an objective of international economic policy. By contrast, smaller trade-dependent and foreign investment-dependent economies required exchange rate stability when trade was prosperous. They required currency adjustment when foreign capital inflows reached unsustainable levels or when foreign markets were severely depressed.[6] Again Williams's message is amplified: there is no *one* set of appropriate rules for all countries in an international financial order. Everything depends on a nation's economic size and degree of openness. The Tripartite Agreement of 1936 is an acknowledgement of this message. It represented, in comparison with BW, a small step towards making international currency stabilization work.[7] The alternative for Williams was not worth contemplating for it involved relinquishing an international approach altogether in favour of nations pursuing their own narrow, short-term economic interests, minimizing external contractionary impacts on their economies and maximizing the domestic advantages from external expansionary forces.

Williams's reaction to Bretton Woods and his alternative

While John Williams was a renowned monetary expert, his formal participation at the BW meetings was not requested. The testimony he gave on this issue to the Senate Committee on Banking and Currency in 1945 makes interesting reading.

> *Senator Taft:* Mr Williams, is it fair to ask if you were invited to be a delegate at Bretton Woods?
>
> *Mr Williams:* I wasn't invited to be a delegate. I wasn't invited to attend in any capacity, but I was informed indirectly that they would be glad to have me attend if I would stay within the President's instruction to the delegates.
>
> *Senator Taft:* And that was, to conform, to support the basis of the experts' report?
>
> *Mr Williams:* To support the experts' report. And I declined to do so, because I had fault to find with the experts' report and wanted to continue to be free to think about the problem.
>
> (Williams 1945b: 332)

In fact Williams's position on creating an international financial order had been well advertised in a series of articles published at about the same time as the Keynes and White plans had been presented. And Williams was clearly opposed to a grand blueprint of the kind which was forthcoming at BW. He favoured incremental alterations in existing arrangements until postwar economic recovery in Great Britain and reconstruction in Europe had been completed. After that, he proposed a large country-specific plan to stabilize the currencies of 'key' industrial nations. In short, Williams openly opposed what the BW Agreement represented, namely 'a multiple purpose plan ... for the transition period as well as for the long run' (1944a: 106).

The BW Agreement embodied enthusiasm for the international rule of law. It was on the face of it legally even-handed but in practice asymmetric in its effects on some countries undergoing balance of payments adjustment. Williams's key currency plan did not share much enthusiasm for the enforceability of international law in the financial realm; instead, it focused on the economic and political realities, first as they unravelled in the interwar years and, second, as they were generally expected to unfold from 1944 onwards. However, he rightly complained that before the BW Agreement 'no other plan' outside the experts' plans 'is likely to get an adequate hearing'. In several contributions to the literature Williams offered an alternative plan, a critical review of the experts' (Keynes and White) plans and an assessment of the final BW Agreement (Williams 1943: 150).[8]

Williams agreed with three preconceptions forming the background to BW discussion:

1 international economic collaboration was essential;
2 short-term capital movements needed official management; and
3 freely flexible exchange rates were potentially destructive of trade and income so that stabilization of at least some key exchange rates was a priority.

Otherwise, BW deliberations were founded on overly 'ambitious' objectives; specifically they were prosecuting an elaborate currency plan under very uncertain, abnormal economic conditions, ignoring the problems of transition from wartime to peacetime economy. Other or better means for constructing a lasting international financial architecture might be conceived at a later stage (Williams 1943: 143, 150, 1944c: 184).[9]

What is quite apparent from our discussion of Williams's view on interwar currency experience is that he could not accept, in practice, the equality of all national currencies as a point of departure for an international financial agreement. Currencies were not equally usable in any imperfect international financial system observable in reality; they were only hypothetically equal on the drafting boards of BW architects. In establishing a genuinely international system of currency relations, rather than one centred on the four leading currencies which really mattered in international trade invoicing and payments, the BW Agreement ignored the very real likelihood that all currencies would not ultimately be freely convertible into all others. As a corollary, the equality of currencies' principle at BW had its counterpart in the gold standard notion of the equality of countries – economic size did not matter after all. Williams elaborated: the 'difficulty for me is that I have long believed that there is another kind of approach to the problem.... This is what might be called the key countries, or central countries, approach'. In contrast, the plans and briefing papers setting the BW architectural agenda 'have a closer family relationship with ... textbook type of gold standard, which implied that monetary stability was maintained by the compensatory action of a large number of countries of equal economic weight'. Furthermore, Williams's main differences with BW architects turned on

> the conception of how trade and finance are organized in the world, and of the importance of stabilizing the truly international currencies whose behaviour dominates and determines what happens to all the others. Though the organization of trade and finance has undergone much change since the nineteenth century, it still seems true that

> stabilization of the leading currencies with reference to each other, combined with cooperation among the countries concerned for the promotion of their own internal stability, would be the best foundation for monetary and economic stability throughout the world.[10]

The architects of BW envisioned the postwar international financial order as symmetrical, with many equal national currencies. The IMF was to act as a central coordinating organization, holding gold and national currencies to supplement national reserves, as the case demanded. Williams's alternative doctrine understood the international financial situation as one constituted by several genuinely international currencies used as vehicles for international transactions and as stores of value for international investment purposes, with remaining currencies having only national significance. He predicted that the IMF would be swamped with a 'miscellany' of forty-four member-country currencies most of which had no prospect, at least in the immediate postwar years, of being used as international means of payment (or stores of value).[11]

Instead of seeking to construct a world of convertible currencies at one fell swoop within the governance of a new global institution, Williams wished to create an organized currency hierarchy. At the apex of the hierarchy was the US–UK currency exchange rate which ought to be fixed (but not for ever unchanging in value) in relation to gold. All restrictions on the movement of gold would be relaxed as economic conditions stabilized in the postwar years. Gold's credibility was important if it was to be useful in the postwar financial order. Since 'a lot of people believe' in gold, its role as a key currency anchor could be retained. Nevertheless, gold was not an essential element in any international financial order. In the 1945 testimony to the Senate Committee on Banking and Currency, he was quite prepared to view the US gold reserve and the gold backing of Federal Reserve notes as an anachronism. He could envisage the evolution of the international financial order to a point where gold's monetary role could become redundant (Williams 1945b: 352).[12]

The success or failure of the BW 'experiment', as Williams often called it, would depend on the ability of policymakers and the governing board of the IMF to uphold exchange rate provisions in the BW Agreement. In short, these BW provisions were vague and easily interpreted in different ways. Williams had always favoured a liberal policy on exchange rate setting. He expected key countries to coordinate their foreign exchange market interventions along with their monetary and fiscal policies so as to minimize resort to major currency realignments. For smaller, open, industrialized economies and 'younger countries', his exchange rate policy prescriptions differed. These non-key countries exhibited macroeconomic conditions primarily reflecting business cycles in 'great world markets, for which they are only secondarily responsible'. Therefore, non-key countries 'should be permitted to vary their currencies' as their balance of payments positions dictated. As long as key countries maintain 'a state of proper economic health', such currency variations should be occasional rather than regular (Williams 1943: 152–3).[13] The 'fundamental disequilibrium' condition in the BW Agreement was, for Williams, quite meaningless. He preferred a loose currency policy, insisting on exchange rate stability for key countries and greater variability for non-key countries. To be sure, balance of payments adjustment would still be required between key countries and this should be a collaborative, 'two-sided' affair (Williams 1944d: 194).[14] Economic conditions in other countries showed greater variability and divergence so it was imperative that more flexibility be permitted in exchange rate policy than is allowed in the BW Agreement.[15] Indeed, premature stabilization of a weak, small-country currency would likely be a waste of financial resources. Nevertheless, 'exchange rate variation' had to be used with caution in all cases because it could not simply be a means of escaping internal price adjustments – it only speeds up and changes their point of impact in the economy. On the other hand, alternative methods of balance of payments adjustment such as bilateral, discriminating trade deals and exchange controls on current account transactions attempt mistakenly to 'run away' from necessary price and cost changes (Williams 1945a: 128).

In respect of exchange rate policy and policies designed to correct international payments imbalances, Williams 'would rather proceed on the post-war problem of adjustment case by case without rules' (1945a: 127). This attitude diverges sharply from the BW Agreement. He was afraid of descent into 'legalism' in which a member country set forth its own interpretation of some rather broad BW principles such as 'fundamental disequilibrium' in its balance of payments and then committed resources to defending this interpretation on legalistic grounds. In Williams's key currency architecture there is no need for a set of binding, transparent rules or a centralized international governing agency such as the IMF. Tedious procedures, currency quotas and voting mechanisms are dispensed with. Williams's scepticism regarding rules for economic policy and international policy in particular derived from his reading of interwar experience. Historical research on 'international cooperative organisations provides many illustrations of how nations can find both the means and motives for defeating their purposes'. The self-interest of national policymakers often required preservation of domestic policy objectives and power to determine the direction of day-to-day national policies. The BW Agreement seemed to presume a harmony of interests between national policymakers' objectives and the rules and guidelines in the IMF Articles of Agreement (Williams 1944c: 183).

Williams had no quarrel with the BW emphasis on the preservation of national autonomy in designing economic policy. However, the UK pound sterling–US dollar exchange rate required urgent stabilization postwar, not least because these two pivotal currencies were the predominant means of international payment, facilitating a large proportion of world trade. In these two countries some sacrifice of national policy autonomy would be required to effect exchange rate stabilization. The BW Agreement promised to be a 'currency stabilization plan in name only', precisely because internal economic conditions across countries were so uncertain in 1944 (Williams 1944c: 199). A linchpin needed to be established and, in Williams's view, that could only be effectively constructed by careful negotiation – even a rule-based bilateral stabilization agreement – between policymakers in the United States and Great Britain. The long-term objective was to secure stability but not immutability in the UK pound sterling–US dollar exchange rate.

That the IMF did not function as a lending agency was a major weakness in the BW Agreement. Great Britain desperately required international liquidity in 1944–5 to finance its large current account deficit, and stabilize sterling. The sterling problem was best resolved by the world's largest creditor – the United States – facilitating an agreement to eliminate Great Britain's exchange restrictions on current account transactions which were a major obstacle to the expansion of international trade after the war. Great Britain would require a loan from the United States to assist in this process and bring sterling (and the London financial centre) back to the apex of the international financial system.[16] Key currency stability therefore required a financial commitment from the United States conditional upon Great Britain supporting activist coordination of official exchange market interventions utilizing each country's stabilization reserve funds. Exchange controls on capital transactions would still be permitted. A loan would in effect be an investment in the maintenance of the US economy and keep up the level of demand in the international economy in the immediate postwar years (Williams 1945b: 354).[17] At the BW meeting Keynes demurred, sniping at the link between the key currency proposal and the Anglo-American loan idea. He remarked that it involved burdening Great Britain with a large US dollar debt in the interests of stabilizing the pound–dollar exchange rate while letting 'the rest of the world go hang'.[18] Keynes preferred a multipurpose loan both for transitional reconstruction of productive capacity in Great Britain and for assisting in trade expansion. In Keynes's mind, rather than debt or charity, Great Britain needed a world in which trade was expanding. For Williams these outcomes were not mutually exclusive.

In Williams's scheme some sharing of the obligations of currency stabilization between the United States and Great Britain would have to be agreed upon. British internal policies – 'social security and public works' were singled out – would likely place upward pressure on costs and thereby impact negatively on export competitiveness. Moreover, British commitment to the immediate realization of full employment under the influence of William Beveridge's plan 'won't solve the ... problem' and the effect 'would certainly be to increase ... imports'. It was on Britain's effective use of a bilateral loan from the United States for postwar reconstruction and IMF resources (for currency account and currency management) that the prospects for the BW financial order hinged. Williams was hardly convinced that the IMF promoted effective policies ensuring British policymakers would use financial resources wisely. IMF loan conditions and bilateral loan conditions in 1945 promised to be too weak to promote currency stabilization. In the BW negotiations, 'under the guise of an international agreement', the British delegation was 'trying to get a maximum of national freedom' (Williams 1945a: 131, 1945b: 343–8, 358, 364–5). In the event, the IMF principles were exceedingly permissive in giving national policymakers (including British policymakers) autonomy. Williams strongly objected. The key currency countries, or a country that was very likely to evolve into one, must bear a greater burden of international responsibility and tailor their policies to their pivotal role in the international order.

With the IMF in operation during 1945, Williams's rhetoric became more openly damning:

> Now, the dollar is the international usable currency. Now see the absurd position ... that we would be in: Because of policies which the British are pursuing, the dollar becomes scarce. We then make the hard choice between making the dollar available [through the IMF], thus financing whatever they want to do, or of having the Fund declare the dollar scarce and letting the nations go back to exchange control.
>
> (1945b: 357)

The scarce currency clause in the BW Agreement was an admission that the IMF's working balance of dollars could rapidly be exhausted postwar. This would be tantamount to giving the 'rest of the world *carte blanche* to resume exchange control and trade discrimination as before'. With the very spectre of a dollar shortage it 'ought to be made clear that the recapture of dollars would require the maintenance of exchange control, not merely for the transition period but permanently, and for current account transactions as well as for capital transactions' (Williams 1945a: 127, 128–9). As it happened, post-BW the long retention of exchange controls for all purposes seemed to confirm Williams's prediction. Operationally, it was difficult to distinguish between capital movements for current transactions and those for speculative, capital account purposes. The BW Agreement indicated a desire to expedite the relaxation of capital controls on foreign exchange used for current account transactions over a transition period, with retention of controls on speculative capital flows. However, 'as any foreign exchange operator would recognize it is a matter of utmost difficulty to differentiate between current account and capital transactions and ... the differentiations would have to be made after, rather than prior to, the fact' (Williams 1944a: 115 note 2).

The responsibilities of the United States as a major creditor country to maintain high levels of output and employment, greater openness to international trade, and an adequate level of foreign investment should not be downplayed. Satisfying these responsibilities would minimize the drain of US dollars from the IMF. Periods of US dollar scarcity were not regarded as a strong possibility by the BW architects so long as policymakers in the United States lived up to their obligations to adopt policies in concert with the nation's creditor position. According to one respected BW commentator, the 'realities of the situation' obtaining at the end of 1945 'make it entirely unlikely that, if the United States maintains reasonable balance, there will be a scarcity of dollars' (Bernstein 1945: 14).[19] For Williams all this was just wishful thinking. It was not obvious that policymakers in the United States must fully and immediately comply with BW obligations on all the dimensions listed above. It was more realistic to expect accurate perception in the United States of more limited bilateral financial responsibilities to Great Britain as a key currency partner than to some amorphous international body of countries. A more modest quantum of international financial goodwill was therefore required in the key currency architecture.

Principal criticisms of the key currency architecture[20]

By promoting a new international financial architecture in harmony with the immediate needs of the world economy in the postwar reconstruction and recovery phase, Williams offered a challenging alternative. As we have seen already, British economists – Keynes and Keynesians in particular – rejected the key currency view out of hand (or out of pride?). Dennis Robertson (1943: 355) feared that weaker nations, 'left in sorry condition' postwar, would not be capable of full participation in an organized international financial system; they would be left 'to scramble back' to full participation in world commerce 'as best they may'. Yet Williams did not dismiss the problems of smaller, weaker, open economies and less developed countries. They were to be accorded greater flexibility and freedom *not* to have to define currency par values so quickly (in terms of gold or the US dollar) as required by IMF rules, and thereby limit fluctuations in their currencies prematurely. They would gradually align their currencies to previously stabilized key currencies as postwar recovery was completed and as a more normal degree of external balance between key countries was approximated. There is one point, however, in favour of BW arrangements on which Williams remained silent: if smaller, non-key country deficits (or surpluses) become more than just temporary, then exchange rate adjustments would be desirable. In particular, deficit persistence would favour currency depreciation so as to limit the flow of less usable currencies into the IMF; this was the mechanism which the BW financial order relied upon to damp down demand for US dollars. And countries would not be allowed to accumulate US dollars indefinitely unless they had a favourable balance of payments with the world as a whole (Bourneuf 1944: 843).[21]

For Williams the difficulty with the IMF was that the weaker deficit nations with inadequate gold and foreign currency reserves would likely place unsustainable demands on the IMF for US dollars in return for currencies 'with which the Fund would have become glutted'. The rules establishing the IMF quota arrangements did not guarantee that the Fund would avoid becoming 'waterlogged' by unusable currencies. US import payments would be likely to exacerbate the situation. While weaker deficit nations would pay for US imports using the IMF's supply of dollars, US imports would not replace those dollars even in the happy situation where the US external accounts were in near perfect balance (with no tendency for gold or foreign currency to flow in or out of the United States). In fact the US would not have occasion to approach the IMF to obtain foreign currencies. Conventions in foreign exchange invoicing prevailing in the late 1940s obviated the necessity for widespread use of smaller-country currencies. Instead, private market participants used the US dollar and pound sterling as vehicle currencies – as media of exchange in merchandise trade – to execute transactions (Williams 1944a: 111–12, 1945a: 126). The economies of scale involved in using vehicle currencies and transaction cost savings enjoyed therefrom are now well known (Hartmann 1999).[22]

Another critic claimed that Williams was interested in creating a damaging, hegemonic arrangement between the United States and Great Britain, when in fact only 3 per cent of world trade was transacted between the two countries. However, this summary rejection of the key currency approach concluded by trivializing Williams's position: 'as competitors or consumers of the products of other countries every currency in the world is a key currency to nearly every other country in the world' (Mikesell 1945: 574). This view blindly neglected the existence of key currencies in international finance. Once again such claims overlooked the fact that the US dollar and sterling were used as vehicle currencies partly out of convention and partly because fully developed financial institutions were concentrated in efficient, financial decision centres – namely New York and London.

Williams's vision for the international financial order involved using a currency agreement between the United States and Great Britain ratifying the leadership of the New York and London financial centres. Unlike the BW Agreement which would create and guide the process of multilateral currency convertibility and exchange rate stabilization, Williams envisioned an international system pivoting on broad, deep, lightly regulated financial markets in the two already renowned international financial centres. The current account deficit and net debtor positions of Great Britain made it difficult to generate confidence in sterling as a key currency in 1945 – though, if it were strongly aligned with the US dollar it could import some credibility and that would be a sound point of departure in encouraging international currency stabilization in the postwar world. Concern was expressed over the structure imposed on the international financial order by a bilateral, hegemonic arrangement. International money, in this view, was more than a neutral facilitator – a medium of exchange or unit of account – for assisting merchandise trade; it also determined the direction of trade. The key currency plan ran against the desire of BW architects to design international finance in a manner conducive to freer multilateral trade. International trade may be driven into narrow channels consistent with a putative isolationist bias or at least a regional bias inherent in bilateral currency stabilization plans (Mikesell 1945: 572, 575).[23] The threat posed by Williams's scheme to the idea of immediate multilateralism could not be entertained by BW architects wedded to multilateral currency convertibility and trade as a rallying point for an international blueprint. As well, Williams's colleague at Harvard, Alvin Hansen, argued that the creation of a key currency agreement between the United States and Great Britain, in which ongoing consultation took place between key-country policymakers almost exclusively, could be a deterrent to smaller countries, keeping them out of an active role in international commerce indefinitely. Nevertheless Hansen acknowledged 'an important core truth in the key country approach.... The fact is that the International Monetary Fund cannot succeed except on the basis of the closest collaboration of the key countries'. Hansen predicted that the IMF would operate to 'devolve basically and fundamentally on the key countries' (Hansen 1945a: 85–6). The potential for financial domination and even international financial imperialism growing out of Williams's plan also violated the policy autonomy principle giving impetus to the agreement reached at BW.

Williams was also criticized for apparently having too much interest in establishing a single standard for making international payments and too little in establishing and enforcing an orderly international system of foreign exchange practices which would promote rapid expansion in trade and investment. A definite policy sequence is evident in Williams's doctrine: first, promote international cooperation and consultation between existing (or prewar) key currency nations; second, allow monetary and exchange rate stabilization to follow naturally elsewhere; and third, as evidenced by extensive historical research, foreign investment will expand, thereby reducing trade imbalances and divergent national growth rates (Williams 1953: 163).

Distilling the 'right' exchange rate settings straight out of the BW Agreement for all countries and currencies was, for Williams, like constructing an architectural design applicable to all environmental conditions. Creating broadly workable standards for making international payments was obviously a priority postwar though as one critic noted, gold and US dollars already served as conventional vehicles for international trade, with other currencies fluctuating with respect to them. Therefore 'of fundamental importance to the commercial operations of trading countries is that the values of their currencies remain stable in relation to one another' (Mikesell 1945: 569). Only the BW Agreement embraced the financial operations of all countries. The demonstrable economic importance of the United States was uppermost in Williams's mind. Beyond gold, a wider key currency was urgently needed and had to be deliberately created by policymakers – it would not emerge spontaneously. There was no point in reinforcing the fiction that all currencies were somehow equal. In the BW financial order the cumulative advantages of economic power and technological progress which the United States was likely to enjoy postwar could only result in a chronic dollar shortage. This is, in fact, what he believed had occurred by 1948 (Williams 1948b: 77). By effecting a key currency agreement with Great Britain in early postwar years, the dollar shortage might have been mitigated and key currency stabilization would have greatly expanded trade and encouraged greater cross-border investment flows. There is a sense in which Williams sidesteps, rather than solves, the scarce currency issue. For the key currencies could become scarce, especially if the key currency system is confined to two currencies. How do additional key currency reserves move into national foreign reserves in non-key countries? As Kaldor warned, there is an inconsistency in key currency doctrine:

> To be widely acceptable as international reserve, a currency must be *strong*, in the sense that nobody seriously contemplates its devaluation. But to make a contribution to the stock of reserves owned by other countries, a currency must be *weak*, in the sense that the country in question must have a deficit in its balance of payments. As the history of the dollar illustrates, these two conditions for contributing to the working of the world monetary system may be in conflict.
>
> (1964: 134, his emphasis)[24]

A special loan (or grant) to Great Britain was an important element in the establishment of a key Anglo-American currency agreement, but the precise function of the loan (or grant) confounded commentators. The key currency architecture had as its centrepiece a currency stabilization plan – at least in the minds of those who favoured the alternative BW Agreement. For them, transitional funding to meet Britain's war debts and reconstruction needs was surely a separate matter. Indeed, the BW Agreement does not refer to such special transitional funding. In the BW financial order, Great Britain was obliged to make a significant exchange rate adjustment if its current account deficit persisted. Internal policy reforms would also be required. Now the favoured mix of policies for economic adjustment was not fully articulated by Williams in any single article on the key currency architecture. However, as demonstrated in the next section, we can discern a coherent set of key currency-supporting macroeconomic policies and microeconomic reforms which were thought appropriate for both the United States and Great Britain in a bilateral currency agreement.

Other policies essential to the key currency architecture

On its own, the key currency plan was not sufficient to create a permissive environment for global economic expansion. The national economic policy mix in major industrial countries committed to the key currency arrangement had to be selected in tandem with any attempt to moderate fluctuations in the US dollar–pound sterling exchange rates. Williams complained frequently, as the BW Agreement underwent successive drafts, that the architects of BW 'watered down and finally left out altogether any reference to corrective economic measures essential to its operation' (1944a: 114). On the other hand, certain economic indicators would have to be demonstrated in order to ensure that key currencies remained key currencies. In particular, policies would need to be designed to yield relatively low rates of inflation and low variability in the rate of change in the domestic price levels in key countries. These low inflation outcomes would reduce the costs of using a key currency internationally and increase confidence in its use as a medium or vehicle of exchange, unit of account and store of value in national reserve holdings. Contrariwise, inflation increases the costs of holding a currency by reducing its purchasing power. Internal economic policies would have to be stable and consistent in order to reinforce key currency status.

Cooperation between the United States and Great Britain on internal economic policies, including monetary and fiscal policies, was of paramount importance if Williams's plan was to be successful. Ideally, key countries should coordinate their monetary and fiscal policies to maintain employment and exchange rate stability. Like the BW architects, Williams believed in both full employment as a legitimate policy objective and a liberal multilateral system of international payments, but his financial architecture exhibits more patience in respect of reaching these objectives.

Williams noticed a disturbing pattern of policy preferences in countries adjusting to balance of payments difficulties after 1945: 'trade restrictions first, exchange controls second, and exchange-rate variation third'. Unfortunately, the BW Agreement did not cover trade policy even though the spirit of the Agreement was in favour of liberalization. Williams's approach was favourable to trade restrictions in the postwar reconstruction period to conserve foreign exchange and achieve external balance. In the case of Great Britain – a key currency country – loans from the United States should not be conditional on *immediate* restoration of free sterling convertibility and freer multilateral trade (Williams 1947b: 87).[25]

While the restoration and maintenance of a high level of employment was desirable in key countries and elsewhere, Williams is always mildly sceptical towards much favoured Keynesian panaceas. A first consideration is internal policy in key countries – it was the principal determinant of international financial and currency stability in postwar years. A postwar 'program for world stability' turned immediately on acknowledging the preponderant size in economic terms of the American economy. Moreover, tendencies towards payments imbalances in the world economy have their 'roots in the growing predominance of the American economy' (Williams 1954: 15). Therefore, a clear position needed to be established at the outset on the various dimensions of economic policies appropriate for the United States as a key transmitter of economic change and prosperity. In this connection, Williams's position may be summarized as follows:[26]

1 internal (federal) budget: employ contracyclical deficit spending but resist long-run deficits;
2 public works: continue to fund socially necessary projects and public housing;
3 public debt: manage so as to shift more into the portfolios of non-bank private investors;
4 employment: no government guarantee of full employment;
5 income tax: reduce where possible on low-income groups;
6 corporate tax: reduce and permit averaging over several years and repeal excess profit tax laws;
7 monetary policy: manipulate interest rates and use direct controls over consumer credit and farm mortgage credit but do not resort to government direction of private investment;
8 wages policy: maintain wage rates after the war and allow rises in line with labour productivity;
9 trade policy: reduce US tariffs eventually;
10 international investment policy: support IBRD and government loans to foreign countries, especially key currency partners;
11 exchange controls: do not regulate capital movements motivated by current account transactions.

This list is exhaustive so far as Williams's thinking is concerned *after* the establishment of the BW financial order. There is no question that, in promoting the key currency architecture before BW, international policies in the key countries (the United States and Great Britain) would need coordination to avoid inflationary pressures. Trade and investment restrictions between the key countries would also have to be eased. Domestic policies to counter unemployment would have to be framed with a view to the level of output and employment but these could not be presented without considering the state of the current account in the balance of international payments. The case of Great Britain in this connection was crucial. The British could not simply rely on US dollar credits indefinitely and rest on their laurels. Major structural changes in the British economy had to be made to assure long-run stability of the US dollar–UK sterling exchange rate. Williams's general, though not popular, position was clear: key countries collaborate on monetary, fiscal and trade policy to effect immediate economic expansion towards full employment. If necessary for honouring the principle of 'two-sided' adjustment, the United States should be comfortable with internal budget deficits, taking into account economic conditions not only at home but also in Great Britain. He did not 'believe that an unbalanced budget is inconsistent with a stable currency' arrangement with Great Britain. Indeed, a continually increasing fiscal deficit which was 'small in relation to the increase in national income' may be substantial and necessary in the key currency arrangement (Williams 1945a: 128, 1945b: 351).

Monetary policy independence between *key* countries would be minimal; at least there would have to be strong activist monetary policy coordination between the United States and Great Britain.[27] Elsewhere, less sacrifice of independence would be required. A supranational monetary institution was not necessary to announce formal rules of the monetary policy game in a two-country arrangement. Guidelines for financing payments imbalances would deserve consideration to ensure key currency exchange rate stability. Continuous consultation and mutual agreement between policymakers in key countries in the light of changing economic conditions were recommended as the chief route to currency stability, economic expansion and freer trade. A strong, credible architecture of currency stabilization and economic growth could then be created internationally, and smaller countries would coalesce as monetary satellites around the key countries. A liberal trade and investment policy in the United States, and active key country participation in IBRD programmes, would support rather than undermine a key currency architecture. As it happened, such participation especially by the United States also gave support to the BW financial order.

Williams (1948a) doubted the efficacy of Keynesian ideas and policies since these policies could have made his key currency architecture, including the policies he thought were appropriate to it, less palatable at the time. Alvin Hansen's position on the widespread applicability of the 'new' Keynesian economics was more widely accepted in the United States in the 1940s and 1950s. As for Great Britain, Williams saw little room for continuing 'the internal program of nationalization and economic planning' and he insisted on 'a changed attitude not only by the [British] government but by the whole country toward its way of life' (1947a: 61). All this was uttered after the key currency proposal was set aside. We can scarcely escape the conclusion that Williams's expression of these long-held views indicates how difficult it might have been for him to promote an Anglo-American agreement genuinely to coordinate their policies along the lines required for key currency stabilization. He remained a mild critic of those who insisted on 'too full employment' since it 'can have crippling effects': it rigidified the economic structure and invited regular 'inflationary outbursts'. Furthermore, while he was not enamoured of the potency of monetary policy, Williams was strongly opposed to an 'all-out easy monetary policy, such as some Keynesians have favored, designed to saturate liquidity preference'. The inflation risks in such a policy were too high.[28] Reliance on easy monetary policies also submerged the concerns of classical economists who tended to emphasize policies for increasing productivity, and necessary supply-side changes which were especially appropriate for the British economy. In short, there were important supply-side causes for 'fundamental disequilibrium' in the balance of payments. These causes could be directly addressed either by internal microeconomic policies or indirectly by exchange rate variations (Williams 1954: 18, 1948: 20).[28] The manipulation of the macroeconomy by general monetary and fiscal measures, while useful in particular for disinflationary purposes in deficit countries, was not enough on its own to effect durable balance of payments adjustment.

Summary and assessment

Williams's principal policy guidelines for countries involved in a key currency agreement, are summarized in Table 4.1. In Williams's work these guidelines applied specifically to policymakers in the United States and Great Britain who might be contemplating an Anglo-American agreement to stabilize the US dollar–UK sterling exchange rate.

John Williams produced a viable alternative to BW and determinedly adhered to his minority view throughout the 1940s. He did not seem perturbed by a key currency architecture based on a hierarchical order of currencies relying in turn on the hegemony arising out of an Anglo-American agreement stabilizing the US dollar–UK pound exchange rate. Up to the mid-1940s the key currency idea appeared to many commentators and critics as a form of American philanthropy towards Great Britain. It was after all vitally dependent on the United States advancing significant dollar credits. In the long run a successful key currency arrangement would ramify throughout the existing international financial system, propelling other small nations' currencies into orbit around a relatively fixed key currency exchange rate. These other currencies would only attain durable convertibility status by being linked to a key currency. So the international financial architecture should be framed as follows: Anglo-American leadership comes first; smaller countries then have time to make the necessary economic adjustments and fall into line. The fact of economic size and financial power could not be wished away by smaller countries.

A multiple or multipolar key currency arrangement was also envisaged as a possible evolutionary outcome, provided other key currencies could be formed. The precise determination of key currency status and the process involved in supplanting one or other key currency over time is not

Table 4.1 Summary: Williams's key currency policy guidelines

Policy instrument	*Time horizon*	*Primary assignment*	*Secondary assignment*	*Guidelines*
Exchange rate policy				
i) Key countries	All	External balance		• Fixed rate between key currencies
ii) Other countries	Short term	Internal balance	External balance	• Flexible rates in transition from war
	Medium–long term	External balance		• Fixed rate, pegging against key currency
Exchange controls				
i) All countries	Medium–long term	–	–	• Abolish on current account transactions
ii) Non-key countries	Short term	Internal balance	External balance	• Retain to protect development capital • Retain until currency stabilized
Official reserves	All	External balance	Internal balance	• Use key currencies as intervention currencies • Gold may be dispensed with in long run
Monetary policy	All	External balance	Internal balance	• Price stability objective paramount • Active coordination of interest rate policies to support exchange rate/exchange market interventions
Fiscal policy	All	Internal balance	–	• Run budget deficits if necessary in short term as contracyclical instrument
Trade policy	Short term	External balance	–	• Retain restrictions in postwar transition to conserve foreign exchange
	Medium–long term	External balance	–	• Liberalize
Investment policy	Short term	External balance	–	• Special loan to Great Britain to help stabilize US dollar–pound rate
	Medium–long term			• Promote IBRD for development purposes

contemplated in Williams's writing.[29] Several judgements in his works *are* clear: a key currency cannot simply be chosen anew by economists or policymakers, though relative national economic size and stable, consistent policies are important in predicting, confirming and reinforcing key currency status. Williams does not underestimate the historical, geopolitical and institutional forces responsible for the existence of a key currency such as the US dollar.

Williams strove to differentiate his proposal from the BW Agreement. Once the BW Agreement had been reached he distinguished between the immediate need for international financial institutions such as the IBRD which could deal with problems of postwar transition and European reconstruction (estimating a five-year transition) and a postponed IMF-type organization for later international monetary consultation and macroeconomic stabilization. To some extent Williams was predicting that in addition to the US dollar and gold, sterling would (and should) once again retain its status as an international currency post-1945. International monetary policymakers had a central role: if they had the opportunity to create a key currency financial architecture they would not merely ratify the status of sterling; they would expedite its return by deliberate agreement. Whether this could have convinced private financial market participants is an open question. There is no mistaking Williams's belief that key currencies may be found or confirmed – unlike BW architects who dismissed the idea as unrealistic in the impending postwar financial world. As it happened, one key currency emerged in postwar years – namely the US dollar standard – in spite of the principles of currency equality in the BW Agreement.

The implicit economic rationale in the key currency proposal is the reduction of transaction costs in the use of one or two key or vehicle currencies. And such an outcome would surely have assisted postwar trade and growth. Altogether, Williams did not hold to the notion that a complete international financial order could be designed in an optimal manner and implemented at one instant. The modern, late twentieth-century concept of optimality used in economic analysis and in international finance would not have seemed useful to Williams; it would have been reminiscent of the philosophy underwriting the BW blueprint. By contrast, his attempt to design an alternative international financial architecture was based on an entirely different outlook encapsulated in the following passage:

> We have submerged the concrete in the abstract, the short-run in the long-run. We have thought too much in terms of broad (and even doctrinaire) principles and not enough about the kind of world to which they would apply. We have been preoccupied with organizational form and procedures which could operate successfully only when more normal conditions have been achieved.
>
> (Williams 1947a: 57)

Obviously this is an implicit criticism of the approach used by BW architects. Williams's doctrine understood the historical and institutional contingencies (as of 1944) restricting any viable international financial plan; it was a more realistic doctrine alive to the protracted economic difficulties likely in the postwar transition period. On the other hand the key currency architecture was not so well tuned to the strong sense of idealism and optimism prevailing in the United States and Great Britain.[30] As we have already seen, leading architects of international finance at the time, including Williams's Harvard contemporary Alvin Hansen, unquestionably believed that it was firmly within the grasp of economists to create and recreate the postwar international financial order as they saw fit. John Williams was no exception.

5 Frank Graham on international money and exchange rates

> I like to emphasise ... that international finance must be the handmaiden of international trade and that, when she forgot her function and set up on her own account, she made a sorry mess of things.
>
> (Graham 1943b: 335)

Graham's critique of gold standards

Frank Graham, an economics professor at Princeton University, produced the most severe and, some would argue, the most heretical criticism of the BW financial order. For the 1940s he independently offered an unconventional set of exchange rate alternatives along with integrated macroeconomic policies designed to achieve dominant contemporary economic goals, especially full employment. He was the only economist immediately before, during and after the BW negotiations to conceive internally consistent 'fundamentals of monetary policies' (Graham 1943a) complementing his exchange rate alternatives.

Like all leading economists thinking and writing about international financial problems in this early period up to 1950 coinciding with the BW Agreement, Graham formulated views on both the operation of the automatic gold standard order which prevailed before 1914, and the more 'managed' gold standard order prevailing in the 1920s which collapsed in the early 1930s. These views coloured his perspective on the most appropriate post-Second World War international financial framework. For Graham, the 'international gold standard, as we knew it in the past, was *inherently* unstable' (1940a: 19, his emphasis). There was, in his mind, no justification for restoring a gold standard as of right when Second World War hostilities ceased. Graham's reading of the pre-1914 gold standard and that which prevailed in the 1920s, along with their international financial repercussions, is quite distinctive in comparison with other prominent economists' views considered in this book. It was a reading which first considered a generic gold standard as a set of formal rules (and not as a collection of practices imperfectly executed in a real international financial system). A review of Graham's arguments on this score is therefore in order.

The most attractive feature of a generic gold standard is that it allows and requires the redemption of bank money or government-produced money for a fixed amount of gold. Graham posits an international financial order made up of countries issuing paper currencies (and not pure gold currencies). Therefore individuals can exchange their notes and coins (currency) at the officially defined price of gold per ounce. This rule regulated the production of fiduciary (trust-based) currency. The supply of currency is thus limited by public demand. For example, if the public's desire for currency increased, it would present gold in return for receipt of currency (or vice versa). Monetary authorities (private banks or central banks, depending on the case) purchase more gold to back the issuance of currency.

Several different sources of public demand for currency might be identified:

1 an increased demand to purchase goods requiring currency (rather than gold which could not act as a direct medium of exchange for goods);
2 international sales of domestically produced goods yielding gold inflows from abroad and requiring conversion of gold into domestic currency; and
3 international forces in the gold market resulting in increased gold production which in turn is presented for conversion into one currency or another (i.e. the monetary value of the gold supply increases).

An important implication of (3) above is that the supply of gold could not be determined by private bank officials, central bankers, government officials or politicians; it responded to cost conditions in the gold-mining industry (affected in turn by mining technology) relative to gold's international market price. Gold supply could be notoriously price inelastic. Nonetheless, gold standards are basically automatic in their operation. Gold storage costs may be significant because inventories must be held as an anchor to back the issue of currency.

One scenario is worth rehearsing here to illustrate a gold standard's operation. What if the demand for currency to finance the exchange of goods and services at both the domestic and international level could outstrip the supply of gold? Since gold backing is required for the issuance of currency and demand is increasing at a faster rate, then the price of gold would rise in relation to the goods and services being exchanged. In other words, the prices of goods and services must deflate *relative* to gold in order for a gold standard to operate effectively. Crucially, also, the value of gold affected the value of currencies in circulation. Major gold discoveries and new mining technologies influenced the supply of gold, and non-monetary uses of gold could affect its demand. The relative price of gold (i.e. relative to goods and services) could change on any of these grounds.

In short, the relative price of gold was not necessarily stable; that is, its *real value* could not be fixed.

In protesting against the operation of an international gold standard, Graham (1940a) proceeds directly to the heart of the matter. He takes for granted what we have stated in the foregoing paragraph. Next he asserts that fixing the money price of gold without being able to control its relative (real) value is problematic. National commodity price levels could not obviously be 'stabilized' – for example, changed at a constant rate or moved in unison internationally just because a gold standard is operating. Thus Graham perceived, quite correctly, that a gold standard (as opposed to a system of pure gold currencies) was inherently unstable. For the realistic case of government monopoly over the production of currency *and* in deflationary circumstances described in the last paragraph,

> Governments adopting the gold standard agreed ... to give a fixed weight of gold per unit of convertible legal tender to all persons presenting such legal tender.... The consequence was that, however great the demand for gold, its price, in the surrogates actually used as money, could not rise. When the money price of gold could not rise, while its value in terms of commodities is soaring, the note issuing authorities were thrust into the uncomfortable position of guaranteeing to sell, at a fixed price per unit, unlimited quantities of a metal of steadily rising real value.
>
> (Graham 1940a: 17)

The existence of currency serving as substitute for gold weakened one-to-one correspondence between changes in a nation's gold stock and national currency supplies. The causes of the 1929–33 depression are located squarely in the inherent instability of the international gold standard coupled with the stark reality of an inelastic gold supply. It was irrelevant whether currencies were convertible directly into gold or indirectly convertible (by being pegged to other gold-convertible currencies). The real value of gold rose in terms of goods and services from the early 1930s; this was a self-feeding process rather than a one-time event. Therefore it was irrational to buy goods or gold-linked currencies – better to hoard gold because its purchasing power was increasing. As Graham explained:

> To buy goods with gold, or gold currencies, was to invite a loss of money. To hold what were, in all probability, *ad interim* gold currencies was likely to be still more disastrous. The result was such pressure to secure gold as made the world forget that, if man cannot live by bread alone, he has still less chance of living by gold.
>
> (Graham 1940a: 17)

Gold was not a very stable anchor for fiduciary currencies after all, especially if one accepts Graham's admission of business cycles (including deflationary shocks) into the analysis. By extension, currency stability under a gold standard is repeatedly threatened when major economic shocks occur.[1]

Another feature of gold standards is the ironic flight to liquidity in deflationary phases of the business cycle which lead to increased production of a metal with few other uses than to provide a reserve or safe haven for panic-stricken market participants. Internationally, production and trade were affected badly in the 1920s and early 1930s by linking currencies to gold. First, exchange rates had to be considered as prices of currencies where currencies are regarded as having much in common with the prices of other commodities. Graham recognized the essential identity between currencies and commodities. Though unusual for the time, this was profoundly important for his later work on exchange rate policy and international finance (Graham 1940a: 26).[2] A fixed currency exchange rate against another currency which is 'anchored' by gold is unsustainable if a rise in the gold value of a currency (as with any other commodity) is precluded. Second, in a deflation the domestic money price of gold should rise to reflect that money's greater purchasing power over goods and services. Given that the money price of gold is fixed for each national currency, gold sales could be pressed to the point where the monetary authority's reserve is exhausted. In fact, gold reserves are not unlimited; the gold industry is not able instantly or smoothly to respond to an increased demand for its product by increasing output. The policy rules of a gold standard are not writ large for all market participants to appreciate – some will want to profit in deflationary conditions, from gold's inelastic supply. In other words, the

> policy adopted gives notice to both bulls and bears that, with a currency at or near its maximum in its gold price, it is dangerous to buy, and to establish a maximum gold price is, therefore, to lead the dice in favor of the bear speculator whenever that price is approximated. The gold price of the paper monetary unit can then move only downward, and the currency is thus thrust into the same precarious position as is inevitable to the maintenance of a gold standard with limited reserves.
> (1940a: 20–1)

The currency experiences of the interwar period amply demonstrated to Graham that bear speculators are bound to profit in an attack on a gold-linked currency. Official gold standard rules forestall speculators' losses. Speculators may convert their gold holdings *back* to a preferred national currency at any time for a fixed price. Any ongoing deflation affecting that currency would not, for speculators, have any downside while a potential inflation of the national price level would offer a profit.[3]

Perversely, any attempt to *manage* the fixed exchange rate rule of a gold standard with a plan to reduce the gold value of a currency unit would be futile; it would add grist to the mill of the 'bear speculator [who] has then only to sell the currency short for gold, in the confident expectation of presently buying it back at a lower gold price' (Graham 1940a: 21). When market participants possess a high degree of preference for liquidity – where liquidity means holding pure gold reserves as against holding currency substitutes – a gold standard regime is inherently unstable. Fixing the price of gold in one or another currency could not avert changes in the purchasing power of a currency because gold's relative price may change for many reasons. For instance, gold supply can be increased only slowly. This problem is brought into sharp focus when there are major macroeconomic shocks.

In several insightful articles during the 1940s Graham paid more attention to substitution effects and relative price effects attendant on gold standards. He neglected income and employment effects. Proponents of gold standards found it quite acceptable to plump for fixed exchange rates. Currencies anchored by gold could not be revalued. All adjustments had to take place in national price levels as, theoretically, gold moved from country to country in response to balance of payments discrepancies and disturbances. Again, in theory, money supplies would fluctuate directly and proportionally with net gold movements. In a deflationary economic downturn the process of substitution away from goods and services and paper currencies to gold hoardings does not reverse itself quickly or, what amounts to the same thing, the demand for money and the supply of money in a country experiencing deflation would not automatically adjust to equality. Adjustment may take place *in time* but only after a long time and after significant falls in nominal income and employment. 'The gold standard', wrote Graham (1944: 422), 'always operated in the right direction, but not with sufficient power or speed'. Thus, whenever individuals in a country showed an increasing preference for gold as a liquid reserve, they would give up domestic currency in return and the price level would fall. In theory again, the

> mining of gold was stimulated in compensation of the unemployment with which other industries were then afflicted. But the relative unimportance of gold-mining as an employer of labour, or its complete absence in many economies, reduced this compensation to negligible importance everywhere but in South Africa.
>
> (Graham 1944: 422–3)

Protracted employment instability had to be tolerated in almost every other country, especially those which did not exhibit 'a thoroughgoing flexibility' in all domestic prices, wages and interest rates. By the standards of policy goal-setting in the 1940s and later, Graham was well aware of the fact that employment stabilization had to be considered in any architectural scheme for the international financial order. A gold standard order could not promise high employment and output stabilization in the long run. Graham regretted that, despite attempts to manage the gold standard in the 1920s in order to overcome some of its limitations, gold 'still commands from Demos, and even more from Plutos, a somewhat superstitious reverence' (1940a: 24). And economists should not pander to such obvious irrationalities. However, he was comfortable with the idea – which incidentally Keynes inveighed against strongly – that domestic economic policy should be subordinated to the economic circumstances *external* to a nation.[4] Relying on the 'impersonal forces' of an international commodity standard for national currencies was not, in itself, undesirable. A commodity standard or anchor for currency issuance was not, as Keynes claimed, 'in error' for submitting national macroeconomic policies, especially monetary policy, to dictation by economic factors outside the control of politicians and their economic advisers (Graham 1944: 424).[5] Only the basis upon which the commodity standard had been constructed may be flawed. The task remained for economists to find a more appropriate commodity standard.

Heretical pronouncements on BW principles

Frank Graham's critique of the single commodity gold standard for the international financial order paled by comparison with his caustic remarks on the BW Agreement. He quickly perceived all the reasons for the eventual breakdown of the BW system. First he critically appraised leading proposals predating the BW Agreement and then he denounced the Agreement itself.

As outlined in Chapter 2 above, exchange rate stabilization was a key BW concern. In fact it could be argued that this stabilization objective became a singular architectural preoccupation from which all other elements of the BW financial order followed. Graham certainly saw it this way: the par value, fixed exchange rate was an 'unalterable desideratum' in various proposals for fundamental international financial reform leading up to the BW Conference (Graham 1943a: 7). It was as if the exchange rate choice had been made in a vacuum. He proceeded to demonstrate that without constancy in the relationship between national price levels, choosing fixed exchange rates created anomalies against which adjustments would have to be made. At first glance, there is nothing startling in this recognition, for the BW architects appreciated the point; they included a 'fundamental disequilibrium' adjustment guideline in the Agreement. Graham, however, went further. In his exhaustive classification there were four possible exchange rate alternatives that could be 'stable' whereas only one option was given serious consideration at BW.[6] The classification is contained in Table 5.1.

While Graham (1943a) did not use the term, Table 5.1, which uses his terminology, is concerned with *real* exchange rates. The real exchange rate

Table 5.1 Graham's exchange rate choices

Domestic purchasing power of national currencies (as determined by national price levels)	*Appropriate exchange rate*
1 Moves independently among nations	Proportionately fluctuating
2 Moves in unison – same direction and magnitude in given time periods	Fixed
3 Moves in some nations and not in others	Proportionately fluctuating
4 Remains stable in all nations	Fixed

is the variable economists should consider when advising on exchange rate choices. Ultimately a currency is only 'valuable' if it has purchasing power over domestic goods. With price levels in other countries taken as given and unchanging, the real value of a nation's currency changes with changes in the domestic price level. As the purchasing power (or real value) of a national currency changes with price level changes, so too would the relative price of the currency in terms of other currencies (the real exchange rate).

In Graham's analysis of exchange rate choices it is vital that the relationship between national price levels be ascertained. Do national policymakers endeavour by agreement, cooperation or policy coordination to conduct monetary policy in order to reach a modicum of constancy between national price levels? Do they do this without considering the impact on output and employment which may vary from country to country? Or is this outcome forced on all nations 'cooperating' in the BW-type fixed, adjustable exchange rate system? Otherwise, if complete monetary independence is permitted, might spontaneous coordination of monetary policies produce either price levels that move in unison (Graham's option 2) or the stable price level outcome (Graham's option 4) (see Table 5.1)? For Graham, monetary policy independence was more likely to produce *in*constancy between national price levels; currency purchasing powers would fluctuate and flexible exchange rates would be ineluctable.

BW principles imply either choice 2 or 4 in Table 5.1 though it was not clear which choice was being promoted at BW. BW architects appeared to leave the choice open.[7] The pre-1914 gold standard fits nicely into choice 4; in theory, national monetary policies were subordinated to gold movements, and price levels were stabilized over the long run. For the BW financial order, the fixed, adjustable exchange rate principle allowed much discretion for national policymakers. The principle was a compromise between rigidity and flexibility because it permitted national price level divergence over long time periods. Only later, when a 'fundamental disequilibrium' in the current account of the balance of payments was observed should the exchange rate be realigned. From Graham's standpoint, the compromise did not make for a coherent, plausible doctrine. Long lags between exchange rate realignments made the BW rule less credible, especially to participants in currency markets and international capital markets. The rule was tantamount either to postponing exchange rate changes until a financial crisis appeared or to maintaining a rate until a change was imminent, thereby issuing in 'cumulative dislocation in the structure of international trade and finance'. Here he attributed to the devastating international crisis in the early 1930s an international exchange rate regime which remained fixed in the face of diverging (and falling) price levels. It was not that fixed exchange rates were undesirable, only that they 'were inappropriate to the varying national monetary policies that then prevailed' (Graham 1943a: 6, 10).[8]

Two institutional developments could bolster the BW exchange rate rule: exchange controls and adherence to a policy of international cooperation. Graham (1940a: 27) viewed exchange controls as a pernicious route to exchange rate stability. Short-term capital movements 'quite unassociated with trade' may well be rationally motivated in the knowledge that transaction costs are low, that a given currency is being supported artificially, or that a currency's movement will persistently be one-way if left free to adjust or if a broadly expected adjustment in the exchange rate occurs so that a profit will be enjoyed. In a fixed exchange rate world, short-term financial flows tend to concentrate on one side of the market, thus exhibiting a bandwagon effect. The BW Agreement, in Graham's mind, depended on exchange controls to thwart bandwagon effects. By 1949 such controls had become 'widely current' and this suggested that 'the countries imposing them are aiming at totalitarianism, or bilateralism'. The extreme contemporary example was the pre-1945 German practice of rigid controls on currency convertibility – controls so strong that all currency exchange was handled by government. Less drastic controls only delayed inevitable currency realignments unless national price levels are held constant by government decree (Graham 1949: 11, 19 note 12).

The BW idea of international monetary cooperation was far too nebulous for Graham. There was no place for cooperation between nations on exchange rate policy in isolation. Narrow forms of policy cooperation would not produce international financial stability in the long run. Cooperative exchange rate policies lacked robust, lasting enforcement characteristics. The BW Agreement, setting par values of the 'right' exchange rates, was not enforceable; countries could simply resist IMF membership or exit membership when it suited national interests. If Graham's fundamental proposition that congruent monetary policies are required to maintain broad constancy in the relationship between national price levels (and thence secure fixed exchange rates) is accepted, it is inexplicable that the architects of the BW Agreement omitted explicit guidelines on the conduct of domestic monetary policy in member countries. Appropriately aligned monetary policies are the known route to price level stability, whereas in the BW financial order that outcome could arise as a happy accident. Along with the BW architects, Graham was inclined to 'look with a sceptical eye on an international organisation which would bind all [countries] to a single monetary scheme'. Yet Graham was critical of the BW Agreement and post-BW discussions on the grounds that they left some 'remote implications' that nations must conduct monetary policy 'in line with some unprescribed and uncertain norm' (1943a: 31, 1949: 18). It appeared likely that the norm would evolve out of a central tendency issuing from a hegemonic, large, industrialized and international creditor nation such as the United States. And since post-BW the US dollar became fixed in relation to gold (in a manner not inconsistent with the BW Agreement), IMF member nations pegging their currencies to the US dollar were unlikely to vary (indirectly) the gold value of their currencies. There would be pressure, therefore, to maintain monetary policies consistent with that of the United States. Similarities with the international gold standard did not go unnoticed.[9]

If the BW Agreement was to have any lasting force, Graham predicted that the call for monetary cooperation would ultimately bring hegemony to the international financial order. Two of his remarks deserve serious study in this connection. First:

> Because the pressure to be exerted on countries with currencies that show a tendency toward relative depreciation is, on the whole, greater than that contemplated for countries with currencies on the appreciated side, the upshot would presumably be an effort to enforce on all countries the policy of the currently more deflationary, or less inflationary country.
>
> (1943a: 18)

While there is nothing inherently wrong with the above outcome, it made a mockery of the BW call for 'cooperation'. Second:

> If we wish to ... abolish [exchange] controls, and still maintain fixed exchange rates we shall put all other polities in thrall to the monetary policy of the pecuniarily most powerful, or deflationary, country since they will all be forced to adjust to the monetary policy, however bad, of the said pecuniarily powerful, or deflationary, country.
>
> (1949: 11)

If a country was to remain an active member of the BW order, unilateral action on monetary policy was not only frowned upon because of an unwritten understanding to 'cooperate'; unilateral monetary action was denied if a nation was to play a meaningful role in an international financial system dominated by one or two powerful nations. The substitution of employment policy for monetary policy in the immediately foregoing passage changes nothing fundamentally. In any case a full employment policy requires an accommodating monetary policy.

Graham's focus on price level changes between countries produced an alternative prediction for instability, contrasting with the deflationary bias scenario which he thought might possibly unravel in the BW financial order. A nation independently pursuing a policy of monetary rectitude could find its price levels deflating more, or inflating less, than those of its main trading partners. Its currency could be deemed 'scarce' as defined by the BW Article of Agreement on scarce currencies. Instead of being allowed to upwardly revalue its currency, its 'scarce' currency would be rationed through the IMF. Discriminatory action against that country's export industries would follow under BW rules. Trade patterns would then be distorted. While discriminatory trade policies may be a temporary measure, 'they put a premium on progressive, and universal, inflationary practices'. A country with a 'scarce' currency would have an incentive to keep pace with the general rate of inflation elsewhere or otherwise run the risk of losing access to export markets. In short, the BW exchange rate rule could produce an inflationary bias. Graham attributed the bias in this direction to BW architects' reading of the 1930s' experience which was 'so impressed on [their] consciousness ... that they completely failed to take into account the evils of *in*flation'. The BW scarce currency provision indirectly encouraged nations to go 'on an inflationary junket' (Graham 1949: 12, his emphasis). Here Graham's attitude is heavily influenced by his own reading of the 1920s' experience and especially episodes of hyperinflation.[10] Also, by 1949 he was convinced that the widely observed US dollar scarcity was caused by a fixed exchange rate system in which the United States was playing a central role – a role potentially exacerbated by the BW scarce currency philosophy.

The BW Agreement was founded on national economic policy independence but the system which evolved in reality demanded for its durability certain agreed notional monetary policy norms. For the system to succeed, policies must be coordinated 'on a covenanted basis' and specify a straightforward price level or general price index target for each member country (Graham 1949: 14). The monetary policy independence asserted at BW to protect domestic economic management prosecuted in the interests of achieving high levels of employment was illusory in view of the ruling international financial order. Uncoordinated monetary policies not referenced to a price index target, non-discriminatory multilateral trade, free currency convertibility and fixed exchange rates grudgingly protected by ad hoc exchange controls were a precarious combination. Yet the BW Agreement gave unfortunate indication that these policies were perfectly compatible. In Frank Graham's harsh judgement, no rallying call for international cooperation could disguise the misleading impression of policy compatibility. Graham was one of the very few economists in the mid-twentieth century to look sceptically on the idea of international financial cooperation.

The commodity reserve standard proposal

> we might lift the world with a real lever, we shall never lift it with a broken reed.
>
> (Graham 1943b: 334)

The 1940s offered many economists an opportunity to provide constructive ideas for redesigning the international financial order. Graham took advantage of this opportunity. He was wary of the effects of flexible exchange rates, especially when exchange rate movements were volatile. The adverse effects of volatile exchange rates on international trade was an issue which, as we saw in Chapter 2, many economists including BW architects believed had been proved by incontrovertible evidence in the 1930s. Graham did not expressly throw his weight behind this judgement. Nevertheless, before the BW Agreement was drafted, Graham proposed the international adoption of a commodity reserve standard (CRS) for nations' currencies. This CRS relied on monetary reconstruction as a first step towards achieving exchange rate stability, enhancing international trade and ensuring global price stability.[11]

The essential idea behind the CRS was that a currency should be issued solely in exchange for a fixed combination of warehouse receipts for a basket of storable commodities. National moneys would be valuable in terms of a basket of commodities. For Graham, a nation should aim to produce 'a rationally conceived currency' (1940b: 6). As such, the gold standard was a rational, single commodity standard for currency issuance. Graham (1941) proposed that a currency be defined in terms of so much wheat, so much rubber, so many ounces of gold and silver, copper and so forth. The ultimate objective was to establish a currency standard for the international economy based upon a designated composite of widely available, widely used raw materials and storable commodities. This is precisely why other leading contemporary economists understood the CRS idea as a fundamental point of departure for genuine monetary reconstruction (Hayek 1943; Friedman 1951).

At the national level one might envisage currency being issued against a chosen set of storable commodities. National law would prescribe units of each commodity to be included in a composite commodity 'basket'. A defined unit or fraction of a commodity 'basket' would be made equivalent to a national currency unit (e.g. one US dollar); it would be exchangeable at a fixed (currency) price when the law was enacted. Following Irving Fisher (1935), Graham favoured a 100 per cent reserve backing rule – whether cash reserves or commodity-equivalent reserves – for monetary authorities and banking systems adopting a CRS.[12] Each unit of a commodity basket would be referenced to the average market price of the group of commodities composing the basket over a preceding period of years. In the meantime and into the future, the *relative* prices of chosen individual commodities would freely vary; only the aggregate price would be fixed. Legal tender currency would be issued by monetary authorities against the deposit of warehouse receipts or vice versa. There are close resemblances here to the contemporary practice on gold trading exchanges. Thus, for example, the US dollar 'would, in effect, be a warehouse certificate having all the desirable characteristics of a gold certificate and of gold-secured money – gold backing, redeemability, limitation of issue – plus certain highly important qualities now lacking in our money' (Graham 1942: 95).

Like gold certificates, composite commodity certificates backing currency issues would be impersonal, non-political and automatically issued. Automaticity would have two favourable stabilizing effects. First, in an inflationary boom, raw materials would be withdrawn from the reserve in return for money – currency would in effect be cancelled, thereby reducing the money supply and counteracting inflationary tendencies. Second, in a period of depression, liquidity in the form of cash is in heavy demand and the requirement for commodity warehouse certificates (or receipts) must be increased as more currency is issued. Industries producing commodities included in the composite unit would be stimulated, thereby absorbing unemployment and increasing investment. All this should counteract deflationary tendencies. Unlike gold-based commodity standards, the broader composite commodity standard would have a much greater impact on the economy during the ebb and flow of monetary demand. The real economic responses would necessitate changes in the production of many useful commodities and not just precious metals.[13] Furthermore, the

> money paid out in the process of production of the goods gathered into the warehouses could be spent, if at all, only on other goods and, together with the expenditures of the recipients of payments in the process of manufacture of these other goods would raise the prices of such goods above costs of production.
>
> (Graham 1942: 99)

Irrespective of the public's preferences for liquidity at any time, there would be no general restraint on output and employment in adopting a CRS as backing for the issue of currency. A CRS would have strong anticyclical potential and protect economies from major monetary shocks linked to macroeconomic mismanagement. Nevertheless, a severe, prolonged depression might legitimately require relaxation of the 100 per cent commodity reserve requirement; unbacked currency might have to be issued perhaps in payment for a government's public works though only 'until prices rose sufficiently' (Graham 1942: 103).[14]

When extended to the international realm, the CRS idea had some major implications: fixed exchange rates between currencies could be maintained in those countries adopting a common CRS for monetary policy and currency issues. National price levels would move in unison with one another. As in the national case, the price level of the composite commodity unit backing currency issues would be fixed while relative commodity prices denominated in any one currency would vary as before. Graham suggested that a major industrialized country should take a lead in establishing a CRS for its own currency as part of the transition to wider adoption. Gold would still have a place in the transition so that existing monetary arrangements and conventions would not be disturbed. The value of gold, in terms of the chosen composite group of commodities in a CRS, could be stabilized:

> The procedure is precisely that of the gold standard except that it applies to a group of important raw materials of industry rather than to a single, and not very important, commodity. If, in addition, the country or countries inaugurating such purchases should, as of yore, offer to buy and sell gold freely, i.e., at a fixed price, the value of gold in terms of the composite of commodities would be fixed, or, to put it the other way round, the gold price level of the group of commodities would be unchanging.
>
> (1943a: 21)

The international price of the composite unit of commodities would have to be monitored by a leading central bank or international agency. Composite commodity warehouse receipts would only be bought or sold by central banks adopting a CRS when the aggregate price of the composite was, respectively, falling or rising. In particular, given widespread expectation of a significant economic downturn after 1945, introduction of a CRS would protect a much greater segment of world industry and income than a system anchored to gold alone. As in the national case, an international financial order built upon a CRS among like-minded nations would have built-in stabilizing effects on incomes, price levels and currencies.

Graham considered the IMF a suitable candidate for a policy-coordinating role in administering an international CRS. Indeed, the IMF or BIS could formally designate an international composite 'unit' of raw materials against which national currencies might be issued and their value fixed (Graham 1944: 425). Later in the BW period, during the 1960s, prominent advocates of the CRS idea – Nicholas Kaldor, Albert Hart and Jan Tinbergen – proposed that the IMF or another international agency create a new international currency unit (the 'bancor') defined as the value of a basket of key primary commodities with a given composition.[15]

In the early 1940s up to the creation of the BW Agreement and associated institutions, Graham saw no way of escaping the logic of a CRS. Gold must have a subsidiary role in securing international financial stability and the most challenging task was to widen the commodity base beyond gold; that base was to act as an anchor for national currencies and relationships between them. A generally stable international currency order needed anchoring. Wholly unanchored mediums of exchange and units of international account carried with them not only greater instability in currency exchange rates; they risked greater indiscipline in the conduct of monetary policy. The nationalization of money following the demise of the gold standard brought with it a great danger – 'any groups that can get control of the monetary system will have totalitarian power over the lives and fortunes of their fellows, without a clear recognition of responsibility' (Graham 1944: 426). It was this political issue which Keynes (1944) addressed in his response to Graham. Keynes railed against commodity standards, including the gold standard, because they purportedly subjected domestic wages and employment policies instantly to the discipline of external price levels. A broader CRS has fine credentials in principle because it adheres to monetary purity, though in practice it imposed international price stability and thence currency stability without leaving room for national policy variations and it submitted national wage policies in particular to 'outside dictation' (Keynes 1943b: 187). The latter influence could potentially be explosive and ultimately render a CRS politically infeasible:

> I doubt the political wisdom of appearing, more than is inevitable in any orderly system, to impose an external pressure on national standards and therefore on wage levels. Of course, I do not want to see money wages forever soaring upwards to a level to which real wages cannot follow. It is one of the chief tasks ahead of our statesmanship to find a way to prevent this. But we must solve it in our own domestic way, feeling that we are free men, free to be wise or foolish. The suggestion of *external* pressure will make the difficult psychological and political problem of making good sense prevail still more difficult.
>
> (Keynes 1944: 429–30, his emphasis)

In Keynes's view, writing on the eve of BW discussions, why waste breath on a scheme which many countries would likely reject? Graham disagreed: countries using a CRS could choose to have independent policies leading to less stable domestic price levels; in that event, their price levels would not move in unison with others adopting a CRS. As well, exchange rates between currencies would adjust accordingly.[16] In theory, currencies would move in direct correspondence with variation in the *local* currency price of the international composite commodity unit relative to the fixed price of this unit in other currencies. In other words, exchange rates would perfectly reflect relative purchasing power of currencies over the composite commodity.[17] There is nothing, therefore, in the CRS scheme requiring countries to submit passively to external price pressures as Keynes had insisted. Ultimately there is no substitute for a disciplined monetary policy in a world financial order organized around a CRS. Graham's (1944: 429) conclusions went strongly against Keynes on this score:

> Any unemployment that may result from this cause is an inevitable phase of freedom. It would be as fatal to freedom to insist that, to avoid any unemployment whatever, the enterpriser must pay whatever monetary wages organised workers may demand, and that the State must so shape its monetary policy as to make this possible, as it would be to insist, to the same end, that workers must accept whatever monetary wage a fascist group of employers might see fit to impose.

There is a copious literature on the strengths and weaknesses of CRS proposals.[18] A CRS for currency issuance is costly because, unlike fiat money, it involves expenditure on storage, maintenance, administration and depreciation of a commodity stock.[19] Furthermore, with ongoing economic growth the supply of international money, that is liquid assets (currencies) linked to a CRS, would need to grow in tandem, thus creating a demand for growth in commodity reserves. More of the world's resources would need to be devoted to producing and storing the relevant commodities which act as currency anchors under a CRS.

While Graham's case for a CRS is compelling when considered in isolation, for reasons that are not explained he gave up on the idea after 1944. Clearly, BW institutions and principles, once created, rendered the CRS idea redundant. BW assumed that monetary authorities wished to regulate the supply of fiat money at will so as to accommodate active fiscal policy in the interests of reaching full employment without too much delay. The CRS was, by contrast, a fundamental financial reform whereas the BW system evolved to create a narrow, indirect commodity exchange standard (gold) for the US dollar which remained for a long time at the centre of the whole BW edifice.

A plan for full employment and price stability after BW

> the only rational course is the adoption of a system of freely flexible exchange rates in a free market for both goods and currencies.
>
> (Graham 1949: 14)

1 Exchange rates post-BW

By the late 1940s Graham's lack of interest in the CRS derived from the grand design that was born out of BW. In order to mount a realistic critique and provide a constructive alternative to the BW order, he started and ended with monetary policy. To pursue active exchange rate management as proposed at BW, congruent monetary policies had to be formulated between members of the BW order. That was no small task and only likely to be carried out adventitiously. Graham's first premise was that the BW fixed, adjustable exchange rate rule ran the risk of allowing speculation as a one-way currency bet on nations exhibiting tendencies towards 'fundamental disequilibrium' in the current account of the balance of payments. The BW order encouraged postponement and perhaps slowing of adjustment to international disturbances; in this it intensified rather than eliminated international payments problems.

As established in the BW Agreement and as then widely desired if countries were left free to choose their own monetary policies and monetary standards in an *un*coordinated manner, the international financial order must assume the following character:

a allow exchange rates an immediate functional role in economic adjustment; that is, let them move in correspondence with the relative purchasing powers of currency in each country; and
b tie at least one national money 'somewhere ... to goods on a stable basis' (Graham 1943a: 29, 31).

By 1949 Graham was willing to go the whole way and promote flexible exchange rates irrespective of the existence of a leading currency which may or may not be tied to gold or a basket of several commodities.

> Appropriately flexible exchange rates are not nearly so disturbing to business as fluctuating commodity price levels, and, when national price levels are moving at different paces and, perhaps, in opposite directions, flexible exchange rates will counter, rather than fortify, the aberrations in commodity price relationships.
>
> (Graham 1949: 13)[20]

As well, institutions would spontaneously develop under a system of flexible exchange rates, for example futures markets in currency – which could reduce uncertainty.

2 *Monetary policy: international implications*

In Graham's financial architecture, as before, the domestic price level relative to foreign price levels is the critical variable. National monetary policy would initially be chosen uncooperatively on the basis of macroeconomic targets in each country or region. Exchange rates could be aligned and remain fixed between countries with broadly similar monetary policies and economic structures or between countries consciously coordinating their monetary policies on a covenanted basis. Exchange rates would remain stable, given both external price level movements and monetary policies in other countries if national monetary policy was set to the following *rule*: attain and maintain domestic price level stability (Graham 1949: 13). Internal monetary stability begets exchange rate stability – these are complementary and mutually supportive. Therefore, domestic price level instability such as a high and accelerating rate of inflation eventually thwarts exchange rate stability. On the other hand an internationally stable price level promotes currency stability and reduces the risk of domestic price level variations.

Policy measures designed to influence the balance of payments, such as managed exchange rates, tariffs and the like, could not properly be understood without specifying the monetary consequences of those measures. Graham held what was only later to be dubbed the 'monetary approach to the balance of payments' (Frenkel and Johnson 1976). This approach was mostly associated with the Chicago tradition in economic theory (which we shall discuss at length in Chapter 7). The essence of the monetary approach turned on the proposition that domestic credit conditions established by monetary policy were vital determinants of the balance of international payments at any moment. By contrast, a stringent Keynesian approach, of the kind we have attributed to Alvin Hansen in Chapter 3, would have focused on the interdependence between international adjustment through the balance of payments and domestic income and employment. Graham's monetary approach had the advantage of simplicity though he did not deny the importance of non-monetary factors such as productivity changes. His monetary approach leads directly, in a fixed exchange rate world, to the determination of the overall current account balance (or imbalance) as the difference between changes in the demand for money and changes in net domestic assets. Changes in domestic credit (strongly influenced by monetary policy) act as a catalyst for that difference. Graham understood the issue straightforwardly: 'Provided the monetary income of a country is kept in the appropriate proportion with its real output [relative to world income and output in each case], I do not see how its international accounts can get out of balance'.[21]

If there is an imbalance between international receipts and payments, Graham would have replied that there is no substitute for monetary policy in correcting the imbalance – appropriate monetary action would be successful. Of course monetary action would not obviate the need for price and wage flexibility; the latter would enhance the speed of correction. These flexibilities Graham took for granted in an era when, as mere observation so often demonstrated, wages, prices and interest rates were rigid.

3 Fiscal policy

Graham's proposals on fiscal policy were heavily influenced by disdain for inflation which, in turn, as noted earlier, results from a particular reading of country experiences in the 1920s. Unlike his position on monetary policy his conviction was that fiscal policy must have a truly national focus with no substantive international implications.

Ad hoc public works schemes, subsidies to consumers and socialization of investment were generally unacceptable. Furthermore, the imposition of taxation and expansion of government debt should be severely circumscribed by the need to prevent inflation. Yet 'the creation and maintenance of full employment, along with a stable price level, must lie with the national government'. Keynesian 'pump-priming' initiatives involving extraordinary government expenditures were flawed (Graham 1946: 40–1). First, money spent under special government outlays may come into the hands of those who do not spend it. Second, expectations among private market participants are not changed by 'ephemeral' government fiscal actions, private investment will not respond positively to a 'momentary flare-up in consumers' goods industries' encouraged by additional government expenditure and, in sum, even 'persistence in pump-priming is ... of little avail without assurance of its indefinite continuation'. Third, if continuation of additional government outlays was indeed assured, much government expenditure is nevertheless 'unproductive' in that it either involves emergency relief or infrastructure construction which receives no '*quid pro quo*' in a saleable form, that is no direct monetary return of principal or interest to offset the outlays. A steady progression in government debt ensues unless taxation is increased to finance such expenditures (Graham 1942: 88).

Whereas day-to-day frictional unemployment was a temporary phenomenon that did not require government assistance, cyclical and chronic unemployment must have a planned government response. In accepting the need for government action, Graham was left with few traditional fiscal policy tools to complete the task. With acuteness and originality, he made fiscal policy the servant of a consistently applied monetary initiative. In general, as already discussed, monetary policy per se should be conducted strictly to achieve price stability in an economy where the banking system held to a 100 per cent deposit reserve requirement. In the capitalist monetary economy the advent of depression created price instability on the downside so a monetary policy response might be necessary. Individuals in depression conditions prefer to demand more money than goods and, since private profit-making commercial banks tend to err on the conservative side, their risk-averse lending policies also contribute to the depression conditions. Therefore, in extreme deflationary contexts, government action using monetary means is by far the best response.

The centrepiece of Graham's scheme is the free issue of government credits to finance producers' inventories that are not readily saleable in a depression. With the United States as an example, an official list of 'standard storable goods' would be created by a newly constituted Federal Recovery Corporation (FRC). Obtaining credits from the Federal Reserve

Banks (FRBs), the FRC would purchase liens over any unsold inventory of officially listed storable goods held by manufacturers and agriculturalists. The purchase price would be sufficient to cover variable costs (only) of production plus storage and insurance costs.[22] Inventory finance would be interest free and would be forthcoming from a newly issued deposit credit to producers' accounts at commercial banks. The FRBs must damp subsequent credit multiplier effects by insisting on the 100 per cent bank reserve ratios. The countercyclical element in the FRC proposal amounts to boosting producers' money incomes which they expend on workers' labour and supplies of raw materials. The tendency for wages and prices to fall will be counteracted, while real goods continue to be produced. Titles to the goods would remain with producers as long as production is continued. Producers could sell the goods to any private buyer at any time and price and then repay the lien.

Naturally, consumers' preferences can change. The FRC would adjust its official list accordingly:

> The FRC will shift the emphasis of its purchase of liens, to correspond with evolving demand, whenever it appears that it is accumulating an excessive volume of liens on any good *in relation to other commodities*. But, so long as depression, deflation, and unemployment continue to threaten, it will be under statutory obligation to keep its *aggregate* purchases at the level necessary to maintain full industrial activity.
>
> (Graham 1946: 46, his emphasis)

A reservoir of goods will absorb excess supplies in depression; aggregate national expenditure on output will be kept in close relationship to the money costs of production; the price level of storable goods will be stabilized, thereby exerting a strong stabilizing influence on the general price level. Employment will also decline less than it might have otherwise. The reservoir's composition will act as a signal to producers of demand fluctuations and of future exploitable production opportunities.

In a response to Graham's enthusiasm for government creation of a commodity reserve, Keynes (1944: 430) warned that buffer stocks 'can so easily be turned into producers' ramps'. Another danger in supporting raw materials' production and manufacturing is the neglect of services. Resources would necessarily be diverted into the production of storable goods by the FRC even if the demand for services collapsed during a depression. In a spirit reminiscent of Adam Smith and like-minded classical economists, Graham maintained: 'we must produce additional storable goods when the demand for services declines, if we are not to suffer productive resources to run to waste'. And, he continued, 'no society has ever been brought to destitution in the possession of large and well-distributed stocks of goods'. Graham criticized the arguments of the

'Keynesian school of economists' because they asserted that private savings were outrunning the propensity to invest those savings – *ergo*, unemployment should be prevented by cajoling or coercing private individuals to invest directly in certain types of production (1946: 54, 56–8, 60). Preferably, governments should place more money in private hands in return for a lien on storable goods, thereby augmenting private purchasing power. Employment would be maintained in those industries on the official list. The reservoir of financed inventory would expand during a depression; little inflation would be forthcoming in an economic recovery as long as there were goods to be sold from the reservoir at or above pre-existing costs of production with the proceeds being withdrawn from circulation (as liens are repayed to the FRBs via the FRC).

Two matters raised by the 1944 British White Paper on employment drew Graham's bitter comments in the light of his FRC plan. Full employment could be attained without inflation, without ad hoc public works expenditure or greater tariff protection or export subsidies. The common national fear of imports often induced distortionary trade policies which were completely irrational in Graham's mind. As for public works, these should be judged on their merits and not be instituted as countercyclical projects simply to soak up unemployment. For example, the Tennessee Valley developments in the 1930s made good economic sense irrespective of the level of unemployment. Any slackening in the demand for exports should not lead to bans or restrictions on imports. Instead, under Graham's FRC plan falling export demand would be reflected in a larger reservoir held under lien by the FRC; domestic demand and employment would be supported in the short run. Rising export demand could be supported by withdrawals from the reservoir without being associated with rising domestic prices for the exportable goods. Graham conceded that the United States was less dependent than Great Britain on foreign trade and on employment in tradable goods industries. The FRC reservoir principle made more sense as a short-run policy response – as 'protection' against comparatively small fluctuations in foreign demand. Long-run adjustments in production for export must still be made though this would be assisted by analysis conducted by the FRC which would subsequently adjust its official list of storable goods against which liens would be offered.

Altogether, Graham's 'fiscal' policy initiative for financing inventories was radical in formulation and monetary in operation. Once established, the FRC did not require short-run fine-tuning or arbitrary action by government officials to direct investment or to create a public works project come what may. The FRC plan required minimal administration; it stabilized price levels and producers' incomes and obviated the need for special tax levies to promote employment relief schemes in a depression. In addition, the FRC would not lead to exorbitant growth in public debt and it was consistent with a liberal trade policy.

Conclusion

For Frank Graham, economic theory was a vehicle for transporting economists towards conclusions on economic policy. His policy reformist intent is no better illustrated than in the CRS idea, in the flexible exchange rate proposal and in the FRC initiative. According to one obituary, 'he worked unstintingly to secure the adoption of social and economic reform' (Whittlesey 1952: 442). Friedrich Hayek's (1945: 177) adulation is also worthy of repeating in this regard: 'We can surely agree with him in regretting the neglect of political economy which has accompanied the preoccupation with pure economics; and we must be gratified for the distinguished contribution he has made to the former'.

The Graham doctrine for the international financial order is summarized in Table 5.2. It is a rule-based programme for *both* national economic policy *and* policies for the international financial order.

The rules binding national economic policy in the above table (p. 100) had implications for the international financial architecture. For example, the 100 per cent monetary reserve requirement and balanced budget rule would have assisted in maintaining domestic price stability and, if groups of nations interacting in the international realm followed these rules closely, exchange rate stability would have been unproblematic even if a flexible exchange rate regime had been widely adopted. An international agency established to create an international CRS was his first preference. Again, the CRS was a rule-based institutional arrangement aimed at minimizing day-to-day political interference, thus turning the international order into an automatic mechanism.

Residing at the core of Graham's CRS doctrine was a requirement that a spontaneous consensus develop among nations on a credible set of guidelines for the conduct of monetary policy. Graham conceded that in the postwar 'nationally-minded world' such a consensus might never materialize (1943a: 8). In that case, barring acceptance of a CRS, fully flexible exchange rates and independent monetary policies were logical and preferable. In the event, policy synchronization might only emerge accidentally. Liquidity problems expected in the IMF scarce currency provisions were completely resolvable by adopting flexible exchange rates. Failing that, a 100 per cent reserve requirement and a price stability objective enshrined in national monetary policy in all IMF member countries would indirectly ensure exchange rate stability. Internal balance, in Graham's essentially pre-Keynesian perspective, must follow automatically and it would not require a macroeconomic policy bias towards inflation to bring into effect.

Any loose form of international cooperation and policy coordination that might evolve after BW could only be effective if it was designed around monetary policies limiting policymakers' incentive to inflate. From that imperative everything else follows in Graham's doctrine. Positive

Table 5.2 Summary: Graham's rule-based scheme for economic policy

Policy instrument	*Time horizon*	*Primary assignment*	*Secondary assignment*	*Rules*
Exchange rate policy	All	External balance External balance	–	a) Flexible exchange rates *OR* b) Fixed rate CRS standard
Exchange controls	All	–	–	• Liberalize
Official reserves	Short term Medium–long term	Exchange rate stability External balance	External balance	• If fixed exchange rate: adopt CRS and manipulate commodity reserves
Monetary policy	All	Internal balance	External balance	• 100% reserve requirement • Target price level stability without reference to targets in other countries
Fiscal policy: a) Tax and expenditure policy	All	Internal balance	–	• Target balanced budget
AND b) Inventory financing	All	Internal balance	–	• Create countercyclical commodity reservoir to maintain employment
Trade policy	All	–	–	• Liberalize
Investment policy	All	–	–	• Leave to market forces

demonstration effects from the experience of implementing low inflation-achieving monetary and fiscal policies must be relied upon to encourage international consultation, cooperation and policy coordination. In particular the main content of inter-country consultation would need to focus on the conduct of monetary policy. Graham's doctrine therefore reduces to the following consistent trilogy:

1 flexible exchange rates;
2 independent national monetary policies;
3 freer trade and international capital mobility.

That Graham did not succeed in drawing wide attention to the defects of the BW Agreement is scarcely surprising given the overriding consensus formed in 1944 on the desirability of fixed exchange rates and managed international money. His perspective did not provoke extensive debate among contemporary economists, though Keynes, Hayek and Friedman noted the importance of some of his ideas. Later in the debates on international finance his contribution did not rate a mention. It was not until the 1950s that economists began seriously to consider flexible exchange rates and then only reluctantly in response to Friedman (1953). The practicability of Graham's proposals for national economic policy which would support his vision for the international financial order was certainly questionable. For instance, balanced budget thinking had been discarded in the mainstream of economic thought in the 1930s and the 100 per cent reserve requirement for domestic commercial banks seemed too conservative. In the postwar world, most economists were deeply suspicious of 'automatic' market processes. With policymakers, politicians and their constituencies demanding widespread government economic management to create and maintain full employment, Graham's original doctrine was destined to fall by the wayside.

6 Robert Triffin's supranational central bank

A plan to stabilize liquidity

> The enormous expansion of the objectives and techniques of state intervention in economic life seems to be incompatible with the restoration and maintenance of [currency] convertibility on the basis of uncoordinated national decisions and policies of several scores of independent sovereign states. . . . A collective organization and effective standard are particularly essential . . . if we are to eschew . . . pitfalls . . . sadly demonstrated by events in the early 1930s.
>
> (Triffin 1957: 303)

Intellectual background

Robert Triffin cultivated an interest in international financial problems during studies at the University of Louvain, Belgium, in the late 1930s. Born in Belgium, Triffin was a US resident and citizen for all of his professional life as an economist. After a period of study in Harvard where he was influenced by John Williams and Alvin Hansen, he produced some important research on central banking, exchange controls and banking systems in less developed countries first as head of the Latin American Unit at the Federal Reserve Board and later as Chief of the Exchange Control Division at the IMF. From the time he assumed a professorship at Yale in 1951 until his retirement in 1978, Triffin devoted his energies to international economic problems and, specifically, to reforming the international financial order.[1]

To begin with, we can foreshadow some of the chapter's conclusions and locate Triffin in the doctrinal line-up presented in the previous four chapters. Along with the BW architects, Triffin shared a deep distrust for free international capital markets and free exchange rates. From the late 1950s the BW system (as opposed to the ideal order in the BW blueprint) had evolved into a *de facto* key currency arrangement (James 1996: 155–6). This evolution drew Triffin's fervid denunciation. Indeed, his international financial reform proposals were to run completely counter to the key currency ideas promoted by his Harvard instructor, John Williams. That Triffin not once in his extensive writings cited the contributions of

Williams favourably on this subject perhaps attests to his dissatisfaction with Williams's ideas.[2]

The key currency approach had been dismissed in one ill-tempered comment by Keynes because it supposedly looked after the interests of the United States and Great Britain while letting the rest of the world 'go hang'. Likewise, Triffin harboured profound misgivings about the necessary conditions enabling the key currency approach to work. The rehabilitation of sterling was an essential prerequisite and the Anglo-American loan agreement in 1946 was supposed to help reinstate sterling as a key currency. Unfortunately, the loan 'was too niggardly, however, to allow war-impoverished Britain to bear alone the burden placed on its shoulders' (Triffin 1957: 142). The loan proved so inadequate that sterling was not restored to its leadership status as a widely convertible currency until the late 1950s.

In the meantime there was something rather perverse about allowing the international financial system to be operated along single, US dollar key currency lines. The BW order permitted an outcome such as to make life better in the short term for the 'rich men's club' of leading industrial countries such as the United States. And it did not, on Triffin's prognosis, serve the broader aims of stability, peace and economic prosperity for all countries in the long run. To consider how he arrived at this conclusion we need to review his early work up to the late 1940s on the international gold standard pre-1914, on interwar financial events and on the BW Agreement.

Triffin's revisionist views on the operation of the gold standard

Triffin's assessment of the classical gold standard *in operation*, rather than the pure textbook doctrine which rationalized that standard, coloured his perspective on what ought to be done post-1945 to change the international financial architecture. Prior to 1914, central bankers, policymakers and most economists agreed that currencies should have a commodity (preferably gold) basis and that international payments imbalances must be settled by shipments of gold. The textbook depiction of how gold standards in general operated was, in Triffin's 'revisionist' perspective, full of mythmaking.[3] One of the more enduring myths was that gold, as a form of international money, managed itself, with central banks simply reacting passively as ancillary facilitators of the monetary forces propelled by nations' payments imbalances. Thus,

> International balance, if disturbed, would be restored because of the effects of the ensuing domestic contraction or expansion on relative cost and interest levels at home and abroad and the resulting shifts in trade and capital movements. The automatic monetary contraction

> produced by gold exports would raise interest rates and attract capital from abroad. It would at the same time exert a downward pressure on domestic prices and costs, thus stimulating exports and discouraging imports. Both of these movements – capital and trade – would tend to correct the balance of payments deficit in which they originated.
>
> (Triffin 1947a: 48)

A surplus would also be self-corrective but the process would begin with gold imports. Gold flows would affect price levels in trading nations; gold inflows would raise price levels and vice versa. Relative prices between trading nations would change and thereby change competitiveness. The amount of gold in each country automatically tends towards an equilibrium at which exports and imports of goods balance. In short, payments imbalances were automatically adjusted in the long run. All this was a faithful rendering of David Hume's classical, price-specie flow doctrine which remained entrenched in textbooks on the subject well into the twentieth century.[4] In its unadulterated form the classical explanation of the automatic adjustment process leaves 'no room for national sovereignty over currency or money'. Furthermore, gold as *the* accepted international money is 'impervious to national manipulation or management' (Triffin 1947a: 49). In honouring the tacit rules of the classical gold standard order, central banks could use discount rate policies and open market operations to expedite the self-correcting effects of market forces upon which the gold standard was founded. In doing so, they were to depart from the purest form of the rules, though the effects appeared innocuous. Interest rates would rise as credit was tightened in deficit countries and the opposite would occur in surplus countries. While logically consistent, this 'simplified digest' of the theory of international adjustment in an international financial order based on gold was far from being descriptively accurate.[5]

The existence of central banks in the nineteenth century, coupled with deposit banking and legislated fractional reserve private banking systems, created very real conflicts between central bank practice and the classical, Humean doctrine or the automatic gold standard and its associated rules. The incidence and degree of monetary volatility in national economies was influenced by existing banking institutions and superstructure. Using the Bank of England as an example, Triffin demonstrated how, operating on a narrow gold base, the Bank interfered in the pure gold standard process and greatly increased monetary disturbances by comparison with what would have occurred under a pure gold standard. The Bank 'was led to follow credit policies which not only permitted but also reinforced' the automatic economic responses resulting from the retirement or disbursement (as the case required) of its legal tender notes in exchange for gold. The fractional reserve banking effects were pronounced. For instance, using an official ratio of 33 per cent, any net change in the gold reserve held by a central bank was able to create a threefold change in the credit base. Yet under the pure Humean gold standard rule, international payments imbalances 'produced only an equivalent amount of expansion or contraction in the monetary circulation'; it did not foster some multiple change in either direction. While consistent with the requisite direction of gold flows and economic adjustment dictated by a pure gold standard, such responses were exaggerated by existing monetary institutions and practices (Triffin 1947a: 52). Bank of England officials defended multiple contraction or expansion as a way of speeding up economic adjustment so as to conserve international gold reserves. However, a gold standard purist would maintain that much greater domestic monetary instability resulted: investment activities were deleteriously affected and output fluctuations became needlessly pronounced.

Just as John Williams had seen the gold standard pre-1914 as a sterling standard, Triffin made the very same claim but with a crucial twist which set his approach on a collision course with Williams's. The gold movements initiated (say) by rising British interest rates brought changes in Great Britain's balance of payments but not through major effects on the British economy; the greatest impact was felt by Great Britain's trading partners, especially the agricultural and raw materials-producing countries. Capital flows accentuated these effects – flowing towards the latter countries in times of prosperity and away in times of depression. Major financial centres and countries, far from being equal in the balance of payments adjustment process, were fair weather friends to small exporting countries. Triffin (1947a: 60) was beginning to formulate a critique of the key country, key currency doctrine as it played out in practice during the gold standard era. The financial centres could in fact 'shift part of the burden of adjustment upon the weaker countries in the world economy'. The 'sterling standard' rather than the pure gold standard offered a salutary lesson: larger countries (in an economic sense) could transmit cyclical fluctuations – price, income and employment changes – on to other, smaller countries less able to defend themselves without resorting to protectionist trade policies and foreign exchange controls.

A broad feature of nineteenth- and early twentieth-century experience, which could not be explained by textbook explanations of the gold standard, related to parallel cyclical movements in imports and exports for *one* country compared with trade movements for other trading countries. Such parallel movements (as against divergent movements) were commonly observed between surplus and deficit countries.[6] Balance of payments disturbances are explained by the pure classical approach in terms of cost and price disparities between one country and the rest of the world. All trading countries were co-equal as far as their trading capabilities were concerned. Obviously this was not a realistic assumption for the actual operation of the gold standard up to 1914. Triffin (1947a: 55–6) observed that many of the 'most spectacular disequilibria in the balance of payments are world-wide in scope', showing parallel cyclical patterns rather than divergent, single-country (or regional) price and cost maladjustments. Up to 1914, large cyclical fluctuations tended to be synchronous in all major industrial countries, circumstances that classical doctrine was not equipped to explain.[7] It was therefore scarcely surprising for Triffin that even the manufactured rules of the gold standard game were increasingly violated, all the more so from the 1920s onwards.

With increasing national monetary management after 1920, international gold movements which financed trade imbalances had a diminishing influence on domestic monetary expansion and contraction. The total value of money could no longer be controlled by gold movements. Now the gold standard as such was definitely not operating smoothly; national stabilization policies alongside more rigid wages and prices thwarted the self-correcting changes in price and cost competitiveness usually associated with the gold standard mechanism whatever form it assumed in practice. International payments imbalances observed in major cyclical downturns tended to be corrected by general income adjustments rather than price changes.[8]

The dynamics of balance of payments adjustment changed dramatically in the 1920s and 1930s for the following reasons:

1 international capital movements began to dampen, and in some cases stimulate, large and persistent surpluses and deficits in international payments on current account;
2 variations in long-term capital movements were erratic and did not play a stabilizing role in all instances;
3 all countries were not of equal economic size so that smaller, open, more export-dependent economies were increasingly subject to major price and quantity changes, along with associated 'perverse fluctuations' in long-term capital imports (which they needed for economic development) and violent terms of trade changes over the course of any normal business cycle (Triffin 1964a: 7–8);
4 monetary authorities wished more stridently than before to intervene in the adjustment process by emphasizing immediate attainment of domestic policy objectives; and
5 given the alleged shortage of gold to back the growing volume of national currencies and facilitate trade in the 1920s, a broad consensus emerged from various international financial conferences to expand the use of credit money as international reserves to supplement gold.

Major financial centres were to take the lead in respect of (5) above, making their currencies gold convertible. This

> solution was particularly favored and propagandized by British experts who rightly expected to see sterling – the most prestigious cur-

> rency of the largest and oldest trading and financial center of the world – play the major role: it would enable the United Kingdom to finance its deficits and/or strengthen its slender gold reserves through the acceptance of its own paper IOUs as international reserves by other central banks.
>
> (Triffin 1969b: 402)

Currencies became more acceptable as international reserve media. Currency and gold reserves continued to permit fixed exchange rates and give countries more time to make orderly internal adjustments to payments imbalances. Monetary authorities in the 1920s were given an opportunity to play a broader macroeconomic stabilization role pending these adjustments without using exchange control or currency devaluation. The opportunity was widely taken up and applauded by international organizations (Endres and Fleming 1999). Nevertheless, Triffin noticed that 'a dangerous instability was built into the system': one reserve currency could be substituted without delay into another, depending on the view taken by the monetary authorities of a particular currency. Gresham's Law was always in the wings, threatening to apply to one or another key currency used as a reserve.[9] In a situation where gold coexisted with several key reserve currencies (sterling and the US dollar), one key currency could be dispensed with quickly for the other or gold could be demanded, depending on the degree of confidence held in a currency. Without labouring the details here, in Triffin's view the 1920s' gold exchange standard (in which gold was progressively removed or replaced by national currencies masquerading as international money in reserve holdings) had a primary role in the world cyclical downturn of 1929–33. Sterling convertibility into gold (and other currencies) was severely undermined during this period. For that reason alone, national moneys could not sustain a long-term position as international money or as a liquidity stabilizer in the reserves of a central banking authority. Major key currency countries will from time to time fall from grace as economic powers. To rely on the questionable stabilizing capacity of a key currency would not provide the basis for a sound international financial order.[10]

New 'canons' of international financial behaviour: qualified support for BW

When the postwar debate had settled and the BW Agreement had finally been consummated Triffin reflected on these developments, offering 'new canons' for international financial behaviour diverging somewhat from the guidelines established by BW architects. In some cases he offers distinctive interpretations of otherwise vague BW guidelines.[11] The following nine points are prominent:

1 All national currencies have to be 'managed currencies'.
2 Domestic policy goals have primacy in the design of an international order.
3 Policymakers in the largest industrialized countries must assume greater responsibilities in adopting 'anticyclical monetary policies' and in preventing the 'contagious' effects of depression originating in their economies.
4 Domestic demand management policies must be used to counter temporary imbalances in international payments.
5 International reserves should be fully utilized in deficit countries to deal with temporary imbalances and support fixed exchange rates; they should *not* be thought of anachronistically as domestic currency 'backing'.
6 Exchange controls should be actively used 'as an instrument of monetary policy' when temporary foreign exchange shortages make the alternatives either currency devaluation or deflationary policies.
7 A dual exchange rate system should be operated in situations of temporary imbalance to control the use of foreign exchange on current account transactions.[12]
8 'Fundamental disequilibrium' in a country's external accounts may not imply an observed current account *deficit*.
9 Exchange rate 'devaluation is not necessarily the only, or most appropriate remedy for fundamental disequilibrium'.

Of these nine general points of principle, the last four, that is 6–9, depart from or are interesting interpretations of the BW Agreement. We shall discuss each of these in turn. Notable is Triffin's silence when elaborating on point 5, and to a lesser extent point 4, on the adjustment responsibilities of *surplus* countries. This accords well with BW, though the emphasis he placed on the responsibilities of larger industrialized countries seems stronger than what can be found in the BW Agreement.

Prior to reflecting on BW arrangements Triffin had spent most of the period 1943–6 studying Latin American monetary problems. During that time he had been strongly influenced by the work of Raul Prébisch. Later Triffin viewed his own reaction to BW, perhaps in part because of Prébisch's influence, as providing 'some highly unorthodox policy advice for the newly born International Monetary Fund' (1966a: 141).[13] The issue of exchange controls was highly controversial at BW and the IMF Articles of Agreement grudgingly permitted controls on capital account transactions only. Triffin (1947a: 81) demurred; he was wary of the contemporary trend towards 'blind and dogmatic rejection of exchange control'. In small, open economy cases – those with narrow export bases, price inelastic demand for exports and poorly developed capital markets – he recommended active use of exchange control on current and capital account transactions where necessary to avoid income contraction and reduction in import demand. Imports were often needed for investment and development purposes in these countries. Selective controls on expenditures by residents on foreign goods can be preferable to indiscriminate, damaging income adjustments. By late 1946 the IMF had not developed objective criteria for exchange control policy. It was imperative that 'objective rules and principles of policy' were formulated without delay. Rules must be contingent on country circumstances such as balance of payments experience, export trade patterns and level of economic development. In Trifffin's mind, temporary or cyclical disequilibrium in the balance of payments of a particular country referred to abnormal *im*balances in the external accounts and not necessarily major deficits or surpluses; these warranted imposition of exchange controls on both current account, that is ordinary trade, transactions and capital account transactions. The precise criteria for identifying a 'temporary' or 'cyclical' imbalance were elastic – countries with extremely volatile or highly seasonal patterns of export receipts might need higher average foreign exchange reserves per year as a percentage of the 'normal requirements for payments abroad, i.e. the total annual sales of exchange by the banks [including the central bank]', than countries with a less volatile pattern of receipts. Triffin then speculated that an 'objective indication' of an appropriate percentage critical for IMF permission to use exchange control might be derived from a measure of the variation in exchange receipts from the past one or two decades. Where there was insufficient evidence, the 'deficit country should probably be given the benefit of the doubt', receive IMF assistance and be permitted to introduce exchange control as another line of defence so that 'foreseeable deficits' could be financed without resort to devaluation or significant income reductions. The IMF would also need a rule to guard against permanent use of exchange control, including a periodic country review schedule.[14]

Temporary payments imbalances could well be alleviated by multiple currency practices in a manner satisfying the BW Agreement. Triffin proposed some specific rules for such practices, giving greater scope for the use of limited market processes as against haphazard, complex and costly administrative practices. A central bank could permit payments for 'all essential and urgent imports of goods and services and of contractual obligations, dividends, or reasonable amortization on approved foreign investment'. The residual foreign exchange could then be auctioned to the highest bidder wishing to purchase imports from any other country. Multilateralism is preserved, consistent with BW. Bidders would be permitted to purchase any currency in the auction. Indeed, Triffin's 'multiple currency' idea does not constitute a genuine multiple currency practice 'if the term is interpreted to imply the setting up of different exchange premiums as between currencies'. The only discrimination employed is between types of transactions – those for authorized imports and the rest. However, major questions are begged: who decides on the degree of urgency for authorized imports, on what basis, and what administrative machinery would be required for this purpose? Preserving both multilateral and non-discriminatory principles is laudable but the practice of rationing foreign exchange by government administrators, which is what he is in fact advocating, is akin to creating a new form of trade barrier.[15] Nevertheless, multiple currency practices dispense with the need to impose other import restrictions or new and more discriminatory selective tariffs. In Triffin's currency scheme there would be two foreign exchange markets: the official market with a fixed exchange rate and an 'official' free market with a variable exchange rate depending on importers' bids. Triffin (1947a: 70) was pleased to report that in principle the 'higher rates prevailing on the free market in times of crises would, moreover, tend to discourage capital exports and encourage capital imports'. Growth and development in such circumstances would not be so badly affected.

As we saw in Chapter 2, the BW definition of 'fundamental disequilibrium' in a country's balance of payments remained unsatisfactorily opaque. Triffin addressed this matter directly, defining fundamental disequilibrium as

> a maladjustment in a country's economy so grave and persistent that the restoration or maintenance of satisfactory levels of domestic activity, employment, and income would prove incompatible with equilibrium in the balance of payments if not accompanied by extraordinary measures of external defense, such as a change in exchange rates, increased tariffs or exchange control protection.
>
> (1947a: 77–8)

Triffin did not rank exchange rate changes very highly in the list of measures taken to affect economic adjustment from fundamental disequilibrium. Unlike the BW architects, he regarded exchange rate policy as 'a blunt indiscriminate instrument' (1947a: 78). Selective policies designed to target specific payments imbalances on current account would minimize the impact on production, costs and economic activity in general which were only very indirectly connected with these imbalances. Microeconomic policy changes were important here, as were carefully planned exchange controls and international commodity agreements to prevent monopolistic discrimination in markets for food and raw materials and to smooth out prices. Triffin understandably disagreed with Gottfried Haberler's (1944) view (which was a faithful rendering of the BW guidelines) that currency devaluation should be used only when policies designed to alleviate temporary payments imbalances confined to normal conditions lead to an observed *deficit* irrespective of its origin. First, the deficit may be due either to accidental political crises or to economic shocks in commodity markets. Second, tighter monetary and fiscal policies may have limited effectiveness and cause unnecessary hardship. Third, exchange control considered as a dimension of monetary policy must be given time to work in the short to medium term and its corrective effect on the imbalance in the external accounts was likely to be less dependent on creating an economy-wide contraction in income and employment. Fourth, exchange rate changes disrupt the pattern of production, consumption and labour demand, all the more so in countries with narrow production and export bases.

Triffin's definition of 'fundamental disequilibrium' accords with Alvin Hansen's (elaborated in Chapter 3); it could apply when a country was in deep recession with abnormally low output and high unemployment yet 'enjoying' a balance of payments surplus on current account or even something close to external balance. Significant internal imbalances could therefore outweigh balance of payments considerations and point towards major policy changes. The BW financial order drew Triffin's qualified approval for giving primacy to national policy objectives. Table 6.1 on p. 118 fully summarizes Triffin's policy hierarchy. Triffin's policy discussion related mostly to countries tending towards (but not necessarily with) deficits on current account. The desired policy response sequence was: first, use international reserves and domestic compensatory policy to deal with temporary imbalances which depart from 'normal'; second, use exchange controls as an integral part of monetary policy primarily to protect international reserves and the exchange rate setting, and preserve some semblance of internal balance in the second instance. Exchange controls will help minimize economy-wide income contraction in conditions where there is no impending danger of rising inflation. IMF borrowing facilities and multiple currency practices, coupled with recommended microeconomic policy reforms and active participation in international commodity agreements (where applicable), may be used concurrently. If the imbalance persists, give more time for exchange controls to work before resorting to an exchange rate adjustment. Last, if all else fails use deflationary policies. Despite Prébisch's early influence on Triffin's other policy prescriptions there is no room here for a relapse into greater trade policy activism in the direction of increased import protection though multiple currency practices and exchange controls contained obvious protectionist elements. Additional direct trade restrictions other than those in place in the late 1940s were definitely not favoured. In general, he wished for the 'construction of a stable and freer system of world trade' and tighter management of both capital movements and exchange rates (Triffin 1960: 7).[16]

While the foregoing policy response sequence stood the test of time in Triffin's work, by mid-1949 these prescriptions were overshadowed in one of his IMF memoranda. BW, he complained, placed an 'exaggerated emphasis … on exchange-rate stability' (1954: 206).[17] Events were now conspiring to place this BW emphasis in a difficult position. Much expected premature currency devaluations were a non-issue 'in the face of the actual, and reverse, threat of *currency overvaluation*' propped up by 'cancerous' restrictions, misused and long-entrenched exchange controls, rampant bilateralism and trade discrimination. To be sure, the BW objective of exchange stability had been achieved but only because various restrictions and controls had nullified the impact of exchange rates on prices and directed trade into inefficient channels: an 'embarrassing victory' for BW architects (Triffin 1949: 182, 184, 191).[18] Exchange rates as Triffin observed them were stable but not effective.

The key currency convertibility crisis

'Convertibility' was a commonly used term in international finance and its meaning was transformed in the BW order. Triffin had long exhorted fellow economists to provide a meaningful and realistic definition of convertibility. The BW Agreement obliged. Earlier, under a pure gold standard regime, convertibility simply meant the 'material equivalence of the various national currencies in terms of their gold . . . content' (Triffin 1960: 21). With the creation of bank notes, convertibility meant the ability of banks to discharge their paper currency debts in gold which was *the* ultimate legal tender money. The stability of rates of exchange between national moneys was guaranteed with respect to all gold standard countries. Banks remained responsible for converting currency into gold at a fixed rate. A currency became *in*convertible when the issuing bank was not able to honour its gold redemption commitment, whereas private markets may well do so at a different rate than originally promised by that bank. In short, the rate of redemption or rate of exchange would become simultaneously flexible and *un*stable – meaning inconvertible at the old, agreed rate.

It may seem strange that by the 1920s at the earliest and the 1950s at the latest, a request to restore currency 'convertibility' meant, in nineteenth-century gold standard parlance, *in*convertibility, or at least the potential for it. This is because flexible exchange rates between national currencies may not settle down in the market to some stable equilibrium rate for very long. As well, various trade and payments restrictions (e.g. exchange controls), and regulations on capital movements, denied currency holders completely free convertibility. The perniciousness of the other extreme – complete *in*convertibility – was not lost on Triffin (1957: 235):

> True *in*convertibility, i.e. the impossibility of legally converting the national currency into foreign goods or currencies at any exchange rate whatsoever, is a relatively modern phenomenon whose consequences can be incomparably more destructive of international competition than those of mere exchange fluctuations in a free market.

Economic philosophy, institutions and policies had altered the content of the concept of convertibility at BW. Indeed, BW architects wished to incorporate in their notion of convertibility 'feasible goals of international economic policy, susceptible of concrete implementation in a concrete historical environment', thus defining convertibility in 'relative, rather than in absolute terms' (Triffin 1954: 24). The relative aspects which varied between countries and currencies over time included the degree of multilateralism permitted in trade and payments and the extent of stability in international trading activities. BW architects interpreted convertibility precisely in this manner; they realized that practical convertibility aims made room for feasible compromises among these criteria.[19] Triffin approved. So was convertibility not incompatible with the maintenance of *some* trade and payments controls in the BW order? There is an ambiguity here which is not removed in Triffin's work. The acceptable *level* of trade controls is not clarified.[20] And since the removal of currency convertibility restrictions is worthwhile because it will lead to more trade and more efficient utilization of the world's resources, it will not have much point if not accompanied by liberalized trade.

The complete, multilateral clearing of debt and credit balances was not provided for in the initial BW Agreement. In borrowing from the IMF, a member country must exchange its own currency for a currency needed to settle its deficit on current account. Currency inconvertibility in the 1940s and early 1950s did not enable a country to use earnings with some countries to settle deficits with others.[21] Notwithstanding this severe limitation, Triffin believed that BW had at least initially restored workable convertibility by condemning competitive devaluations and eliminating unbridled bilateralism in trade and payments while sanctioning organized payments discrimination only in special circumstances (exchange controls, scarce currencies) and requiring, *eventually*, equal transferability of *all* currencies.[22] By the 1950s Triffin was playing a major role in advancing the cause of regional convertibility in the European Payments Union (EPU). He learned in the process how West European nations were 'highly interdependent (exports to the EPU area account for nearly three fourths of member countries' exports)'. Given this keen, conscious economic interdependence, these countries were better 'able to understand each others' problems and policies', thereby creating favourable conditions for economic growth and regional cooperation on convertibility. For the sterling area countries the same argument applied. Convertibility should be made freer gradually, starting from regional arrangements and leading to greater international convertibility. Key currency agreements, by contrast, set rules to be imposed from above on the rest of the world. That hegemonic approach was emphatically not the best way forward since it would not muster genuine international financial cooperation (Triffin 1954: 212–14, 228, 1956: 387–90).

The BW approach to convertibility was loose enough to allow any national currency – either singular or plural – to evolve into acceptable, convertible international reserve media. Reserve accumulation (or liquidity) was of course pivotal in the BW order. Reserve measurement and adequacy were complex matters; they needed to be developed on a country-by-country basis. Two things were certain: reserves must be higher both in an unstable economic environment and in less developed economies facing more volatile export prices and requiring large, discrete demands for capital imports. Poorer nations were more likely 'to assign lower priority than the more developed countries to a reserve level adequate to eschew or minimize undesirable resort to devaluation or restrictions' (1960: 35). Be that as it may, the BW order had bigger issues to deal with by the end of the 1950s than the problem of poor countries.

The global composition of reserves had become concentrated in a single key currency – too concentrated, on Triffin's reading of the evidence. The problem was not the sufficiency of reserves per se but the excessive dependence on US dollars for the growth of reserves. Monetary authorities had become enamoured of the US dollar, and this posed a danger of instability for the BW order. A hallmark of Triffin (1960) was its strong statistical support base; it provides extensive, data-driven illustrations of the so-called 'dollar crisis'.[23] The actual BW system was founded (as we saw in Chapter 2) on a key currency, gold exchange standard, with the US dollar in particular substituting for a shortage of gold in the reserve holdings of central banks. Those US dollars were always ultimately convertible into gold at US$35 per ounce whenever confidence in the US dollar as a substitute diminished. The US dollar, or any other currency for that matter, was never going to be a perfect substitute for gold.[24] The key currency system was therefore periodically indicted for creating international financial instability.

The world financial situation in the late 1950s became fragile and precarious and it is in this context that the famous 'Triffin dilemma' arose: world economic growth had created a growing demand for convertible currencies (as gold substitutes) to be used for financing international transactions, and to act as liquidity in support of the BW, fixed exchange rate rule. As a proxy world central banker, the United States' authorities had fixed the value of the US dollar to gold; all other currencies could convert into US dollars and then to gold at a fixed rate at any time. As long as the United States could supply dollars to support liquidity demands all would be well, though it must normally run a current account deficit in order to supply sufficient dollars to the rest of the world. When US dollar liabilities increased, the supply of gold to back them did not keep pace. As the ratio of US dollar liabilities to gold fell, the guarantee of convertibility into gold lost credibility.[25] Conversion of US dollars into gold would expedite 'international monetary chaos' if not a 1930s-style liquidity crisis and depression (Triffin 1960: 145). The world financial system would inevitably collapse if dependence on US deficits continued. On the other hand, policymakers in the United States could engineer a set of circumstances which reduced the

United States' demand for imports and cut the trade deficit. However, this response illustrated the other horn of the Triffin dilemma. A US dollar shortage would be precipitated as the deficit was reduced, a liquidity crisis would occur and international trade and growth would decline. In the worst-case scenario, trade restrictions would increase, and deflation and depression would follow (Triffin 1960: 64–77).[26] For Triffin, the dilemma was so compelling and so pressing that he called for immediate reconsideration of the BW Agreement. He takes for granted that IMF finance was insufficient; it was indeed minuscule relative to liquidity supplied by the United States' deficit and by gold in that order. He offered a gloomy prognosis for the lending capacity of the IMF.[27]

A collapse of the US dollar would result in a collapse of the BW order. Imperfectly as it operated in practice, the BW system still contained a rationally designed architectural structure which was potentially fair and just. Triffin concurred that, indeed, exchange rates should be fixed, currencies treated equally, capital movements controlled, the risks of output losses in the balance of payments adjustment process minimized, and trade gradually liberalized in the interests of smaller, less developed countries; finally, the financial imperialism so commonly associated with hegemonic key currency schemes should be expunged. That large-scale intervention was required did not mean interference by heads of state in operational matters including design of the financial architecture. The latter is best left to financial experts, economists and technocrats. International financial diplomacy has a place in treaty-making and pact-building which gives legitimation to a particular international financial architecture and sanctions enforcement procedures.

Cooperative efforts spawned by the so-called 'dollar crisis' from the late 1950s attempted to institute *in*convertibility of key currencies into gold. Triffin dismisses these efforts as mere 'gentlemen's agreements'; they elicited from major central banks loose restraints on gold conversions which were not durable, especially where central bankers were not independent of their political masters. The BW gold exchange standard had in fact become highly politicized at this point. Politicians, alarmed by an impending 'crisis', delved into the day-to-day operations of the BW system. Triffin was unimpressed:

> The survival of the gold-exchange standard has now become dependent on the *political* willingness of foreign countries to finance, through their own monetary issues, the deficits of the countries whose *national* currency is accepted by them as international reserves. Compliance with such a system becomes more precarious every day, because central banks are being called upon to finance debtor countries' policies in which their own governments have no voice, and with which they may profoundly disagree.
>
> (1965b: 349–50, his emphasis)

Central bankers were not able to act and cooperate across countries in accordance with a deeper understanding of the technicalities pertaining to the international financial architecture and its operations. Even worse, governments apparently had no inkling that in acquiescing to certain operations for political reasons, they would be undermining the entire BW architecture.

The supranational bank proposal and its limitations

The architecture of the BW financial order was in desperate need of revision by the early 1960s; it had evolved to a stage of 'utter irrationality' and 'international monetary anarchy'. Why had this alleged outcome come to pass? For Triffin, the universal bogy was the domination of international reserves by key currencies. Speculative switching between these currencies (as confidence in them waxed and waned) proved to be a source of instability. He tirelessly insisted that the 'absurd Monte Carlo roulette game dignified under the name of "gold-exchange standard"' must be brought to a close (1969c: 10).[28]

Three objectives set the background to Triffin's redesigning of the BW architecture: (i) to remove speculative fear and greed by controlling short-term capital flows associated with destabilizing substitutions between key reserve currencies; (ii) to provide a new means of international liquidity not so reliant on the liquidity-creating deficits of key currency countries; and (iii) to remove threats to the stability of the BW order by 'internationalizing', through a central international organization, member countries' currency reserves.[29]

World liquidity was a major pillar of BW; it needed reinforcing so as to sustain the growth of trade and payments. Once it had been reinforced, confidence would become less problematic and balance of payments adjustment issues would be squarely dealt with. Triffin wished to centralize international reserves at a newly constituted, credit-creating IMF. The 'new' IMF would possess more 'modest and feasible' functions than the 'broadly similar' Keynes (1943a) plan for an International Clearing Union presented at the BW Conference. Triffin's 'new' IMF would, he thought, end the practice of key countries 'being able to palm off their short-term IOUs upon the world reserve pool'. Key countries were getting 'too much rope to hang themselves', thereby imperilling the BW order. It was no accident that key countries persistently failed to adjust their external imbalances. The imbalances were 'nearly unavoidable' when a country assumed a reserve currency role; the key country could then escape for long periods the full pressure of its deficits at the cost of accruing greater indebtedness and risking sudden international crises of confidence (Triffin 1969a: 59). Furthermore, key countries such as the United States and Great Britain tended to be insulated against large-scale conversion of past IOUs into gold. As leading economic engines in the world economy, these countries would be able to conduct monetary and fiscal policies with domestic objectives in mind, rather than with concern for the external acceptance of their currencies held by foreign monetary authorities. Triffin proposed to replace key currencies held by monetary authorities by claims against the IMF.[30]

Main architectural renovations

A new charter should be created for the IMF with a facility for member countries by which they would make foreign exchange deposits backed by an IMF gold-value guarantee. The IMF guarantee would protect deposits against exchange rate changes and inconvertibility of the currencies concerned. Each member would agree to hold a fixed (and high) proportion of its international reserves in the form of IMF deposits. Existing capital subscriptions to the IMF (negotiated at BW) would be replaced by this deposit requirement. Such deposits would become genuine international money, expressed in an IMF currency or 'gold units' at an agreed, fixed rate (Triffin 1960: 105). Parities of national currencies would be expressed in gold units. Foreign exchange risk otherwise attached to holding reserves in the form of national currencies would be eliminated. Gold units could be counted as part of member countries' national reserves, though they would be held by the IMF. Interest would be paid on IMF deposits. Interest would act as an inducement, along with the gold value guarantee, encouraging central banks to hold most of their reserves at the IMF.

There were several versions of the so-called Triffin plan. A strong version required compulsory reserve requirements with the IMF in proportion to each country's total international reserves (up to 20 per cent in one version). These reserves could *not* be drawn down, for example, to pay international debts. In any case, all member countries would have to transfer to the IMF three types of assets:

1 existing net creditor claims accumulated on the IMF;
2 foreign exchange holdings – mostly US dollars and UK pounds; and
3 gold (Triffin 1960: 107).

The IMF, like a bank, would hold deposit liabilities in a large reserve pool comprising its lending capacity as well as a clearing fund for international settlements among national central banks and a resource to assist currency stabilization activities of central banks. The IMF would, in short, centralize world reserves. Finally, gold would retain a place in this renovated version of BW; it would help sustain the popular illusion that gold alone could act as an ultimate pillar and barrier against inflation of national currencies, and as a backing for IMF liabilities.[31]

Operational characteristics of the new IMF

The IMF would now control international monetary reserves. It might expand or contract the volume of its assets through open market operations (purchasing and selling securities) in member countries' financial markets; lend to members, subject to specific conditionality requirements; permit operation of limited overdraft facilities and purchase bonds issued by the WB to assist in financing viable projects in less developed countries. The IMF would have new powers to lend reserves and create credit for members on the basis of those reserves (see Table 6.1).

Triffin assumed that the international financial system requires steady growth in currency reserves in line with expanding world trade. The IMF would therefore tend to make more open market purchases of securities (in return for liquidity) than sales as expanding trade and rising economic growth demanded. As indicated in Table 6.1, IMF open market purchases in selected countries increase the reserves of national central banks held at the IMF. The IMF's lending capacity also grows accordingly. Would this practice be inflationary? Not according to Triffin, so long as the IMF set an upper limit to the increase of centralized reserves of the order of '3 to 5 per cent a year' (1960: 103).[32]

The IMF's functions as an international lender for temporary balance of payments imbalances on current account would not change fundamentally. As under the BW Agreement, the IMF could support agreed adjustment policies and permit exchange rate changes as the case demanded to counter persistent deficits. Triffin seemed to favour limiting the maturity and duration of IMF lending and tougher enforceable guidelines so as to allay lingering doubts among some of its members about the safety of its deposit liabilities. He also believed that the IMF's open market operations in different markets could counterbalance 'undesirable movements' of short-term capital.[33]

Table 6.1 The Triffin plan: reserve creation through purchase of securities

	IMF		
Securities purchased in open market	+100	Deposits of central banks	+100

Source: adapted from Machlup (1962: 31), 'T-account set 5'.

Assumptions:

1 An expanded IMF, whose deposit liabilities are part of the member countries' monetary reserves, purchases securities in the open market.
2 The seller of the securities deposits the IMF cashier's cheque with the seller's bank; this bank deposits it with its central bank; and this central bank deposits it on its account with the IMF.
3 The increased credit balances with the IMF constitute increased monetary reserves of the member countries.

The Triffin plan amounted to a credit reserve standard. The requirements were formidable. All IMF member countries must negotiate, cooperate and then adhere to a treaty setting out a reorganized IMF. Just as with the BW Agreement, Triffin believed in 'producing a blueprint' for international financial reform (1969c: 6).[34] Critics of his world central bank idea, which is what his plan was essentially offering, were quick to find fault. We turn next to the most cogent arguments against various versions of Triffin's plan.

Main criticisms of the supranational bank

The first major criticism struck at the heart of Triffin's empirical approach. He always marshalled copious statistical evidence demonstrating impending crises arising from international financial trends. Did he exaggerate the impending liquidity problem and the associated risk of exchange rate instability? The shortfall in supply of world reserves (liquidity) relative to demand was questioned by Altman (1961: 49), for whom the issues were evidential rather than doctrinal:

> [Triffin's] proposals are based upon a simplified view of the statistics on reserves and trade that does not reflect such important factors as the distribution of reserves, the change in the quality of exchange assets, the state of balance of international trade and exchange rates.

Clearly, contemporary market participants were not nervous or alarmed, so perhaps Altman's claims of simplification were valid? In fact the US dollar–gold ratio was in steep decline from the late 1950s, but critics observed through the 1960s that large-scale switching of reserve currencies – such as substituting gold for US dollars – did not occur. As the 1960s wore on, the predicted liquidity crisis remained as much a chimera as ever. A supranational bank constructed for the purpose of expanding international reserves would have been redundant precisely because the United States did not experience a genuine disequilibrium on its balance of payments until the late 1960s at the earliest. In the meantime, the United States did not have a pressing adjustment problem which in the event could have seriously depleted world liquidity. The BW order remained largely intact.

It turned out that Triffin had overlooked the role of the United States as an international financial intermediary disbursing a distinctive 'commodity' called liquidity. The conventions defining 'deficits' are crucial for understanding the role of key reserve currency countries. The important concept in international finance of relevance to key countries such as the United States is the 'international settlements balance'. This balance comprises the current account of the United States plus its balance of capital flows excluding any changes in foreign official (central bank) holdings of short-term claims on residents of the United States (Triffin 1963: 114–15, Isard 1995: 50 note 64). The balance of capital flows is complicated by the fact that loans to non-residents can be offset by non-residents placing their own money in liquid US dollar-denominated assets in markets *outside* the United States. These assets acted as a desired store of value. In Europe during the 1960s markets developed to supply long-term finance and investments denominated in US dollars to enterprises, private savers and governments. The United States, through the 'Euro-dollar market' as it was known, became a financial intermediary *par excellence* with an elastic supply of dollars on offer; it was in fact lending for the medium and long term and borrowing short from the rest of the world. A profitable trade had developed in US dollar-denominated financial assets and liquidity itself – just like any other commodities. A US dollar market evolved, with Europeans generally preferring to hold long-term financial assets with short-term liabilities remaining against them. Europeans on average had high liquidity preference. The opposite profile held for US residents.[35] These financial asset-trading activities did not create a genuine disequilibrium in the United States' balance of payments. Trading on the Euro-dollar market did not undermine confidence in the reserve currency system which placed the US dollar at its centre. That the short-term claims of the rest of the world on the United States increased each year with the development of the Euro-dollar market was not a reason for nervousness. Residents of the United States were not in a position of *net* indebtedness. Indeed, contrary to Triffin's fears, the more the US dollar was used as a reserve asset by foreign savers and as a means of long-term finance for foreign enterprises, the greater the familiarity with that currency and the lower the costs of information, and the lower the transaction costs associated with using it.

The Triffin plan was also subject to scrutiny by another group of critics who were alarmed at the thin layer of confidence provided by the proposed supranational bank's 'gold unit'. No international blueprint could prevent monetary authorities from ultimately abandoning the gold unit, just as they would desert any national currency used as a reserve medium. Gresham's Law could apply so long as attractive alternative reserve media – national moneys and gold – were still available.[36] Triffin attempted to build into his architecture narrow limitations against the danger of excessive depletion of the IMF's gold resources by, in some circumstances, allowing only partial convertibility of the gold unit (1960: 112–13).[37] None of this removed the danger of a gold run on the IMF when a crisis of confidence supervened.[38] Confidence among member countries in the underlying assets of the IMF could ebb and flow since the assets were in part to consist of loans to countries which could have questionable creditworthiness (e.g. less developed countries with dubious productivity records). Rules of IMF loan disbursement and enforceability had not been clearly established in Triffin's plan. The IMF acting like a bank may not be in a position to lend on the same criteria as ordinary commercial banks.[39] Alvin Hansen chimed in with doubts on this score: 'Triffin believes that ideally it is a primary function of an international credit creating institution to provide capital to countries that are capital poor.' On the contrary, for Hansen a 'credit creating bank ... cannot afford to be a foreign-aid, soft-loan agency' (1965: 136).

The sacrifice of monetary policy independence in the Triffin plan was predicted to be greater than under the BW Agreement. According to Leland Yeager (1961: 294) that sacrifice might be equivalent to the loss of independence under the gold standard pre-1914. Two levels of monetary management were involved in Triffin's plan: domestic monetary management and the IMF's international monetary policy. If countries relinquished monetary policy independence completely they would simply conduct a passive policy to keep their balance of payments in balance on current account; exchange rate stability would be assured, though avoidance of periodic deflation would not, depending on price level movements elsewhere. If, as was customary in the 1950s and 1960s, and as intended by Triffin, domestic monetary policy was assigned in part to maintaining high aggregate output and employment then some domestic inflation would have to be accepted. At the international level, the IMF would lend to countries with deficits of a size and duration that might otherwise not have been experienced so as to protect domestic policy goals. Yet the creation of international money, that is IMF 'gold units', could strengthen world demand and raise price levels. Hence the oft-repeated claim that the Triffin plan had an inflationary bias.[40] The delicate balancing act between domestic monetary policy and IMF monetary policy presents a problem for policymakers in Triffin's financial architecture: they must coordinate domestic money and IMF credit creation in order to minimize the effect of rising price levels that go hand in hand with emphasis on Keynesian-type policy goals. Any restriction on IMF credit to deficit countries may well bring more trade restrictions to protect national employment objectives, rather than an international liquidity crisis. Even so, the new IMF as a supranational bank faced the difficult task of preserving the sovereignty of national policy goals while simultaneously attempting to stabilize international liquidity without precipitating greater trade barriers or excessive inflation.

Economic policy coordination among IMF member countries was an indispensable pre-condition for the Triffin plan.[41] Agreed limits on international reserve growth were also vital to minimize inflation. Yet there were no formal limits in the plan, the only real control being the confidence and forethought of IMF officials about their policies. Also crucial was the IMF member countries' willingness to accept the new international gold units.[42] These factors were rather shaky foundations upon which to renovate the BW order.

In sensing that his full-fledged supranational bank and new IMF charter might be ill-fated on political grounds (given the perceived threat to national sovereignty), Triffin searched for other opportunities to apply his ideas at the regional level.[43] His plan could be rendered politically feasible – contemporary European monetary cooperation was an exemplar of the type of financial architecture envisaged by Triffin for the international economy. The EPU had been a prime example of the possibilities and Triffin was instrumental in providing intellectual foundations for this regional arrangement. The EPU was a short step from full monetary and currency unification in Europe, with a European Central Bank *of* central banks likely once political obstacles were overcome. Triffin favoured a European clearing house or centralized reserve fund in which each member central bank would hold a proportion of its international currency reserves.[44]

Concluding reflections on Triffin's policy assignment guidelines

While Triffin's renovation plan for the BW financial order was confounded by complications introduced by private capital flows coupled with competing definitions of a genuine imbalance in the United States' external accounts, his ideas seemed more prophetic from the vantage point of the late 1960s. Vietnam war expenditure, among other things, led to inflation and excessive expenditure in the United States and a significant deficit on the current account of the balance of payments which called for genuine economic adjustment.[45] The international financial order was now more vulnerable to sudden confidence problems inducing massive conversions of key currencies, especially from the US dollar into gold. To dramatize matters, Triffin suggested that the 'divisive and destructive international monetary and economic chaos of the 1930s' could soon be revisited (1969c: 8).[46] Certainly, the outstanding stock of US dollar reserves more than doubled from $16 billion to 33 billion in the ten years 1959–69, and the US price level rose 40 per cent over the same period.[47] High US inflation made US dollar-denominated assets far less attractive than they had been at the beginning of the decade. With the US Federal Reserve willing to trade gold with foreign central banks at US$35 per ounce throughout the 1960s, obviously Gresham's Law would again apply. Speculation in the private gold market focused on the unsustainability of the fixed gold convertibility value of the US dollar; gold was driven out of international monetary reserves and US dollars began to replace it. This central pillar of the BW order finally collapsed on 15 August 1971 when President Nixon ended the US undertaking to trade gold at a fixed rate. Gold prices then increased rapidly, nearly doubling in the next twelve months.[48] The BW gold exchange standard was dismantled and replaced by what Triffin called 'man-made credit-moneys and reserves' (1969b: 480). Contrary to Triffin's original expectations, the collapse of the BW order had little connection with a shortage of international reserves; it had much more to do with undisciplined monetary and fiscal policies in key countries, notably the United States and Great Britain. Indefensible fixed exchange rates were prevalent throughout the 1960s and early 1970s, yet central banks continued to defend them for long periods only to make belated, large, discrete currency adjustments (in some cases before moving to more flexible exchange rates).

Triffin remained adamant throughout the 1960s on the need for centralizing international reserves to preserve both liquidity and confidence. Early initiation and coordination of balance of payments adjustment policies to avoid exchange rate instability must follow centralization. His overall policy assignment guidelines are outlined in Table 6.2.

The normative message embodied in Table 6.2 is that central control of international reserves is desirable to distribute more wisely the fruits of both international investment and expanding international trade. Triffin longed for an international financial order 'that will gradually improve man's control over this crucial basis of his economic life in an increasingly interdependent world' (1969b: 492). Earlier he insisted that international financial stability 'cannot be achieved by a return ... to the ideals of international laissez faire'. Indeed, 'positive action and policy' are required to *establish* an international order. Furthermore, it was to his mind nonsensical to rely on the spontaneous creation of international financial order as a result of the 'happy coincidence of unilateral decisions' (1947b: 179). The unflinching, freely chosen, pursuit of common or 'correct' policies at the national level created instability in the international realm (1957: ix).

The tradeoff for greater collective control over world reserves was significant sacrifice of domestic policy autonomy although in the conditions prevailing during the 1950s and 1960s harmonization of general policy goals did not seem impossibly difficult (e.g. full employment and high rates of economic growth took priority in most IMF member nations). The means and time horizon for reaching these goals were more controversial. An important addition in Table 6.1 compared with parallel tables in previous chapters is inclusion of the incomes policy instrument. Incomes policies comprised price, wage and rent controls in some countries where they were institutionally more applicable and implementable, such as Great Britain in the early 1960s. Triffin (1965a) had no problem recommending such controls where wages and other costs were fuelling historically high inflation rates. Moreover, like BW, timely external financing methods including foreign reserve utilization and IMF finance were preferred to second-best corrective policies such as exchange controls and further trade restrictions. Exchange controls were acceptable provided it could be demonstrated that capital flows were causing disruptions that had little connection with economic fundamentals, that is with the existing degree of price and cost competitiveness evident in a particular country (Triffin 1966b). What is notable about Triffin's contribution compared to other leading architects of

Table 6.2 Triffin's guidelines for national policymakers and the SCB

Policy instrument	*Time horizon*	*Primary assignment*	*Secondary assignment*	*Guidelines*
Exchange rate				
i) SCB	All	–	–	• Fix parities of national currencies against IMF 'gold unit'
ii) All countries	Short term	External balance	–	• Use multiple currency practices
	Medium–long term	External balance	–	• Fixed adjustable exchange rates as under BW (see Table 2.1)
Exchange controls	Short term	Internal balance	–	• Use actively on capital and current account transactions
	Medium–long term	External balance	–	• Use to control speculative capital controls
International reserves				
i) SCB	All	–	–	• Use as credit-creating base • Augment by open market operations
ii) National central banks	Short term	Exchange rate stabilization	–	• Use as buffer for financing current transactions
	Medium–long term	External balance	–	• Use as indicator of 'fundamental disequilibrium' • Deposit as much as possible at SCB
Monetary policy				
i) SCB	All	–	–	• Conduct open market operations, mostly purchasing securities to augment world liquidity
ii) National central banks	Short term	Internal balance	External balance	• Coordinate with SCB • Use anticyclically
	Medium–long term	Internal balance	–	• Coordinate with SCB • Accommodate fiscal policy

Fiscal policy	Short term	Internal balance	External balance	• Support monetary policy sterilization of exchange market interventions
	Medium–long term	Internal balance	–	• Maintain high aggregate domestic expenditure
Trade policy	All	External balance	–	• Liberalize slowly • Liberalize in surplus countries first
Investment policy i) SCB	All	–	–	• SCB to lend widely, not just to deficit countries • Directly support IBRD
ii) All countries	All	Internal balance	–	• As BW, see Table 2.1 • Intervene in capital markets to direct growth
Incomes policy	All	Internal balance	–	• Apply where institutional conditions permit to control inflation

international finance discussed so far in this book is his abiding faith that a collective, centralized design for international finance would extinguish the problem of confidence weakening the existing BW order. Unfortunately, unlike our other architects surveyed thus far, Triffin offered few, if any, clear policy rules for national policymakers and only rather loose guidelines for the custodians of the supranational bank (or new IMF). In remaining implacably opposed to what he considered inevitably *un*stable flexible exchange rates, he completely ignored the very real possibility that the liquidity shortage (dearth of international reserves) could be dissolved in one fell swoop. For some architects of international finance the solution was simple: instituting floating exchange rates internationally.[49] The IMF could then be reassigned exclusively to lender of last resort and crisis management functions as opposed to exchange rate surveillance. Contrary to Triffin's dire predictions, the key currency dollar standard (which he reluctantly endorsed only after the link to gold was severed in August 1971) could look after itself. If policymakers in the United States concentrated on keeping the national inflation rate relatively low, as urged by John Williams in the 1950s, there would be little danger that a United States current account deficit would trigger a flight from the US dollar, forcing interest rates up and bringing widespread economic contraction and deflation. The US dollar would then have enjoyed broader credibility and acceptance as a medium of international exchange and payment, a transaction currency and a store of value.

In summary, Triffin preferred a regime of international finance which emphasized strong, active coordination of macroeconomic policy between nations bound, in turn, by the direction of a supranational central bank or the new IMF. The latter would ultimately control the growth of world reserves. Exchange rates would be fixed though adjustable. There would likely be some joint decision-making between international officials at the IMF and national monetary policymakers because of the interdependencies between credit creation at international and national levels. Within these bounds, national policymaking regimes could be highly activist along Keynesian lines, as before under the BW order. All this amounted to an extension and reformation of the BW architecture rather than a standalone alternative.

For all its logical coherence, like so many other reform proposals, the Triffin plan had become an 'also ran' by the 1970s. Not only were events turning against Triffin's bold plan to centralize international reserves and give the IMF power to create reserves; doctrinal forces in favour of a freer international economy founded on flexible exchange rates, previously unthinkable in the BW order, were becoming more popular and influential. These doctrinal forces gave rise to a completely different architecture for the international financial order, promising to solve the problems experienced during the BW era. We will now consider leading examples of this alternative doctrine.

7 A Chicagoan international financial order

> The U.S. should renounce any commitment to peg exchange rates. We could then eliminate at once the growing restraints that are becoming imposed on what U.S. citizens can do with their dollars. Why should you be free to make any deal you want with a used-car salesman – but not with a Frenchman offering francs?
>
> (Friedman 1968b: 246)

A Chicagoan tradition on international financial reform?

The purpose of this chapter is to investigate the main elements of a Chicagoan view on international economic policy from the 1940s to the 1970s. This task has been made easier by well-established literature both on the stylized modes of thought in the Chicago 'School' of economics (Miller 1962; Reder 1982) and the Chicago 'tradition' of monetary thought pre-1945 (Patinkin 1969; Tavlas 1997; Laidler 1999). That there were common themes in the thinking of University of Chicago economists on BW and on post-BW international financial problems has not yet been demonstrated by those interested in doctrinal lineages in twentieth-century economics.

Unlike the single economist focus of previous chapters, discussion in this chapter will be devoted to leading architects of international finance and policy considered as a group. This group consists of five economists who were trained or taught in Chicago over the period under review: Henry Simons, Jacob Viner, Lloyd Mints, Milton Friedman and Harry Johnson. We shall take for granted that a Chicago 'tradition' was formed on the subject of the international financial architecture even if the economist identified would not have found this designation meaningful at the time.[1] While their thinking on the architecture may have been specially focused on a contemporary aspect of the BW system or policy we still find it meaningful to identify common elements in their architectural preferences and normative views on international economic policy. There was definitely an overarching 'Chicago view on economic policy' in general in the postwar decades up to the 1970s which won over many disciples outside Chicago.[2] It is the contention of this chapter that this 'view' also encompassed a common set of ideas on international financial arrangements. However, identifying a common 'view' is not the same thing as distilling a true consensus on specific aspects of the international architecture over the period under review. A genuine 'school' of economists presupposes homogeneous views on a subject over time.[3] This chapter asserts only that there was a Chicago tradition created by five economists over a thirty-year period addressing somewhat different international events and policies including the emerging BW system and its revealed failings over time. The Chicagoan architectural style is winnowed and adapted to changes in environmental conditions. And it was an architectural style doubtless having a locus of influences well beyond Chicago. It was not a rigid doctrine or an unchangeable orthodoxy but a mode of thinking, the details of which will be unravelled below.

Reactions to BW: Simons and Viner

Simons on the primacy of domestic monetary stability

Henry Simons was a professor at the University of Chicago Law School from 1927 to 1946. His work became a focal point for later research at Chicago on monetary problems (Stein 1987). Of prime interest here are his comments on BW discussion and the BW Agreement though his early article, 'Rules versus authorities on monetary policy' (1936), is also highly relevant for what it implies for managing instability in international finance. Simons was committed throughout his relatively short life as a professional economist to developing a 'positive program for laissez faire' both in the United States and internationally (Simons 1934).

For Simons, the catastrophic economic events in the early 1930s had monetary causes.[4] Thus major institutional changes were required for capitalist economies following the depression of the 1930s and these turned mainly on monetary policy. In general, a capitalist economy based on a 'liberal creed' requires organization of economic life through individual action '*in a game with definite rules*' (Simons 1936: 160, his emphasis). Business enterprises in such an economy have enough problems to cope with in the market without facing uncertainties associated with speculating on the future of monetary policy conducted by an inscrutable monetary authority. The demise of the international gold standard obviated the need for governments to assume positive responsibility for managing national currencies – this would only make matters worse. A positive approach for creating Simons's competitive economic order allowed for one government monopoly: the privilege of producing fiat money must be an exclusive government function and not left to the impersonal forces of the gold standard or to private banks. This monopoly was later endorsed by other Chicagoans including Friedman (1951:

216–17) and Friedman and Schwartz (1963), but not by contemporary Austrian economists Mises and Hayek (as we shall see in the next chapter).

In seeking rules for constructing viable international monetary arrangements after the depression of the 1930s, 'Our problem is that of defining an adequate monetary system based on simple rules ... [since] we cannot seek merely to return to some arrangement of the past. The monetary problem was never solved in earlier arrangements' (Simons 1936: 163).

The 'automatic' rules of the gold standard were a sham; governments had to define rules for their monetary authorities to buy and sell gold freely at a fixed price and to maintain some proportion between official gold reserves and the amount of national currency in circulation. Gold was in this sense just another fiat currency! Making a rational, enduring agreement on such rules within and between nations was one difficulty. Another problem occurred with unproductive, private hoarding of gold 'in the face of perplexity' which was an expression of irrationality. Yet another issue was the lack of enforceability of gold standard rules at the national level once they were clearly established so that there was 'little prospect that the blame for [their] violation would fall on those really responsible'. This observation applied to both the behaviour of banking authorities and controllers of public finance. In respect of the latter it was not often recognized that government expenditure and various fiscal policy measures had major monetary consequences. Gold standard rules defined simply in terms of the goal of maintaining currency convertibility and redemption could not ultimately control 'reckless accumulation' of public debt (Simons 1944a: 262–3, 1936: 176 note 21).

By the 1930s the total available world supply of gold represented a small fraction of the amount which those creditors holding national currencies might legitimately demand. Simons (1936: 168) was damning and dramatic in response: it was 'beyond diabolical ingenuity' to conceive of such a financial system, national or international, since it seemed 'designed for our economic destruction'. Was there a way out? Only if independent national currencies including the US dollar could be created first on the basis of clear monetary rules. Without labouring the details here, simple monetary rules were preferred to stabilize the United States' price level and prevent wide swings in both inflation and deflation. Exchange rate stability would follow naturally. Ideally, with a stable velocity of money, governments should fix the aggregate quantity of fiat money in circulation. Realistically, Simons was driven to a compromise on empirical grounds, given monetary experience in the early 1930s: a quantity rule, accompanied by unstable velocity would result in an unstable price level.[5] As a first, short-run approximation to reforming national money (with positive spillover effects eventually for exchange rate stability and international monetary order), Simons recommended legislation requiring private banks to hold reserves in currency and deposits at a central bank (in the United States, the Federal Reserve Bank) against 100 per cent of their deposits. This conservative 100 per cent reserve requirement would reduce the banking system's excessive reliance on short-term debt issuance – a practice shown to be highly dangerous in the early 1930s when lenders faced severe declines in security values, banks recalled loans and inevitable speculation occurred over the solvency of banks and the quality of their loans. A second set of monetary recommendations made by Simons concerned government debt which took two forms – currency issued and bonds. Fiscal policy would become a central element of *monetary* management. In fact government taxing and spending were 'ultimate monetary powers' and governments could control the quantity of money indirectly by altering both the size of its debt and the structure of debt as between currency issuance and bond sales or purchases. Since the quantity of money could not and should not be controlled directly, Simons proposed rule-based management of fiscal policy (thence monetary policy) by targeting price index stability. The price index and the operational definition of stability would have to be made clear to all market participants and possibly enshrined in a formal monetary constitution. The policy rule would be 'grounded in expert and popular opinion' and would be binding upon politicians and public officials (Simons 1942: 205, 1936: 183).[6] Simons had no qualms about the fact that all this might be tantamount to committing to 'a real monetary religion' so long as it was workable and minimized uncertainty (1942: 206).

In the international realm the implications of Simons's domestic monetary regime were not all that obvious. Operating an international gold standard did not appear to be a desirable option. Gold standards of any kind give gold producers a 'prodigious subsidy'. By the 1940s the idea of resuscitating the pre-1914 gold standard was akin to accepting a bad, if innocuous, religion. Stabilizing exchange rates to promote international trade no longer required gold:

> Now, monetary gold is almost monopolized by one nation which is also the creditor of almost everybody and the predominant international lender or investor as well [i.e. the United States]. The value of gold is thus merely a fact of the official American gold price and of the commodity value of the dollar, that is, our fiscal policy. We may hitch gold to the dollar if and as we choose. To think of hitching the dollar to gold is almost not to think at all; one does not hitch a train to a caboose!
>
> (Simons 1944a: 263)

With these remarks, Simons turned the role of gold and the international gold standard on its head. Everything in the international financial architecture post-1944 would depend on American fiscal and monetary policy.

These two dimensions of macroeconomic policy were not sundered in Simons's work, for he quite rightly saw fiscal policy as having profound monetary consequences.

The real issue with gold and gold standards was the value of gold; value depended mostly on gold convertibility into national currency and, especially in 1944, to the US dollar (and not conversely). The imminent prospect of tying gold to the US dollar indefinitely was more than an 'innocent deception', for the greenback would be perceived as 'gold-plated' and the international financial order would be founded on a 'dollar standard with a façade of gold'. Some international cooperation might be facilitated by such a move and the United States would have to accept a binding fiscal responsibility to maintain the credibility of the dollar standard. Moreover, if it became 'a really international currency' the US dollar's stabilization would become a 'multilateral responsibility'. Sovereignty issues were, for Simons, just red herrings. A stable US dollar was required for a sound domestic economy in the United States just as much as other nations required a stable international monetary unit for their objectives. There was a harmony of interests between the United States and the rest of the world. The only prerequisite – not to be underestimated – was to find sound rules for domestic monetary and fiscal policy. If the US dollar was stabilized 'in terms of a broad index of domestic prices', then there would be no occasion for major exchange rate realignments. Admittedly, 'large disturbances [in price levels] . . . probably would necessitate *occasional* alterations of exchange rates; but large disturbances are not to be expected with monetary stability in a substantially peaceful world' (1944a: 263–4, his emphasis).

In the light of Simons's proposals for fiscal policy, monetary stability and price level stabilization, he reacted coolly to the BW Agreement. The largest contribution the United States could make to 'the progress of international organization' was to adopt a firm, rule-based monetary and fiscal policy which would lead, in turn, to currency stabilization. He favoured a hegemonic international financial order created and led by the United States. It was therefore vital that macroeconomic policy in the United States be committed to clear, consistent rules which in time would be imported by other nations (Simons 1945a: 39, 1945b: 295).[7] Like his friend Frank Graham in Princeton, Simons was adamant that international collaboration over monetary and fiscal policy could only be loosely organized or planned; regional arrangements were not favoured because they carried 'a collectivist danger'. Successful demonstration by a major industrial nation which had adopted appropriate macropolicy rules was the best way forward. Unlike John Williams's key currency idea incorporating the US dollar and UK sterling at the centre of the international architecture, Simons's doctrine saw the dollar and US economic policy as pivotal (Simons 1943: 241).[8]

Simons (1944a: 261) sneered at the BW discussions:

> The specialists have now been called upon to lay plans for monetary reconstruction. As might be expected, they have responded vigorously and with cultist *esprit*, to this relaxation of their political ostracism. Their prescriptions, naturally enough, center around a supranational bank – which may be good tactics, since everyone defers to the experts and no one much pretends to understand their elaborate institutional contrivances.

The Keynes and White plans used in preliminary BW discussion had little to do with the fundamentals behind policies required to stabilize the US dollar or UK sterling. Simons concentrated his attack on some glaring omissions in BW discussion. First, trade policy was ignored at BW as if international trade and monetary arrangements were unrelated activities. The Keynes and White plans considered together are 'like *Hamlet* without the Prince of Denmark' (Simons 1944a: 226, 1944b, 113).[9] Second, plans for supranational currency stabilization were founded on the exercise of separate monetary powers in national jurisdictions; and these powers are manifest in heterogeneous taxing and spending policies among governments. All was not lost, however. If the BW Agreement was able to stave off bilateralism and totalitarianism by making currency devaluation more orderly, then it might have some point. It might also be a means of international collaboration over macropolicy reform in postwar transition years. What Simons hoped for, contrary to the intentions of BW architects, was that the BW Agreement was a temporary 'stop-gap' while the world waited for a 'radical reduction' in tariff barriers, with American leadership on this score (1943: 243, 1944a: 266).[10]

While granting immediate postwar transition problems in international finance, Simons (1943: 245) looked forward to market-determined exchange rates; that is, to an

> eventually more flexible and less administered system in which the separate currencies of nations or groups of nations are stabilized fiscally in terms of internal price levels and freely traded, without fixed parities, in organized, unmanipulated foreign-exchange markets. Such arrangements, however, perhaps cannot be recommended as a proximate objective, since with them it might be nearly impossible to prevent (or to define) arbitrary, governmental rate manipulation.

In an article written not long before his death, Simons reflected on the BW Agreement, hoping that, after postwar transition and reconstruction, the IMF would not be so focused on exchange rate stabilization. Given his preference for flexible exchange rules, the IMF could then 'evolve into a flexible agency for coordinating national programs of monetary-fiscal stability'. This was a portentous remark in the light of events after 1971. Finally, and consistent with his free trade orientation, the only point of international lending out of supranational institutions such as the IBRD must be to *require* reduction in trade barriers as a loan condition (Simons 1945b: 295).

Viner's support for rule-following international financial institutions

Jacob Viner taught at Chicago from the 1930s to 1946. That did not make his position on the international financial architecture identical to Henry Simons's though there were notable similarities, particularly in the emphasis Viner accorded to constructing that architecture on the basis of clear rules. More than Simons, Viner delved into the details of the BW Agreement.

Viner insisted that the global monetary system 'will have to be deliberately designed and ... operated under strictly international auspices'. Difficulties in reaching agreement on technical details must not deter the planners. Though the IMF had power to enforce its general rules, the 'rules ... are for the most part ambiguous, elastic ... or, if they are rigorous enough, are sapped of their coercive power by elaborate series of escape clauses' (Viner 1943: 195). Before the BW Agreement was reached he preferred a modified international gold standard to a world of flexible or arbitrarily controlled exchange rates. Orderly, planned exchange rate adjustments were desirable in order to avoid beggar-thy-neighbour policies, impending depressions or world-wide deflation. Intervention must be sanctioned by a supranational authority. Moreover, changes in the monetary value of gold should be allowed occasionally, as required by the authority guided by a clear rule embodied in a formal international agreement.[11] Disappointment is expressed over the Keynes and White plans because they had the effect of imposing more rigidity on exchange rates than was necessary (Viner 1943: 205–6).

After BW, comprehensive, entrenched exchange controls persisted; Viner regarded these as pernicious and only worthwhile in 'genuine emergencies'. Full currency convertibility, removal of controls on capital and current account transactions should be immediate – not postponed indefinitely. In effect, Viner pleaded for free trade unrestricted by arbitrary exchange controls (Viner 1943: 212, 1944: 236).[12] Altogether, the BW exchange rate rule is condemned as being opaque; it created uncertainty given that realignments were effectively to become the subject of 'international mass-meeting' before being sanctioned. Exchange rate policy required 'stricter and more guarded' operational criteria. Otherwise the BW rule promised 'a speculators' paradise' (Viner 1946: 325).

Implicit throughout Viner's scattered remarks on fiscal policy is disapproval of its inflexible character which in turn makes fiscal policy a culprit for inflation at the national level. International coordination of fiscal policy is not practicable given the unwillingness of policymakers to transfer fiscal prerogatives to an external agency. In this his position was close to Simons's. And, like Simons, on monetary policy Viner was concerned about the absence of discussion of monetary discipline in the BW Agreement. There was no clear sanction to control participating nations which chose to embark on loose monetary policies leading to an 'inflationary spree'. When nations freely adopted strong monetary discipline their currencies could come under the scarce currency provisions of the IMF articles. These nations might be placed in 'a monetary quarantine' by these provisions and have exchange or other controls imposed against them. While American monetary sovereignty was to be maintained in any event, there was no guarantee that monetary policy in the United States would not have an inflationary bias acting as a bad example for other nations (Viner 1944: 237–8). As if in a state of resignation, Viner places little emphasis on international collaboration over monetary policy. Presumably his demand for more precise, transparent operational criteria for exchange rate policy contains at least tacit instructions for monetary policy.

Consistent with his rule-based preference for exchange rate policy, Viner desired a more precise, transparent formulation for international investment policy. If capital was to be allocated by the IBRD a clear economic rationale for intervention in capital markets was required. The IMF's exchange rate stabilization function was essentially 'cycle dampening' if it operated according to the letter of the BW Articles of Agreement. However, in a crisis, exchange rates have 'a questionable and indeterminate relationship to the lasting values [that would obtain] under free-exchange-market conditions of the countries involved'. In that case the IMF would merely act as a 'relief agency'. The IMF was definitely not designed to correct perceived capital market failures – that task fell to the IBRD. Where international capital was used to prevent mass unemployment a completely different supranational institution was required (Viner 1947b: 339).[13]

Also problematic was the IBRD's charter which addressed the supply of capital but made no reference to appropriate timing of loans with respect to the business cycle. The IBRD utilized a technique of organizing loans that could decrease the private capital market's enthusiasm for lending by permitting the Bank to redeem loans at par before maturity. This would 'weaken the marketability of such loans where the appeal to the investor lies wholly or predominantly in the Bank's guarantee and not at all or only slightly in the credit standing of the borrowers'. An adverse selection effect would arise when only high credit risk borrowers have strong incentives to use the Bank, and the bonds issued by the Bank would reflect its credit rating and not the credit standing of actual borrowers. Furthermore, without a transparent, common international legal framework protecting the rights of creditors and debtors, the allocation of finance would inevitably be subject to the risks of moral hazard (Viner 1944: 245, 1947a: 296–7).[14]

Without a clearer international rule-based financial architecture arising out of BW, Viner equivocated. In his conception, perhaps BW was just a harmless short-term agreement: did it amount to no more than 'a modified version of American philanthropy' rather than hegemony? A charity to be 'dispensed at American discretion, rather than a genuine international authority'? Perhaps also, in the long run the unregulated character of trade, payments and capital flows in the nineteenth century based on *laissez-faire* was optimal after all? On the benefits of *laissez-faire* he reflected nostalgically: 'despite that fact that it was motivated by private profit, it was one of the great blessings which cupidity has procured for mankind' (Viner 1950: 378, 1949: 327). Here he draws back towards the Chicagoan outlook also promoted by Henry Simons.

By the time Viner had settled in Princeton after leaving Chicago in 1946, he had observed the BW system in operation for several years. Prevailing economic policies were not, in his mind, going to give up their strong nationalist bias; western industrialized economies were predominantly planned and market processes heavily restricted. In sharp contrast to the prevailing view from Chicago, the pragmatic thinker in Viner emerged. The international financial architecture could not be expected to be constructed spontaneously – it must be the result of detailed rules and precise planning, Exceptions and escape clauses Viner accepted as commonplace. If a recognizable international financial *order* is to arise it will be established 'by means of day-to-day negotiation, whose outstanding characteristics will be its dependence on compromise, on piecemeal adjustments where the pressures are greatest, and on avowed or disguised improvisation' (1950: 378).

Milton Friedman's case for flexible exchange rates

Widespread antipathy towards flexible exchange rates after BW did not deter Friedman. In 1950, while a consultant to the US Economic Cooperation Administration – the organization responsible for channelling Marshall aid to Europe – Friedman made a comprehensive case for flexible exchange rates. 'Flexibility' for Friedman meant freely floating. Though he referred explicitly to European currencies in his article on the subject, Friedman intended the case to apply more widely.[15]

Friedman rehearsed the basic principles behind flexible exchange rates: they are not ends in themselves, just prices that clear markets and in this case prices that balance the international balance of payments. An incipient surplus in the balance of payments will be accompanied by an excess demand for domestic currency and the exchange rate against foreign currency will tend to rise (relative to some pre-existing rate) until the excess demand (and surplus) is eliminated. This process has a direct counterpart if there is an incipient deficit, when the exchange rate tends to fall. Monetary authorities would not need to accumulate foreign exchange reserves to support a fixed exchange rate, thereby, in principle, contributing to a more efficient allocation of world capital (Friedman 1953: 160–2). By contrast, under the BW Agreement, while the 'use of monetary reserves as the sole reliance to meet small and temporary strains on the balance of payments . . . is an understandable objective of economic policy . . . it is not a realistic, feasible or desirable policy' (Friedman 1953: 172).

As for realism, it is seldom clear in advance whether a balance of payments 'strain' is temporary or permanent. As for feasibility, reserves may have to be very large if they are to be relied upon exclusively to meet 'temporary' changes in the balance of payments; the duration of such changes cannot always be determined in advance. As for desirability, corrective economic adjustments to payments imbalances may be postponed too long because adjustments are politically unpalatable; as a result reserves are relied upon to thwart adjustments, forcing more drastic policy changes when reserves are depleted.

Friedman dealt directly with the main arguments of conventional BW doctrine against flexible exchange rates. The bogy of uncertainty and instability associated with flexible rates is not inherent to flexibility. Usually, instability is a symptom of domestic economic imbalances rather than a cause. By comparison, the BW fixed rate rule can perpetuate imbalances and introduce instability in times of economic stress. The fact that there will be uncertainty as to the prices of tradable goods is accepted, but can be met by hedging facilities in foreign exchange markets. Some hedging costs will, of course, have to be borne by individual traders. As well, futures markets in foreign exchange are inhabited by speculators who can bear the bulk of the uncertainty whereas the BW rule merely transforms the uncertainty faced by traders. Uncertainty manifests itself in other forms: under BW there will be uncertainty about the commitment of monetary authorities to supporting the fixed rate; fears about administrative manipulation of both the fixed rate and various uses of foreign exchange; and doubts about the workability of policies designed to restrict foreign exchange trading to current account transactions and specific capital account convertibility needs. The hoary BW position that foreign exchange markets operating freely will lead to destabilizing speculation is seen by Friedman as an empirical question unsubstantiated by BW supporters (e.g. Ragnar Nurkse). The 'cavalier rejection of a system of flexible rates' in the late 1940s had much to do with oversimplification of the consequences of 'hot' money flows between countries and a misreading of currency experiences in the 1930s (Friedman 1953: 176).[16] In most cases, speculative currency activity was a symptom of existing economic fundamentals; it correctly anticipated inevitable currency movements rather than acting as a cause of changes in the values of most European currencies during the interwar years. What was wrong with 'destabilizing' speculation in these cases if it confers net economic benefits by hastening correction of the imbalances already evident?[17] At the very least Friedman was not asserting the omniscience of foreign exchange market participants, as Richard Kahn (1973: 181) later alleged; Friedman only had sublime faith in their ability to react effectively to major economic imbalances. While the BW doctrine on exchange rates had conquered the economics profession by the 1950s, in Friedman's view this conversion must have occurred by a leap of faith, for the evidence from currency experience in the interwar years did not provide compelling justification for fixed exchange rates.

The second main area of consensus at BW was that flexible exchange rates were likely to transmit inflation from abroad to the domestic economy, thereby disrupting internal balance. Would countries lose control of their price levels? For Friedman, this is not a valid objection to flexible exchange rates. Flexible rates can enable a country to neutralize international price disturbances. It all depends on the starting point. Of course a country which adopted stimulatory demand management policies to increase employment will expand income, and this will tend to increase the demand for imports, lower the value of the (assumed flexible) currency, and raise the domestic price of foreign goods and hence the national price level. However, if the starting point was a national *recession* then there would have been some initial downward pressure on the demand for imports and on domestic prices through a flexible exchange rate. In a situation where a declining exchange rate engendered domestic wage and price spirals as organized labour demanded compensation for a rise in the cost of living, this was an outcome of special institutional impediments to economic adjustment and not the fault of flexible exchange rates. In Friedman's view the causes of inflation were more likely to be found in undisciplined monetary and fiscal policies and inappropriate wages policy. Indeed, currency depreciation in a flexible exchange rate regime 'is then an obvious result of inflation rather than a cause' (Friedman 1953: 181). On the other hand, if exchange rates are fixed and inflation is repressed by direct price and wage controls this only leads to major, more disturbing, changes in exchange rates at a later date.

A third argument against flexible exchange rates is that they do not give policymakers time to make adjustments to changing external economic circumstances. Instead, according to this argument, through the operation of the price mechanism flexible exchange rates force immediate allocative changes in the domestic economy which may not be appropriate in the long run. Friedman conceded that this is an 'exceedingly difficult question'; it must be considered relative to alternative proposals at BW, that is the fixed adjustable exchange rate rule:

> there seems no reason to expect the timing or pace of adjustment under the assumed conditions [flexible exchange rates] is to be systematically biased in one direction or the other from the optimum or to expect that the other techniques of adaptation – through internal

> price changes, direct controls, and the use of monetary reserves with rigid exchange rates – would lead to a more optimum pace and timing of adjustment.
>
> (Friedman 1953: 185)

Unfortunately, Friedman does not set out criteria for defining the 'optimum'. Discontinuous exchange rate changes or even general expectations of such changes under the BW rule were potentially more disruptive than orderly, continuous changes. That any slowing down of internal economic adjustments to external imbalances should be regarded as desirable or an 'improvement' wrought by fixed exchange rates seemed perverse to Friedman (1953: 186).[18]

Friedman tirelessly applied a simple model of demand and supply in which price is fixed. Thus, in retrospect, the par values of exchange rules fixed after the BW Agreement made the US dollar too cheap in terms of foreign currencies. Hence the scarce dollar problem arose in the 1950s. By the 1960s par values were too slow to change to the new economic circumstances and the US dollar became overvalued. To make matters worse, fixed exchange rates inhibited freer trade. Trade policy liberalization was hampered by all manner of foreign exchange controls and by restraints on currency convertibility. Opportunities for trade expansion were severely crimped in the BW architecture. With the BW exchange rate rule, changes in conditions of trade could be met only by internal prices and monetary conditions, or 'changes in reserves, internal prices and monetary conditions, or direct controls over imports, exports and other exchange transactions' (Friedman 1953: 196).[19]

Friedman's expressed preference throughout his case for flexible exchange rates is a national economy with sufficient price flexibility to make large exchange rate changes *un*necessary – in fact also the ultimate objective of the BW architects. Later in the BW era he commented on the formal equivalence between a system of floating exchange rates and an international currency union (where exchange rates between union members remain fixed and currencies are transferred automatically across national borders): 'for they are members of the same species even though superficially they appear different. Both are free market mechanisms for interregional or international payments. . . . Both exclude any administrative or political intermediary in payments between markets of different areas' (Friedman 1968d: 271).

What did all this mean for the IMF? Flexible exchange rates would obviously require 'a major rewriting of the statutes of the IMF' if Friedman's case was accepted. The IMF would not be emasculated. On the contrary, it might remain as a lender of short-term funds perhaps in a 'last resort' capacity, though Friedman insisted that it must lend 'along commercial lines' and not at concessional rates. In a world of fully convertible, floating currencies the IMF might also have a tutelage role, giving advice to member nations on monetary and fiscal policy (Friedman 1953: 190, 191). It should not escape us that these are precisely the main roles the IMF assumed in the international financial architecture that evolved spontaneously after the collapse of the BW order in the 1970s.

Friedman's views on the desirability of flexible exchange rates never changed from the 1950s to the 1970s.[20] His later reflections on the subject were more circumspect in separating the exchange rate choices for a single country from those available to the international community. By the 1960s he was more adamant that gold had a minor role to play as international money or as backing for key currencies; gold 'is now at most window dressing, not the king pin of the monetary system that determines the quantity of money'. Gold would have no special monetary role in his international financial architecture. To be sure, he determined that a system of fixed exchange rates based on a gold standard was far preferable to the BW system which used some national currencies ('paper gold') as international reserves as well – for the latter were of variable quality and their credibility became hostage to the vagaries of discretionary, national monetary policies in key currency countries (1967a: 7).[21] Simply raising the US dollar price of gold as recommended by some economists in the 1960s to counterbalance loose monetary policy in the United States and its growing external deficit did not fundamentally alter the causes of this imbalance. A central bank which replicated a pure gold standard mechanism might be useful, however, because it could correct the deficit by reducing money supply growth, thereby lowering income and prices or letting these macroeconomic variables rise less rapidly than in other countries. The demand for foreign exchange by US residents would then decline.[22]

In the latter half of the 1960s Friedman became more vociferous in appealing for independent United States' action to float the US dollar, cease official gold purchases or sales at $35 per ounce and eliminate all controls over bank lending and private investment. A stable, non-inflationary United States' monetary policy would do the rest; the US dollar would be taken up widely as an international vehicle currency. Unilateral action was therefore quite acceptable to provide a lead to other countries which could either float their currencies or else peg them to the US dollar. In choosing the latter course, other countries would have to harmonize their monetary policies with United States' policy in order to keep their exchange rate fixed. They would also have to add US dollars to their reserves when in current account surplus and take dollars away from their reserves when in current account deficit. The final choice for these other countries was less about faithfully following a doctrine and more about adapting to circumstances.

> For many countries, it would make a good deal of sense to link their currencies to the dollar. These are countries that have a large foreign

> trade sector, are closely linked economically to the U.S. and are not likely on their own to have a more effective internal monetary policy than the U.S.
>
> (Friedman 1969a: 365)

There is nothing dogmatic about Friedman's case for flexible exchange rates. He would have agreed with leading contemporary commentators: 'what is relevant is not the question of fixed versus flexible rates in principle, *but which is better for a particular political or economic unit*' (Officer and Willett 1969: 224, emphasis in original).[23]

That Friedman had solved the international liquidity problem for major industrialized economies in one fell swoop just seemed too good to be true. Flexible exchange rates for these countries meant that official foreign exchange interventions (and thus reserves) were unnecessary. Speculators would be relied upon to dampen short-term currency fluctuations. Moreover, 'the frustrating and ineffective negotiations for a new international liquidity arrangement' in the 1960s would be swept aside, as would the 'frantic scurrying of high government officials from capital to capital ... lining up emergency loans to support one or other currency' (Friedman 1967a: 16, 17). Yet there is still an unanswered question: what policy preconditions, what monetary and fiscal policy framework, were appropriate for stabilizing both the national and the international economy in a world of flexible exchange rates?

Friedman's monetary and fiscal framework for international stability

In *Monetary Policy for a Competitive Society* the University of Chicago monetary economist Lloyd Mints (1950: vii) paid tribute to Simons and Friedman. Well before Friedman's (1953) article on flexible exchange rates the view was widely held in Chicago that monetary policy mistakes and subsequent monetary disorder had a greater influence on international trade and payments than exchange rate fluctuations in the interwar years. This was an entirely different perspective from that offered by Ragnar Nurkse and the BW architects. In typical Chicago style Mints championed flexible exchange rates and freer trade; asserted the stabilizing effects of currency speculation; denounced the practice of discretionary government action in the conduct of monetary and fiscal policy; and criticized the effects of fractional reserve banking. The BW system is condemned – it was a source of financial disorder:

> The worst of all possible systems is that which we now have. It cannot be surprising if the current combination of fractional reserve banking, (limited) convertibility into gold, unlimited purchases of gold at a fixed price, discretionary management by numerous monetary author-

> ities, and the resulting uncertainty with respect to monetary policy ... leads to frequent periods of unemployment and crisis.
>
> (Mints 1950: 113)

Mints also worried incessantly about political control over money supplies. In a frank address to the Mont Pelerin Society in 1965, Friedman chimed in on the subject of the 'Political economy of international monetary arrangements' (Friedman 1968d), emphasizing the undesirability of a small number of individuals, not directly responsible to an electorate, having so much power over economic activity through their control over money supplies. In the international sphere IMF officials are not answerable, even indirectly, to the authority of a politically elected executive, so granting them power over the international monetary architecture (say, through a Triffin-style scheme for a world central bank) raises serious questions about democratic accountability. Further, a 'benevolent dictatorship by a technically skilled and disinterested oligarchy of central bankers' through some world monetary authority was not only unacceptable on political grounds; such financial collectivism on an international scale was probably not economically sustainable or enforceable in the long term (Friedman 1968d: 273, 276).

Friedman broadly concurred with Mints on monetary policy. If international economic stability is achievable, specific monetary arrangements between countries and within regions must be permitted to evolve without deliberate design. In particular, it was of 'profound importance' to make sure that 'monetary policy can prevent money itself from being a major source of economic disturbance' (Friedman 1968c: 12). The priority given to avoiding monetary policy mistakes derived from a lifelong interest in United States' monetary history.[24]

From the outset, Friedman (1951) assumes that pure fiat currency systems in national jurisdictions are the norm. The well-intentioned actions of monetary authorities in these circumstances, especially in the larger nations, often destabilized the international economy. It was important that architects of international finance take a longer view and prepare a monetary and fiscal framework supportive of a flexible exchange rate world. In that world, national monetary policy would be set free to target domestic policy objectives and achieve internal balance.

Private bank creation of money is best controlled by applying Simons's 100 per cent reserve requirement. Discretionary action by central banks would be eliminated; open market sales or purchases of government bonds would cease, as would all controls over private lending. What would remain? In short, 'the chief function of the monetary authorities [would be] the creation of money to meet government deficits or the retirement of money when the government has a surplus' (Friedman 1948: 136). Government expenditure would be financed by tax revenues or the creation of additional fiat money (equivalent to zero-interest-bearing securities from the government's point of view). The aim of sound fiscal policy would be to avoid large variations in government expenditure. The idea of a balanced, stable government budget over any normal business cycle was central to Friedman's (1948) policy framework. Fiscal policy activism is unacceptable. There would be clear expenditure rules applying when cyclical fluctuations in aggregate demand occurred. Transfer payments from the social security system would be preordained by a definite, stable, transparent set of rules; the absolute level of government outlays would still vary in aggregate over a business cycle – rising according to existing transfer payment rules in recession and falling in economic recoveries. Taxes would be progressive on income and tax receipts would naturally vary with cyclical fluctuations in aggregate economic activity. Any structural changes in the tax system should be rule-based and transparent: they 'should reflect changes in the level of public services or transfer payments the community chooses to have'. No credence was accorded to Hansen's doctrine of secular stagnation – a state which would have rendered Friedman's policy framework redundant (Friedman 1948: 138).[25]

After agonizing over the various referents for the conduct of monetary policy in this long-term policy framework, Friedman opted for a steady monetary growth rate rule. Monetary policy would target the growth rate of a specified monetary aggregate in order to achieve internal balance given flexible exchange rates. Controlling the monetary aggregate would be referenced to the growth of real output. More precisely, in his *Program for Monetary Stability* Friedman stated his rule for monetary policy: 'The simpler rule is that the stock of money be increased at a fixed rate year-in year-out without any variation in the rate of increase to meet cyclical needs' (1959: 90).[26]

The objective was to eliminate central bank action in adjusting the stock of money to short-term fluctuations in economic activity. With fractional reserve banking prohibited, in a context where aggregate demand and employment declines, government tax revenue would fall and the internal deficit would automatically be financed by newly created money. Existing institutional conditions which might thwart this framework – for example price and wage rigidities – were short-term irritations duly acknowledged by Friedman as major obstacles to achieving internal balance (including full employment). He also granted that explicit control of the quantity of money by governments, and money creation to meet government deficits, might give rise to irresponsible actions, though the principle of a stable, balanced budget over the duration of a full business cycle would be a controlling factor (1948: 155).

Leaving aside perennial issues concerning the definition of the 'stock of money', determining the precise rate of money growth must assume stability in the velocity of monetary circulation and a constant, reliable relationship between the money stock and other macroeconomic variables such as consumption, investment and employment. The *international* implications of Friedman's constant money growth rate rule are of prime interest here. Policymakers in different countries would have to commit in advance to a system of flexible exchange rates and a constant money growth rate rule – this would be the extent of international 'cooperation' in Friedman's international architecture. Currency market expectations would be stabilized; there would be little reason to force exchange rates to fluctuate wildly unless domestic policy rules were violated. Flexible exchange rates would leave 'maximum leeway' for national monetary and fiscal policy. Any international agreements would be simple by comparison with BW, and occur spontaneously or 'inadvertently' as a result of each nation choosing a constant money growth rate rule for monetary policy (Friedman 1959: 77, 1968d: 278). Adherence to gold on the part of any leading currency country including the United States would be purely nominal; at best, gold would function as a placebo for those worrying about a world in which sovereign governments demanded some semblance of control over economic processes – a control they indeed seriously desired in the 1950s and 1960s. In a world dominated by fiat money, gold, like an old soldier, would not die; it might just fade away.[27] Even so, freeing the price and market for gold provided the best guarantee against governments abjuring the constant money growth rate rule. Looking towards the 1960s, Friedman was rightly perturbed that the fixed price of gold in terms of US dollars would lead to greater trade protectionism in a situation where the US dollar was becoming overvalued. Rather than requiring costly negotiations over international coordination of monetary policies, flexible exchange rates and a free gold market supported independent monetary management within national borders and *voluntary* cooperation between nations over international issues.[28]

Friedman's recommendations ran against the grain of popular Keynesian thinking in that his monetary policy was not supposed to be accommodative of a contracyclical fiscal policy and should not be adjusted in order to meet a specific, short-term employment objective. For Friedman, such policies were fruitless in the long term. While not fully certain, the delayed consequences of a monetary and fiscal policy aimed at reducing unemployment to a specific level and keeping it there were likely to manifest themselves in a higher rate of inflation.[29] On the other hand, freely flexible exchange rates would be the sole policy tool for targeting the balance of payments: they would insulate an economy from major changes in foreign demand. Flexible exchange rates alter the relative prices of foreign and domestic goods; export returns in local currency terms will *tend* to be maintained, as will the external balance, irrespective of the direction of foreign supply and demand shifts. Overall, the case in logic for flexible exchange rates seemed complete in the context of Friedman's monetary and fiscal frameworks.

Harry Johnson's renewed case for flexible exchange rates

In taking up the case for flexible exchange rates in the 1960s, Harry Johnson continued faithfully in the Chicago tradition on international economic policy that began with Henry Simons. Johnson (1969a: 199) lamented that the case was 'consistently ridiculed if not dismissed out of hand' by other economists and policymakers.

All the contemporary plans for international financial reform were reviewed and found wanting. The BW financial order was in a parlous state by the 1960s.[30] Three central problems had to be confronted. First, Johnson agreed with Triffin: international liquidity was threatened by the conversion of national currencies into gold at the fixed price of US$35; the growth of gold supplies was potentially insufficient to keep pace with the demands of monetary authorities to increase their gold reserves, even with allowable reductions of US gold holdings. The impending gold shortage could ultimately force countries to respond to international payments deficits by trade restrictions or deflation. Second, and compounding the gold shortage problem, the expansion of US foreign liabilities and balance of payments deficit reduced confidence in the US dollar; foreigners were lending real resources to the United States which could be used by residents of that country to raise unproductive domestic expenditure (e.g. military spending) or be recycled as foreign aid and foreign lending. Perversely, the international financial influence of the United States had in fact grown, along with its balance of payments deficit. US policymakers were therefore understandably reluctant to abandon the BW system and the fixed US dollar link to gold. Third, as a consequence of all this, the United States was 'dangerously vulnerable' to short-term shifts in confidence in the US dollar, subsequent short-term capital movements and the demands of foreign monetary authorities to convert US dollar liabilities into gold (Johnson 1962: 370–4). In a commentary on the 1961 Report of the United States Commission on Money and Credit, Johnson warned that conversion of US dollar liabilities into gold would perpetuate 'the ... chronic problems of international liquidity' (1963: 138).

Extending the BW fixed exchange rate system along the lines of Triffin's plan must lead to inevitable policy compromises which in Johnson's mind only weakened the BW order. As we saw in Chapter 6, Triffin's plan for 'replacing' gold with an international credit currency implicitly acknowledged that gold would have to remain an ultimate reserve at least as a transition measure:

> The Triffin plan is therefore something of a halfway house between the gold exchange standard [against the US dollar] and the establishment of a genuine international credit currency entailing the demonetization of gold. Its outlines are apparently the result of a compromise between a clear appreciation of the basic defect of the gold exchange

> standard – relying on the expansion of credit money to provide increments to international reserves while retaining gold as the ultimate international medium of exchange – and the desire for a negotiable scheme, the prerequisite for which at present is the retention of gold as the ultimate standard of value. The compromise runs the risk of reproducing the problems of the gold exchange standard in another form, before . . . the next logical step of abandoning gold altogether.
>
> (Johnson 1962: 389)

Like Friedman, Johnson very early on saw the strong theoretical and practical case for flexible ('floating') exchange rates. And he saw the implementation of such a system dispensing altogether with gold. Conveniently usable, interest-bearing currency substitutes for non-interest-bearing commodities such as gold would be preferred by reserve-holding countries. Empirical grounds for debate still remained over the effects of so-called destabilizing speculation in foreign exchange markets, whereas fixed exchange rates supposedly minimized speculation (Johnson 1967: 27).[31] However, there were no grounds for believing that BW could stop one-way betting against officially pegged rates by speculators without major, disruptive changes in exchange rates. Furthermore, the 'commonly held belief that the fixed rate system exercises "discipline"' on policy-makers, thereby preventing the pursuit of irresponsible policies, was 'a pernicious myth' perpetuated in the BW order. The BW Agreement enabled countries to use exchange controls, trade policy interventions and devaluation. Not only were there no deterrents or enforcement mechanisms to punish countries for not adhering to the BW rule; there was 'no international mechanism for compensating those who suffer from adhering to the rules', while other countries take no share in the burden of adjustment (Johnson 1969a: 205).

If policymakers in the Keynesian era are driven to achieve internal balance as a first priority, Johnson (1969a) reasoned, then why not adopt flexible exchange rates which offer monetary and fiscal policy independence without the need to restrict international trade and the movement of capital? Of course, flexible exchange rates are not a panacea; they will not remove the need for occasional structural economic change to correct persistent payments imbalances. Sources of disturbance would still remain: government policies could lead to excessive inflation, thereby inducing exchange rate changes, and changes in tastes, technology and other underlying economic conditions could also lead to shifts in the exchange rate. Crucially, responses to these shifts would be market determined. The balance of payments constraint on macroeconomic policy formation would disappear while governments would be free to use monetary and fiscal policy for internal balance. As well, the pressure to introduce ad hoc trade policy and payments restrictions to protect national foreign exchange reserves would be removed.

Like Friedman, Johnson saw no strong reason why *all* countries should adopt flexible rates. A new international financial architecture could emerge out of the defective BW system in which some major currencies floated and others remained pegged and strictly convertible to one or other of those floating rates. Developing countries, for example, could make their currencies more useful and stable by pegging to a major floating currency. By being joined to a larger, deeper currency market, a smaller developing country may benefit from the positive effects on trade and foreign investment. The currency of a 'banana republic', for instance, 'will be more useful if it is stable in terms of command over bananas; and exchange flexibility would give little scope for autonomous domestic policy' (Johnson 1969a: 206). Johnson (1966) canvasses the other international monetary reform possibilities which could benefit less developed countries. In theory, he understood proposals to convert the IMF into a world central bank, including Triffin's plan, as being conducive to channelling more liquidity into those countries. However, in practice, if a world central bank *à la* Triffin possessed liabilities which were conveniently and easily convertible into gold, as seemed to be the case for all Triffin-style plans, such initiatives would not especially benefit less developed countries.[32] The only realistic hope for *all* countries was a move to flexible exchange rates by major economic powers.

Johnson was convinced that the BW financial order could be maintained only by widespread government intervention in international trade and payments. Thus the appearance of an integrated international financial order wrought by the BW Agreement was now just that – an appearance purchased at the expense of international restrictions. The original architects of BW never expected that the exchange value of currencies would 'become a political symbol, devaluation a stigma of national disgrace and defeat and appreciation a symbol of surrender to pressure from other countries'. BW avoided the classical gold standard deflation–inflation mechanism of balance of payments adjustment and now the IMF exchange rate mechanism was being avoided by policymakers. The core policy problem was ignorance of the *monetary* effects of balance of payments disequilibrium. A payments deficit according to Johnson's monetary interpretation was simply 'an attempt by residents to dispose of unwanted domestic money by spending it'. To avoid inevitable reduction in domestic money and interest rate rises, BW adjustment policies turned on the use of official reserves rather than ongoing exchange rate changes. Liquidity demands grew rapidly with the growth of international trade and the BW system 'demanded a U.S. deficit during the 1960s to provide the rest of the world with reserves' (Johnson 1969b: 307, 309). The United States, as a reserve currency country, started to inflate at an 'immodest pace' from 1965 onwards. The monetary implications for other nations of a 'vastly enlarged' outflow of US dollars were seriously destabilizing to the fixed exchange rate system by forcing unwanted inflation on the international economy. All this culminated in the 'dollar crisis' of 1971 in which the link to gold was officially severed (Johnson 1972b: 18, 1972a).

A rash of proposals barring fully flexible exchange rates were forthcoming in the last decade of the BW era. Most of the proposals sought to provide additional reserves ('liquidity') without relying on large US deficits and without the need to change the price of gold or promulgate a credit-creating world central bank and so forth. All of these options, thought Johnson, could have been avoided by adopting flexible exchange rates. Finally, gold was 'fossilized' into the BW system but with genuinely flexible exchange rates it should have no significant monetary function (Johnson 1972b: 10). We have come full circle: Friedman's earlier conclusion for 1950 had now been reiterated for the later 1960s and early 1970s.

Policy assignment rules for a Chicagoan international financial order

Friedman and Johnson kept alive a vigorous and fertile Chicagoan monetary tradition which had lessons for the design of the international financial architecture. It was a tradition founded on the general rule that policymakers in separate countries freely choose to provide a stable monetary background for their economies. For the international financial architecture there was only one major policy prescription: the adoption of flexible exchange rates for major industrialized economies. Uppermost in the minds of these Chicago economists was the high value accorded to marginal additions to policy sovereignty. Table 7.1 sets out a summary of the principal Chicagoan policy rules; these are a synthesis of the main ideas offered by Simons, Viner, Mints, Friedman and Johnson. However, the table in no way captures the full variety and particular nuances in their policy recommendations which changed with events. Here we wish to underscore points of complementarity in the group surveyed.

Friedman and Johnson supported exchange rate flexibility because it would eliminate international payments imbalances in the long term. All the Chicago economists surveyed in this chapter saw little scope for globally coordinated monetary policy, though all appreciated the need for clear rules for ensuring domestic monetary stability. The speed of adjustment to external imbalances would vary of course, depending on the flexibility of key economic variables (prices, wages, interest rates) and the stability of rule-based monetary and fiscal policies in a country which adopted flexible exchange rates. Then the imbalances, if they occur, must arise from inappropriate trade policies, foreign investment restrictions or random structural disturbances (due to sudden changes in consumer tastes or production technologies or environmental factors) affecting particular nations. However imbalances arose, major exchange rate changes would be confined to those particular nations. Therefore there would scarcely be any need to use trade policy interventions, exchange

Table 7.1 Summary: Chicagoan rule-based programme in the BW era

Policy instrument	*Time horizon*	*Primary assignment*	*Secondary assignment*	*Policy rule*
Exchange rate:				
i) Major countries	All	External balance	–	• Flexible rate
ii) Small less developed countries	Short–medium term	External balance	–	• Fixed rates aligned with a major currency; otherwise flexible rate
Exchange controls	–	–	–	• Eliminate
Official reserves				
i) Major countries	–	–	–	• Unnecessary • Gold to have no monetary role
ii) Small less developed countries	All	–	Internal balance	• Hold intervention reserve in major currency against which exchange rate is fixed • Gold to have no monetary role
Monetary policy	All	–	Internal balance	• Constant growth rate monetary rule for each country or region (Friedman) • 100% private bank reserve requirement (Simons, Mints, Friedman)
Fiscal policy	All	–	Internal balance	• Announce fiscal rules and strongly link to monetary policy • Renounce activist, compensatory fiscal policy
Trade policy	All	External balance	–	• Liberalize
Investment policy	Short–medium term	–	Internal balance	• Use IBRD in postwar transition (Viner) • Use IBRD finance in return for reduction in trade barriers (Simons)
	Long term		Internal balance	• Leave to private capital markets

controls or official reserves to inhibit the allocation of the world's resources.

In the late 1960s it was possible to report that 'the vast majority of academic economists favor greater exchange rate flexibility than existed in the BW order'. There were still significant differences of opinion over the appropriate degree of flexibility (Officer and Willett 1969: 222).[33] Critics would forever point out the somewhat naïve nature of the Chicagoan position on flexible rates. Many economists both during and after the BW era attributed to Friedman and Johnson 'a charming faith in the ability of private markets to get the exchange rate right, and to keep it there' (Cooper 1999: 105). By comparison with the early twenty-first century, it *is* valid to claim that during the BW era good institutional arrangements for the efficient operation of foreign exchange markets such as hedging facilities, forward exchange markets and currency futures and options markets were not well developed or widely available. Yet these institutions could not have emerged without foreign exchange markets being allowed to work freely in the first place. Friedman and Johnson definitely idealized the workings of free foreign exchange markets; they represented these markets as being fundamentally no different from other commodity markets. Why not liken the used car market to the market for French francs? Friedman's intention was to persuade readers of a basic solution and describe the nature of an international financial architecture organized along the lines of flexible exchange rates in a world of fiat currencies without gold dependence. To the Chicagoans, the immediate political feasibility of such an architecture was a secondary problem: first, demonstrate on what basis a new financial order may be constructed. 'The tools of rational economic analysis', wrote Johnson (1969b: 311), 'can only illuminate the issues; ultimately politics has to resolve them'. Chicagoan analysis did not retreat from contemporary policy (as opposed to the day-to-day politics of international financial diplomacy). For the Chicago economists ingeniously grafted their free foreign exchange market proposal and free trade ideas on to the BW era concern to use policies to achieve domestic policy goals such as high growth and low unemployment. Major domestic monetary and fiscal policy instruments could be set by policymakers uniquely to achieve domestic goals without having to be preoccupied with external balance. National monetary independence was the *quid pro quo* for flexible exchange rates. In this, creating domestic monetary and fiscal policy rules increasingly played on the minds of policymakers in the last two decades of the twentieth century when flexible exchange rates became the norm. Many major currencies successfully floated after the collapse of the BW order. The spirit (rather than the detail) of the new international financial architecture since the 1980s is evocative of a general mode of thinking common among the Chicago economists discussed in this chapter. This modern architecture attests to some remarkable prescience in the Chicago tradition on international monetary reform in the BW era.

8 Reconstructing the international gold standard

European perspectives

> The international gold standard works without any action on the part of governments. It is effective real cooperation of all members of the world-embracing market economy. There is no need for any government to interfere in order to make the gold standard work as an international standard.
>
> (Mises 1949: 473)

A genuine gold-based international financial order: the Mises ideal

An Austrian economist, Ludwig von Mises taught at the University of Vienna until 1934, then moved to the Graduate Institute for International Studies in Geneva where he stayed until 1940, subsequently migrating to the United States and completing his career at New York University. The citation accompanying his election as a Distinguished Fellow of the American Economic Association in 1969 began with the following remark:

> A library possessing all the books by Ludwig von Mises would have nineteen volumes if it confined itself to first editions, forty-six volumes if it included all revised editions and foreign translations, and still more if it possessed the *Festschriften* and other volumes containing contributions by him. This stream of publications began in 1902.
>
> (AEA 1969)

The AEA citation also mentions some of Mises's major areas of research and publication in which 'special emphasis' is claimed to have been given to 'international finance', among other subjects. The basic core of Mises's work on international finance was formed in Europe, well before his move to the United States. His reactions to the BW order reflect the presuppositions of this early work. Yet modern followers of Mises and commentators on his work either do not mention his contribution to international monetary theory and policy or fail to find in it much substance or obvious practical value.[1]

So far in this book we have observed very few, if any, economists who remained committed to any type of gold standard. Those who were concerned about anchoring the international financial system to a commodity standard such as Frank Graham, Nicholas Kaldor and Jan Tinbergen could take some solace from the fact that BW rested on an indirect link to gold (via the US dollar). All leading architects of international finance introduced in previous chapters had a particular variety of gold standard in mind when assessing its strengths and (mostly) weaknesses. In the era of the 'classical' gold standard the actual price of gold was fixed at UK£3.85 sterling per ounce up to 1914, though there were several temporary departures from that rate.[2] Throughout the first half of the twentieth century Mises tirelessly reminded economists that the 'classical' standard as it in fact operated was by no means a genuine, ideal gold standard.

In the updated and revised English translation of *The Theory of Money and Credit* (1953) Mises included a new section on monetary reconstruction to take account of contemporary ideas, policies and trends in the post-war international economy. He was driven to restate some of his earlier doctrines to reinforce opposition to the BW architecture. The following list summarizes the 'inflexible' variety of gold standard Mises had in mind as a benchmark against which to assess any *real* gold standard structure:

1 A national monetary system is constructed in which gold coins or claims on gold circulate as money and facilitate exchange.
2 Gold coins are minted by weight and money, or gold substitutes (deposits, bank notes, cheques, bills of exchange) are obligations to pay a certain weight of gold on demand.
3 There should be a 100 per cent gold reserve requirement on all deposits in the banking system.
4 The gold parity of a country's monetary unit is determined by legislation; the gold weight of each monetary unit is unvarying so foreign exchange rates between different national monetary units (currencies) will be fixed by definition.
5 Governments would have a minimal indirect monetary role nationally and internationally: they would merely certify and enforce gold weights and measures, and enforce laws relating to the gold parity.

According to Mises (1953: 471), in 'virtue of the parity law, the unit of the national currency system was practically a definite quantity of the metal gold'. It was therefore of 'no consequence' in principle whether or not money substitutes had been given legal tender status by monetary authorities. Governments have the power to enact legal tender laws and the operation of Gresham's Law will thwart attempts to overissue fiat paper money or other gold substitutes (Mises 1949: 780). Fractional reserve banking regulations would also be fruitless; they would ultimately destroy the pillars of any gold standard structure. Gold redeemability, that is convertibility of gold substitutes into gold, would be regulated by the market, not governments. Mises appeared to believe that various substitutes for gold in circulation, including widely held banknotes, had the comparative advantage of convenience in being usable immediately in commercial transactions. One form of money will not be desirable in all conceivable commercial uses and the market will create substitutes from time to time.

In a mutation of Mises's 'inflexible' gold standard, a gold exchange standard evolved in which little gold was in fact used in everyday commercial transactions (Mises 1923: 22–3). This did not mean that bad money had driven gold out of circulation since up to 1914 at least central banks were active in both buying and selling gold against domestic currency at the legal gold parity for international receipts and payments respectively (Mises 1953: 471–2). Such a flexible gold standard economized on the national use of gold for monetary purposes. For either the inflexible or flexible standard as conceived by Mises, the international implications were straightforward. The gold standard equilibrates the supply and demand for nations' currencies. Gold movements between countries would be activated if the demand and supply of a national currency did not balance. If a nation exports less than it imports its money supply will decrease as gold is demanded outside the country in payment for the excess of imports; internal prices would adjust downwards, including the prices of inputs used in export production, until international trading competitiveness and the trade balance improved.

There would be no fundamental violation of the inflexible standard so long as the gold content of money was not altered from the legal par and so long as individuals had complete freedom to buy and sell gold as they desired. The supply of gold and gold money substitutes would grow in direct relation to the profitability of gold mining and rate of gold discovery (Mises 1949: 471). Critics would argue that under a flexible gold standard, sheer accident could determine whether or not a nation's money supply grows in step with demand for real purchasing power over goods as dictated by productivity and population growth.[3] For Mises, a price level inflation or deflation linked to an oversupply or undersupply of gold at any time (relative to the demand for money) was preferable to discretionary government monetary policy. Better to be dependent on mining technology and geology than unreliable governments. The market would be left free to determine how much money would be produced in the world economy; changes in the purchasing power of currencies would be freed from political interference. As Mises (1953: 416) wrote: 'The excellence of the gold standard is to be seen in the fact that it renders the determination of the monetary unit's purchasing power independent of the policies of governments and political parties.'

While a genuine inflexible gold standard was Mises's first preference he was aware that a textbook gold standard rule could not easily be introduced and enforced in practice. And he suspected that the flexible standard provided scope for discretionary monetary policy.[4] Furthermore, Mises was under no illusion that gold does not have unchanging purchasing power.[5] Gold can be subject to fluctuations in value over the long term. The basic economic story of value determination is intact for gold as any other commodity: the purchasing power (value) of gold is determined by demand and supply. And we

> cannot calculate the intensity with which definite quantitative variations in the ratio of the supply of money and the demand for it operate upon the subjective valuations of individuals and through these indirectly upon the market. This remains a matter of very great uncertainty.
>
> (Mises 1934: 256–7)

As Mises (1949: 470) argued much later, human preferences change, thus changing the relative prices of goods and the demand for money to purchase those goods. So the 'very notion of stability and unchangeability of purchasing power are absurd'. As well as preferences, changes in purchasing power also originate from demand-induced structural changes in production technology, thereby impacting on the supply of consumption goods. With these changes going on, adopting a gold standard does not guarantee economic stability and the absence of business cycles; it only eliminates influences on purchasing power (of gold-backed money) arising from ambitious monetary and fiscal policies. Nevertheless, a gold standard ensures exchange rate stability between national currencies.

Under a gold standard, price levels would, of course, fluctuate over time. The uncertainties and discomfort created thereby gave rise to interventionist, monetary policy actions to prevent changes in the purchasing power of gold (ultimately), but these interventions must, in Mises's view, be arbitrary and destabilizing. To know the broad determinants of the value of money is one thing, to 'bend them to our will' is potentially destructive to any gold standard that may be operative. An *in*flexible gold standard is supremely attractive because the international financial architecture can be formed in a depoliticized manner. Gold will become 'the money of international trade and [a mechanism binding] the supernational economic community of mankind. It cannot be affected by measures of governments whose sovereignty is limited to definite countries' (Mises 1949: 472).

The bastardized interwar gold standard and an alternative to BW

A more flexible gold exchange standard implemented in the interwar years was completely unacceptable to Mises and he admitted a failure to realize its dangerous implications in the 1920s.[6] Mises later saw it as a bastardized gold standard for three main reasons. First, gold parity changes became subject to change without notice under the direction of national central banks. The official price of gold was often raised, along with the pro-inflationary, countercyclical credit expansions promoted by policymakers.[7] That is, currencies were manipulated downwards in the interwar years in order to secure short-term competitive advantage in international trade. Second, central banks exchanged various legal tender money substitutes for gold and held a plethora of foreign currencies in addition to gold in their reserve assets. With the widespread practice of fractional reserve banking, any quantity of domestic money substitutes might be produced and freely exchanged at the official parity against gold or against foreign currency substitutes held in central bank reserves. Official promises to pay embossed on these substitutes were misleading if the gold value of monetary units was altered or easily alterable.[8] Third, central bank policies were not generally consistent with a genuine gold standard; they did not abstain from offsetting the effects of external payments imbalances. Thus, for example, central banks were observed not to have been sufficiently contracting credit (or selling official securities to the public) when gold and gold substitutes were lost from foreign reserve holdings.

On Mises's interpretation of financial events in the 1920s and 1930s, gold was slowly being demonetized. Nations were trying to preserve the appearance of gold while undermining its role in international finance. The risk, soon realized in the 1930s, was that Gresham's Law would come into play. Currency substitutes had no fully convertible anchor (in gold) and their supply was dependent on the whims of monetary policymakers not normally independent of political influence. These policymakers had a propensity to adopt inflationary policies as and when their political masters demanded. An inevitable, latent instability was therefore transmitted to international financial markets. Certainly there was convenience to be enjoyed in holding currency substitutes in official reserves because they obviated the necessity of first converting them to gold. However, currency holdings could now be quickly switched around, depending on perception of, and confidence in, the currency concerned. Occasionally, gold was understandably sought as a hedge against the increasingly uncertain value of banknotes and bank deposits. Abolishing private markets in gold in these circumstances only made matters more uncertain, and the well-known real effects on production and trade in the 1930s were momentous to say the least.[9]

Mises had no faith in the soundness of monetary policy conducted in a fractional, gold reserve banking world when different national governments, with varying policy agendas, had full control over the production of currencies used as gold substitutes. As an advocate of 100 per cent national gold reserve banking, and recognizing the convenience of gold substitutes in international trade and payments, Mises insisted on an automatic one-to-one link between currency issuance and gold reserves. International currency exchange rates would then be fixed indefinitely. The BW financial order also embodied fixed (but adjustable) exchange rates; it preserved the role of gold while at the same time allowing most member nations to escape the discipline on the production of their currencies imposed by a Mises-type 100 per cent gold reserve requirement. The rules of currency exchange and convertibility became an exclusively governmental prerogative under BW. Mises observed with alarm the common practice in the 1950s of governments assuming complete monopoly over foreign exchange dealing. The BW international monetary standard, far from being certain and fixed, was 'illusive' precisely because of threatened changes in the official currency buying and selling rates when a 'fundamental disequilibrium' appeared in a country's balance of payments (Mises 1953: 474). Foreign exchange control over certain types of international transactions led to mispriced currencies which amounted either to imposing an export duty or subsidizing imports depending on whether or not the exchange rate was undervalued or overvalued as against a pure market outcome.[10]

In reviewing both the official Keynes Plan and White Plan submitted at BW, Mises (1946: 216) bemoaned the 'illusion' contained therein that government-created gold substitutes such as bank notes and bank deposits could adequately substitute for real wealth and real capital goods. Whatever happened to rates of interest in money markets under conditions where gold substitutes were widely circulated would have no long-run effect on the production and maintenance of wealth. Interest in Mises's doctrine is not a monetary phenomenon but a *real* rate of return on assets (capital goods) affected by trends in productivity.[11]

The idea of international financial 'cooperation' at BW was just a euphemism for concerted, government-led credit creation. The Keynes Plan is ridiculed for portraying credit expansion as a matter similar to 'turning stone into bread' (as Keynes expressly stated it). For this 'miracle, on closer examination, appears no less questionable than the tricks of Indian fakirs' (Mises 1946: 217).[12] The doctrine Mises attributed to Keynes and the Keynesians on international finance is stated simply: it attempts to remove the external balance of payments constraint from the immediate policy agenda. Widespread government-sponsored credit expansion and manipulation of the domestic money market rate of interest was touted as 'creating an everlasting boom'. Nations would be insulated from money rates of interest that might otherwise be determined by free international financial markets (Mises 1949: 787). While the BW Agreement did not satisfy the most rabid Keynesian bent on promoting a world bank which could create a swathe of credit for use by all member countries, the United States was to become, in effect, that very bank in the BW era. None of this escaped Mises (1949: 475):

> The Bretton Woods Conference was held under very particular circumstances. Most of the participating nations were at the time

> entirely dependent on the benevolence of the United States.... The government of the United States looked upon the monetary arrangements as a scheme for a disguised continuation of lend-lease. The United States was ready to give and the other participants... were ready to take whatever was offered to them.

The United States subsequently began to issue more fiat money on the precarious, superficially credible link that had been created between the US dollar and gold; it was free, wrote Mises sarcastically, to 'pour a horn of plenty over the world' (1949: 474). Increasingly during the BW era, the fiat money supply in the United States grew at rates independent of that country's gold stock and balance of payments position.

Mindful of the difficulties in simply replacing the existing BW international financial order which was slowly imploding, Mises (1953: 481–95) suggested a major reconstruction in three stages, beginning in the United States.

Stage 1

1 Prohibit *additional* credit creation by the central bank.
2 Legislate for a 100 per cent reserve requirement on bank deposits from day one of the reconstruction.
3 Allow free international trade in gold, and free exchange of gold for currency at the national level.

Stage 2

The United States' government must declare a new dollar–gold parity after allowing sufficient time for gold markets to consolidate and adjust to the new free market regime.

Stage 3

1 Establish a 'Conversion Agency' to exchange US dollars for gold on demand (using a gold fund, borrowed interest free from the US Treasury).
2 The US Treasury undertakes to buy all US dollars offered by the Conversion Agency, removing all notes obtained from circulation.
3 The Conversion Agency mints and offers gold coins in exchange for small denomination notes.

What obstacles were in the way of implementing this three-stage reconstruction? Mises saw no economic or technical reasons standing in the way of reviving the role of gold nationally or internationally, though political factors were problematic. Politicians were enamoured of the Keynesian conventional wisdom. Mises (1953: 18) wrote rather despairingly that there could be no question of a major reconstruction of the national or international financial orders 'as long as such fables as that of the blessing of "expansionism" form an integral part of official doctrine and guide the economic policies of nations'.

The international *process* of financial reconstruction is far from clear in Mises's work. Perhaps he thought that other countries would follow the United States once it was demonstrated that the proposed three-stage reform was workable? He was right from a historical point of view to believe that there was nothing sacrosanct about the BW gold price of US$35 per ounce. Given the all-powerful place of the United States in the world economy during the early 1950s, Mises expected fairly quick internationalization of the gold standard once the three-stage reconstruction was accepted by United States' policymakers and legislators. Governments were certainly needed in the Mises scheme to see through the reconstruction process. Later, the international financial order based on gold would look after itself. As one sympathetic Misesian argued, the Mises doctrine leads to the demise of central banking and the eventual construction of a system of national free banking (Ebeling 1985: 51). By contrast, government monopoly over the production of fiat money through an official central bank was accompanied by an incentive to inflate – all the more so if that bank was not politically independent. In Mises's plan, active monetary policy would become an anachronism; monetary authorities would be responsible for administrative tasks: 'enforcing contracts, auctioning the assets of defaulting banks, protecting copyright on bills and coins, prosecuting [both] the emitters of counterfeit coins and fraudulent balance sheets' (McCulloch 1986: 78).

The proposed international gold standard revival together with national free banking would take many years to bring into effect. It could be blocked by 'Washington politicians and Wall Street pundits' who regarded a return to gold as a 'taboo' subject unworthy of serious consideration. In addition, the revival of gold could be postponed because 'professional and journalistic apologists of inflation' represent it falsely as 'an absurd idea' (Mises 1953: 490). Mises's reasoning on the appropriate national and international financial architecture may have seemed archaic in the 1950s. His policy proposals appeared impracticable. Nonetheless, he pressed on uncompromisingly in a hostile intellectual atmosphere which by the mid-1950s had given well-nigh full endorsement to the BW architecture. Mises admitted frankly that his reconstruction plan presumed 'a radical change in economic philosophies'. Yet he saw no middle way, exaggerating the choices available: either the international architecture is to be remade on the 'utopia of the market economy' or continuing acceptance of the BW order leads inevitably to the 'utopia of totalitarian all-round planning' (Mises 1953: 499–500). It was clear after a decade of BW that Mises was not a lone voice. For as BW arrangements started to reveal their limitations in the late 1950s and 1960s other gold standard proponents entered the fray, offering slightly different reconstruction plans.

Mid-twentieth-century gold standard doctrine

1 The French connection

That two key currencies had emerged in the BW era – the US dollar and the pound sterling – did not offer confidence and security in the international economy. Gold and foreign exchange (mostly the two key currencies) became substitutable elements in central bank reserves. The United States as the supreme key currency country fixed the value of its currency to gold at $35 per ounce. By the early 1960s some commentators, particularly those economists in Europe who favoured a return to gold, condemned the key currency system because it was encouraging the United States to overissue its money and take a cavalier position on inflation and a complacent position on internal economic adjustment.

Jacques Rueff was one of the most vociferous critics of the BW order. He had served on various League of Nations' missions to restore financial stability in Greece, Bulgaria and Poland and later played an influential part in the Tripartite Agreement which attempted to create exchange rate stability between France, the United States and Great Britain in the late 1930s.[13] Rueff, along with a leading French monetary economist Charles Rist (1961), voiced serious misgivings about the role of the US dollar as a dominant key currency. Both writers had their views popularized, if not legitimated, in Europe (at least) by French President Charles de Gaulle in 1965:

> We consider that international exchanges must be established, as was the case before the great world-wide disasters, on an unquestionable monetary basis which does not bear the mark of any individual country.
>
> What basis? Actually, it is difficult to envision in this regard any other criterion, any other standard than gold. Yes, gold, which does not change in nature, which can be made either into bars, ingots or coins, which has no nationality, which is considered, in all places and at all times, the immutable and fiduciary value par excellence. Furthermore ... even today no currency has any value except by direct or indirect relation to gold, real or supposed. Doubtless ... the supreme law, the golden rule ... that must be enforced and honored again in international economic relations, is the duty to balance, from one monetary area to another, by effective inflows and outflows of gold, the balance of payments resulting from their exchanges.[14]

Rueff was described by *Fortune* magazine (July 1961: 127) as 'De Gaulle's ... moneyman'. Indeed, throughout the 1950s and 1960s, in a lucid and journalistic manner Rueff proceeded to argue in favour of restoring a gold standard financial order which would not lead to initial deflationary outcomes. Like Triffin, Rist and Rueff warned of dire consequences if action was not taken to reduce the international economy's dependence for liquidity on the growing United States' currency account deficit.[15] That deficit issued more US dollars to supplement the growth of official reserves. In a lecture delivered to a French parliamentary committee Rist (1950: 92–3) foresaw the problem inherent in the BW order which developed much later: 'to select the currency of one country as international currency presents grave consequences. That country would constantly have to be a debtor with regard to the community of the other countries'. More dramatically, Rueff wrote that the western BW member countries were 'risking a credit collapse'. And later he expresses a sense of urgency – for, if a change 'is made *à froid*, before a crisis, the world will have been saved the horror of a new depression' (1961b: 126). Exchange controls, trade restrictions and gold trading embargoes would then ensue; these outcomes would imply an 'immense setback in civilization that must be avoided at any cost' (1967a: 185).

The essence of Rueff's analysis, as opposed to his alarmist rhetoric, pointed to the United States financing its external deficit by increasing its IOUs (as Triffin called them) or international liabilities rather than by losing gold. In other words, from a domestic monetary point of view 'it was as if the deficits had not happened' (Rueff 1961b: 126). Policymakers in the United States were able to pursue inflationary internal policies without much regard to the adjustment burden created thereby for United States' trading partners enjoying an external surplus. The exchange of gold in international settlements for payments imbalances was in fact discouraged by the BW system. The system had therefore been unfortunately misnamed the 'gold–US dollar standard'. Central banks outside the United States were able to create additional money against their US dollar reserves – a currency which was considered, in principle, convertible into gold at a fixed official rate. In other words, surplus countries accumulated dollar reserves that allowed their monetary base to expand. By taking US dollars in settlement for trade with the United States, foreign central banks

> left a large portion of these dollars on deposit in the U.S. where they were generally loaned to American borrowers. The central banks welcomed this new arrangement all the more enthusiastically because it substituted in their accounts revenue-producing assets for entirely unproductive gold bullion or coins. The functioning of the international monetary system was thus reduced to a childish game in which, after each round, the winners return their marbles to the losers.
> (Rueff 1961a: 322)

Foreigners received their own currency for settlement with United States' residents, and foreign central banks in effect issued more national money against dollars that they held and reinvested back in the United States. Credit is therefore expanded in both nations simultaneously, definitely augmenting international liquidity but also giving powerful impetus to world-wide inflation. On the other hand, if United States' liabilities were drastically reduced, world-wide deflation might well ensue. In this view, cumulative imbalances were created by the BW architecture and the world economy would eventually become highly unstable. It is scarcely surprising that Rist also often repeated his call for a new international financial order 'no longer bound by the shackles of Bretton Woods'.[16]

Both Rist and Rueff prescribed a return to gold. Rist had already demonstrated how BW would pave the way for the operation of Gresham's Law – it had already worked surreptitiously to promote gold, even in the early 1950s. In an article on the 'Failure of the International Monetary Fund', Rist (1952b: 188–9) produced data indicating that official holdings had absorbed 21 per cent of total gold production (valued in US dollars) in 1951; the rest had 'vanished into industry or into the hands of private individuals'. Obviously for Rist, these data implied a desire by individuals to possess gold because of their deep suspicion of monetary policies followed by governments; there was nothing irrational about such a desire since it was a form of insurance against bad monetary policy. A latent instability in the international financial order was also implied here: market participants were alive to the precariousness of the US dollar – it was not, in fact, 'as good as gold'. A decade later, Rueff (1961a) demonstrated how a large, persistent United States' external payments deficit made gold an increasingly sought-after asset as confidence in the US dollar declined.

The 'gold rush' of March 1968 represented the nadir of the so-called US dollar–gold exchange standard in the BW order.[17] Before March 1968 BW member countries could issue money against either gold or claims in national currency; claims in US dollars presented to non-US monetary authorities could also be exchanged for gold. US citizens were prohibited from directly substituting gold for their US currency holdings. However, the prohibition was ineffective. For example, dollars 'could also be sold freely in the London gold market' so US citizens 'could obtain at any time, without any justification or controls' gold in return for their US dollars. When the governors of six major central banks agreed in March 1968 to cease supplying gold to the London market and restrict all gold transfers to transactions between monetary authorities, they were merely staving off the collapse of the BW system (Rueff 1970: 181, 183). Private dollar balances outside the United States could no longer be freely converted into gold; they could only be presented to monetary authorities in return for payment in other national currencies of equal value. The BW gold pillar was gradually crumbling – all the more so with greater foreign accumulation of dollar balances.

What solution did the two French economists offer? First, Rueff (1961a: 327) was sure that the chief problem was 'neither exclusively, nor even essentially American'; it was instead located in the fixed link between US dollars and gold and restrictions on gold trading. Additionally there were two subproblems: gold production capacity was not being expanded as much as would otherwise be the case and policymakers in the United States could not act directly on the US dollar price of gold. If the official price of gold was raised, gold production would be increased, thereby counteracting any deflationary bias inherent in returning to an international gold standard. Also, a rise in the price of gold entailed a US dollar devaluation against other countries, both improving US export competitiveness and damping import demand in the United States. While favouring on these grounds a rise in the US dollar price of gold, Rueff was uncertain as to just how much the gold price should increase; he was only convinced that it should be sufficient to allow the United States to repay what it owed in gold to foreign central banks.[18] Second, other participating nations must fix the gold value of their currencies. Currency exchange rates would remain fixed, as under the BW Agreement. However, a free market in gold would be allowed to operate and monetary authorities must agree to buy and sell gold to all individuals at the new official rate. Third, the conduct of monetary policy in each country must be coordinated so that policy changes were aligned. Policy in respect of fiat money supply should be determined by changes in official gold reserves. No central bank should be permitted to lend to the United States or any other debtor country the currency against which it had already created credit in the domestic economy. A gold standard, once adopted, would immediately prevent money creation except against gold or claims against a national currency tied to gold (Rueff 1961c: 124). Fourth, and for practical transition purposes, existing US dollar liabilities may not need immediate settlement (or liquidation). Settlement could be effected 'progressively' (Rueff 1961a: 326). Whatever the precise mechanisms used in advancing towards a pure gold standard, countries already holding substantial gold reserves (and gold producers) would reap windfall gains.[19]

In any event, all new gold standard procedures would be established in transition as determined by an international conference dealing with implementation issues. Here participating countries would become signatories to a new international convention outlining the technicalities associated with the new gold standard. Expert international financial diplomacy would also be required but there would be no call for an international organization such as the IMF.[20]

From the point of view of existing economic circumstances, Rueff's (and Rist's) policy recommendations for international financial reconstruction were directly relevant to impending liquidity shortages in the 1960s and to the United States' deficit problem. By contrast, Mises had for the most part abstracted from these circumstantial problems. We shall reserve judgement on the merits of these various arguments for reviving a gold standard until later in the chapter.

2 Two views from Geneva

In the late 1930s the Graduate Institute of International Studies in Geneva supported Mises's intellectual independence; it nurtured for a long time thereafter a tradition in favour of reintroducing the international gold standard. Michael Heilperin, a professor at the Institute from the 1950s to 1964, produced a distinctive doctrine on gold more attuned to the contingencies associated with the BW financial order.[21] Like Rueff, Heilperin attended the Princeton (1963) and Bellagio (1964) conferences of Economists on International Monetary Arrangements where both argued in favour of a pure gold standard. Heilperin (1964) was moved to write a dissenting note which was appended to the main report on both conferences.

In an initial reaction to the BW Agreement, Heilperin (1945) was impressed by the BW architects' desire to develop a cooperative international financial plan. For Heilperin, the Agreement was a special purpose, emergency plan for a world economy in crisis. Therefore, the idea of a general purpose gold standard would have seemed entirely academic at the time. Observations of the BW system in practice led him to conclude not only that it was biased towards inflation because monetary and fiscal policies were not sufficiently disciplined; it also permitted chronic balance of payments imbalances on the current account (Heilperin 1955). The BW exchange rate rule was not the source of this problem, so greater exchange rate flexibility was not proposed as a solution. Given existing international financial market institutions and financial trading practices, flexible rates introduce greater uncertainty into international trade in goods and services, possibly acting as a deterrent to the expansion of international trade. As well, flexible exchange rates can be inflationary, permitting national monetary policy independence and indefinitely rising price levels sheltered by exchange controls and trade restrictions.[22] In Heilperin's (1952: 170) view, floating exchange rates only work if accompanied by appropriate domestic policies. Nothing encouraged faster international economic adjustment to external imbalances than an outflow (or inflow in the case of surpluses) of foreign exchange reserves in a fixed exchange rate world. There were some vital provisos, however. First, policymakers must renounce exchange controls. Second, central banks must conduct monetary policy directly to reflect (in direction at least), changes in foreign reserves. The problem with the BW architecture was that it embodied a single remedy for a fundamental payments disequilibrium, namely discrete exchange rate adjustment, when ongoing monetary policy changes would have avoided all that. Also, the BW architecture incorporated exchange controls as a 'permanent feature' and trade restrictions were also accepted (Heilperin 1961: 260, 264). Fixed exchange rates under these perverse conditions must inevitably lead to major, persistent international payments imbalances.

Overall it was difficult for Heilperin to envisage 'any useful purpose that would be achieved by trying to reform the IMF as set up at Bretton Woods'. He championed free trade, free international settlements and fixed exchange rates. A self-styled architecture for the international financial order was then put forward, based on the premise that a gold standard must be adapted to the financial environment of the 1960s (Heilperin 1961: 267). Like Mises, Rist and Rueff, Heilperin (1962) saw no alternative other than to raise the price of gold to take account of the extended inflation created by excessive issuance of US dollars in the period from the mid-1950s to the early 1960s. He departed from Mises's ideal in proposing a managed form of gold standard, just as the gold standard before 1914 had in fact been a system of managed, leading gold-linked currencies.[23] Both domestic money and international money are deliberate constructions of a political and legal system and not simply the spontaneous result of market forces. All advanced industrialized economies starting with 'the Atlantic community' must purposively create a gold standard. Unified international management to implement the standard is required from the outset (Heilperin 1962: 108, 154).

After an international agreement is reached, the first phase in introducing a gold standard would necessitate paying all future external deficits on current account in gold. The spread of US dollar liabilities held in foreign central banks would be halted by prohibiting additional accumulation of dollar reserves. Phase two required a doubling of the US dollar price of gold to US$70 per ounce (for the reasons outlined by Rueff) though the exact price change should be a matter of international agreement. The United States must over an agreed period then pay off all its foreign liabilities in gold and all countries must formally agree to make their currencies fully convertible into gold either directly or indirectly, while permitting free gold trading and free private ownership of gold (Heilperin 1962: 154).

At the Bellagio Conference, Heilperin (1964) qualified his gold standard plan for the post-BW financial order, labelling it a 'semi-automatic' approach as opposed to an 'automatic' standard (of the type proposed by Mises). The primary purpose of the Heilperin plan was to use gold more extensively in international finance to remove chronic external payments imbalances. A disciplined national monetary policy was essential to control fiat money production by altering money supplies in the same direction as changes in a nation's gold reserves. The potential for internal imbalances, especially persistent inflation, was limited by such a policy. The precise size of a monetary adjustment is not specified but it should be *no smaller* than the amount of gold loss or gain. There is a residual degree of discretion here to allow monetary policymakers some freedom to adjust monetary conditions at a pace and to a degree suitable for local conditions, where invariably banks were not bound by 100 per cent gold reserve or 100 per cent deposit reserve requirements. In addition, major technological changes which lead to a boost in gold discovery and production may dramatically increase the supply of gold; this surge must be managed by appropriate (downward) changes in the official price of gold as set by cooperating monetary authorities across different countries.

Otherwise, Heilperin was confident that a single, ad hoc increase in the price of gold in the 1960s would bring forth sufficient new supplies of gold to provide growth in international reserves without the need for central banks to hold key currency substitutes. Finally, to ensure adequate, intelligent management of the new gold standard architecture and to coordinate occasional changes in gold parities, a global institution such as the IMF could be part of the structure. If so, the IMF could possibly also be used as an international lender of last resort when particular member nations found themselves in a crisis situation.[24] Many years later at a conference on international adjustment issues, Heilperin (1971: 119) shifted ground, protesting that he had 'never considered . . . the gold standard as the final point in the evolution of monetary affairs'; rather, it was a 'transitional device' towards establishing a world currency managed by a world central bank, possibly along the lines of an improved Triffin plan. Now Heilperin was falling back on a preference for international money – any form of architecture creating a genuinely international money – when, in his perception, the world was heading backward to a 'more deeply involved nationalism'. This preference, indeed concession, is not evident in his earlier work though there are allusions to it in his proposal for allowing greater government discretionary management in the operation of the 'semi-automatic' gold standard.

While Heilperin provided the clearest technical case for a gold standard, Wilhelm Röpke, also a professor from 1937 to 1966 at the Geneva Graduate Institute of International Studies, offered a broader, complementary philosophical case for the revival of gold as the single, genuinely international money.[25] Hayek (1969: 197) noted how Röpke's extensive writings were 'intended for a wider audience' than professional economists. Röpke, according to Hayek, was convinced from an early point in his career that 'an economist who is nothing but an economist cannot be a good economist'.

In arguing for the reconstruction of the international order based on gold, Röpke set out to persuade a wide audience – the general public, fellow economists, politicians and policymakers. He recalled the 'painful experience' of both the 1930s *and* the 1950s when widespread exchange controls and trade restrictions were the order of the day. For Röpke (1960: 246), a gold standard was the 'only possible' pillar upon which to build a viable international financial architecture.[26] An architect of international finance must begin by adopting the correct vision of 'monetary order' and 'international integration' which not only incorporated financial arrangements; integrated trade relations between nations were surely the sole end and purpose of the financial architecture. Any reconstruction must begin from within national jurisdictions. International blueprints are not useful. For example, the BW Agreement incorporated a vision quite alien to international integration; it had sanctioned exchange controls and given further impetus to the forces of international disintegration which first became evident in the interwar years.[27] An improvement in 'philosophical insight' had primacy over events in effecting integration. For in the event of a major economic upheaval the options of collectivist trade and exchange controls might easily look more attractive to policymakers if no clear alternatives were made available to them (Röpke 1960: 246).

Röpke's long-term vision, like that of most of his Geneva economist-contemporaries, was to secure a free market-based world economy. Economic integration is enhanced on this view if markets are allowed to determine prices for money, goods, labour and other inputs in production processes. Markets cannot function in isolation, however. A world market economy based on gold needs a 'stable framework of *political, moral and legal standards* such as will secure international relations in general' (Röpke 1960: 255–6, his emphasis).[28] A gold standard was much more than an automatic mechanism; it was not just a matter of engineering a particular monetary technique because it could not function without a supportive institutional framework. For one thing, it presupposed that committed governments would initiate and maintain a gold standard even if it caused temporary economic hardship. Specifically, Röpke (1961: 231) foresaw that a 'nucleus of countries' whose governments were committed to maximum monetary discipline would gradually adopt a gold standard. For another, it required national market economies with flexible enough prices and wages for economic adjustment to external imbalances to be expedited.

An international architecture based on gold had three principal ideational foundations: freedom, unity and stability.[29] First, freedom from political direction was paramount, for gainful exchange among residents of different nations using different national moneys and subject to different national costs and prices was difficult to achieve in its own right without government regulations complicating matters. There was no escaping a necessary link between a gold standard and freer international trade (than that which obtained under BW). Second, unity in the international financial order was created *de facto* by a gold standard. Even in a world of diverse national fiat moneys created as legal tender, gold becomes international money without the expressed order of any government. Third, stability in currency exchange rates is assured by an 'ingenious "thermostatic" mechanism' of international payments adjustment unique to a gold standard. The mechanism works through the 'opening and closing' of domestic money and credit issuance in strict accordance with changes in gold reserves (Röpke 1960: 202). Government attempts to manipulate exchange rates so as to effect payments adjustment would likely be extraordinary violations of an unwritten pact accompanying a gold standard, thereby harming the unity and stability that go with international economic relations. At the national level such violations usually meant adopting reckless monetary and fiscal policies which disrupted the normal adjustment of cost and price relationships between countries and undermined the principle of comparative advantage upon which all mutually beneficial international trade was founded. International financial disintegration is usually a sign of these deeper violations. In summary, stability in the international financial architecture presupposed a specific orientation of national economic policies. External economic policy must be driven by fixed exchange rates since in a world of heterogeneous fiat currencies, flexible exchange rates will deliver to 'the hyper-nervous foreign exchange market psychological shocks which hamper the adjustment in the balance of payments' (Röpke 1960: 211). Internal economic policies must be stable, gold reserve referenced and ultimately subordinated to ensuring external balance.

Röpke trenchantly dismissed the 'supposed dictates of the "spirit of the age" which, as evidenced by its impact on the majority of economists in the 1950s, amounted to regarding a return to a gold standard as utterly absurd. In not understanding the vital role of gold in providing freedom, unity and stability without the need for complex international agreements, economists often resorted to making facile jokes, for example by pointing to the fact that in 'South Africa gold was dug out of the earth with much toil, only to be buried once more in the vaults of Central Banks'. Röpke replied that it is 'much more senseless and costly to expend much toil in bringing people into the world, and educating them, only to bury them once more, in an unproductive fashion, in foreign exchange offices among mountains of forms' (Röpke 1960: 257, 253). Indeed, exchange controls, associated limits on currency convertibility and gold trading restrictions were given their blessing in the BW Agreement.

Currency convertibility at fixed rates in the BW order was completely incompatible with national monetary policy independence. The policy experience in the first fifteen years of BW indicated that each member country had freedom 'to choose whatever degree of monetary discipline at any given moment seems to lie on the national line of least political and social resistance'. Persistently differing degrees of monetary discipline among member countries led to chronic international payments imbalances, exchange rate crises and drastic exchange rate changes. So much, thought Röpke, for the BW objective of exchange rate stability. In fact, he was moved to conclude that BW had produced 'a world without a monetary system' (Röpke 1961: 228–9).

In a chapter devoted to 'International monetary order' and a section entitled 'Toward a new world economy' Röpke (1960: 221–58) prescribed two major changes on the way to reconstructing international finance along the lines of a gold standard. First, abolish exchange controls on both current account and capital account transactions, perhaps beginning with individual countries and then by positive demonstration effects to whole regions and the rest of the world.[30] Second, restore international liquidity, which by the early 1960s had become an acute problem. Increasing the official price of gold was an essential first step towards a gold standard:

> with the official purchasing price of gold as it is today, the international value of all the gold available has become far too low to bear the strain of free international payments transactions. Should such a rise actually be effected, most of the problems of international liquidity would probably solve themselves, and against this the disadvantages, so often cited, would weigh lightly. It would be a measure calculated to put an end to a state of affairs which, anyhow, cannot be maintained permanently ... – a measure without which the reintroduction of a gold standard is unthinkable. It would of course, be dangerous to present this tension-reducing measure to a world determined to use it for the continuation of its undisciplined economic and monetary policies, instead of for a transition, through internal economic stabilization, to an external monetary freedom.
>
> (Röpke 1960: 258)

Undisciplined economic policies obliquely referred to in this passage are generally Keynesian-inspired inflationary policies targeting the 'will-o'-the-wisp' of full employment (Röpke 1960: 212). Röpke's scathing attack on the post-1944 full employment movement began with a review of the United Nations' report on 'International Measures for Full Employment' (Röpke 1952).[31] From the stance of a committed gold standard adherent, the BW Agreement allowed for greater national autonomy to pursue so-called full employment policies though these often turned out to be open, audacious inflation-generating policies and interventionist policies designed to manipulate international trade in the interests of maintaining full employment. Yet, at the same time, both the architects of BW and the United Nations desired closer international relations and economic policy coordination to achieve high growth and full employment. The irony in all this is brought out by Röpke (1960: 254): 'It was deplored [by BW sympathizers] that the gold standard did not leave to a Government full autonomy with regard to its national economic policy – as if there ever could be such autonomy if there are close international economic interrelations.'

There could be no place for activist international monetary and fiscal policy coordination in a gold standard architecture. Accordingly, international monetary organizations like the IMF and World Bank would be redundant. The 'boundless overestimation of the possibilities of monetary management' at the national and international levels in the 1940s and 1950s was in no small way due to oversimplifications introduced by Keynesian macroeconomics and an associated contempt for the workings of a gold standard. To be sure, all architectural plans for the international financial order exhibited imperfections, including commodity standards. However, the strength of a gold standard is that it supported from the very beginning free multilateral trade and payments. Unlike the BW architecture, a gold standard was not reliant on exchange controls, quotas, foreign trade restrictions and macroeconomic planning in general. BW possessed a fatal flaw: it had artificially separated financial arrangements from policies designed to promote international trade in goods and services – something gold standard proponents like Wilhelm Röpke could scarcely contemplate.

3 The shadow of Friedrich Hayek in Geneva?

In Heilperin's and Röpke's work we find the shadow of Hayek; not the Hayek of the late 1970s, but Hayek the gold standard champion in the late 1930s. In the post-BW years, Hayek argued for an international economy based on monetary denationalization, free international currency competition and free banking.[32] In an earlier era before BW, while occupying an academic position at the London School of Economics, Hayek visited Geneva and delivered a series of influential lectures at the Graduate Institute of International Studies. The lectures were then published as *Monetary Nationalism and International Stability* (Hayek 1937).[33] Hayek made a strong case in principle for the generation of international financial stability by reintroducing a full gold standard.

Hayek had long sought a 'truly international monetary system' or, more precisely, a homogeneous world currency which would be used extensively and its movement determined wholly by the actions of free-trading individuals in different nations. Like Mises, he was not prepared to believe that the pre-1914 gold standard conformed to the 'truly international' ideal. Gold movements were frequently sterilized or neutralized by counterbalancing central bank action, especially by the Bank of England, such that internal economic conditions did not adjust fully or in a timely manner to the flow of external payments (and receipts) (Hayek 1937: 41, 61). The post-1920 gold exchange standard gradually supplanted any semblance of a genuine gold standard since it carried the incentive to hold interest-bearing currency assets instead of non-interest-bearing gold in central bank reserves. And, as we noted earlier in this chapter, central bank currency reserves were more convenient to hold than a commodity like gold because they could be used directly to settle international payments without the necessity of first converting them into gold.

In the fifth lecture in Hayek's Geneva series, he sought to assess the problems involved in establishing an international financial architecture based on a single international money. A 'rationally regulated world monetary system' was difficult to achieve since even gold has serious limitations. Furthermore, in 'a securely established world State with a government immune against the temptation of inflation, it might be absurd to spend enormous effort in extracting gold out of the earth if cheap tokens would render the same service as gold with equal or greater efficiency' (1937: 86). Hayek preferred to be more realistic, however, given that the international economy consisted in a large number of sovereign trading states with different national moneys. A commodity reserve currency of some kind was preferable and gold an obvious candidate because historically it could be demonstrated that a gold standard, while imperfect:

1 creates a unique international money without need to refer national monetary policy to an international monetary authority;
2 makes monetary policy mostly automatic, stable and predictable;
3 secures appropriately fixed exchange rates;
4 makes changes in the supply of national fiat currencies move in the right direction (if not magnitude);
5 encourages gold production to respond in the right direction (if not magnitude).[34]

Reviving a metallic *national* monetary system was not, in Hayek's view, essential (by contrast with Mises's doctrine). An international monetary authority is not necessary because close cooperation between national monetary authorities under harmonized, tacit gold standard rules creates a 'tolerably rational' international financial architecture. In the absence of sufficient cooperation, a mechanical gold standard principle which at least secures some commonality of national monetary changes resembling the ideal international architecture would be far preferable to arbitrarily managed money and independent government action driven by no rule other than national expediency. If gold was unacceptable on its own, a composite commodity standard along the lines suggested by Frank Graham was also acceptable to Hayek. Such a standard, like gold on its own, would make changes in the volume of monetary circulation in the world more predictable. In fact, excerpts from Graham's work, as well as from Hayek's note in favour of Graham's scheme, were included in submissions to the BW Conference but did not receive much attention.[35] That was the last word from Hayek on the subject of international finance until after the collapse of BW in the 1970s.

While Hayek was attracted to the principle of fixed exchange rates under a commodity reserve standard of some kind because this protected international money from day-to-day political forces, he quietly gave up on the idea during the triumph of BW and Keynesianism in the 1950s and 1960s. Perhaps he also took comfort in the notion that the BW architecture was anchored to gold through the US dollar? He may have reasoned that any attempt to sever that link would prove catastrophic.[36] In the event he returned to the debate on international finance in the late 1970s, proposing a new financial order quite different from the commodity standard structure he so vigorously defended in the years leading up to the BW Conference.

Mid-twentieth-century gold standard doctrine: a synthesis?

Fundamental to the BW financial order was the fixed exchange rate rule, and the gold standard architecture incorporated this feature. Otherwise Mises, Rueff, Rist, Heilperin, Röpke and Hayek plumped for a completely different style of international financial architecture. The BW architecture was essentially a 'gold–dollar' system (Gilbert 1968) which harboured instability. All our gold standard architects thought that the BW financial order was biased towards inflation, all the more so in the reserve centre countries, notably the United States. Events in the 1960s seemed to bear out suspicions of inflationary bias since the United States was the only nation absolutely obliged to hold gold reserves. The function of gold as a discipline against inflationary monetary policies was especially relevant to the United States.

All gold standard proponents surveyed in this chapter blur the distinction between gold held as an official reserve asset for exchange rate intervention and stabilization, and gold or other moneys used as an international vehicle currency for international trade. Events in the BW era emphasized that it 'is virtually impossible to limit international money to one unless that money is accepted in monetary transactions in the major countries of the world' (Kindleberger 1989: 56). Simply decreeing one international money, namely the US dollar, invites financial markets to create other, sometimes more convenient forms of money for financing international transactions if the capacity of the single money to finance trade and provide capital is reduced by shifts in confidence. When the United States imposed strict exchange controls to limit gold losses in the 1960s, confidence in the US dollar had already begun to decline.[37] Both central banks' preference for gold in their reserve holdings and private demand for gold increased dramatically. As well, the capacity of the US dollar to act as an international vehicle currency became questionable mostly because of growing suspicion that gold convertibility could not be honoured. The market, according to gold standard adherents, will seek other means of rehabilitating gold.

Rueff and Heilperin made it a core part of their doctrines that, if the centrality of the US dollar in the existing financial architecture was accepted, the dollar could retain a key currency role so long as the dollar price at which the United States Treasury transacts gold was raised significantly. In other words, the US dollar would be devalued against gold and all other currencies. This action seemed far preferable to the imposition of more stringent exchange controls and macroeconomic policies designed to produce a quick, corrective recession in the United States. It is notable that Rueff and Heilperin did not give serious consideration to the revaluation of surplus country currencies (for instance an upward adjustment of some European and Japanese currencies). They, too, seemed captives of the conventional BW wisdom which required the deficit countries to take the initiative in the adjustment process and bear the immediate burden.

The ad hoc action to increase the US dollar price of gold would have the effect of increasing international liquidity pending construction of a genuine gold standard; it should not be read as a policy to resuscitate the BW order, just as a measure to prevent immediate disintegration of a failing architecture.[38] International liquidity in the sense of generating a plentiful supply of US dollars was not a satisfactory substitute for gold, so adjustment of the United States' current account deficit could neither be postponed indefinitely by such a move (though it might be assisted) nor be palmed off to countries enjoying a surplus. By contrast with BW doctrine, gold standard doctrine did not recognize the unique, *long-run* international status of the US dollar or any other fiat currency.

Mises, Rueff and Heilperin were predicting collapse of the BW financial order well before the event. Yet most economists 'almost to the end of the 1950s' thought that BW was sustainable (Gilbert 1968: 37). While there were differences between them on matters of detail, all recognized that a transition period was required to move from BW to a gold standard architecture. Their views echoed Hayek's ideas on the subject first enunciated to a Geneva audience in 1937. Röpke chimed in with a philosophical approach reinforcing gold standard architects' scepticism towards the role of international organizations in the world financial order. Table 8.1 synthesizes major policy assignment rules under a gold standard proposed by writers surveyed in this chapter, taking into account economic events in the 1950s and 1960s.

Table 8.1 minimizes differences between gold standard architects in the mid-twentieth century. Nevertheless, it shows that these economists based their recommendations on definite policy rules. First, the exchange rate is not an active policy instrument. Second, trade and investment policy are completely emasculated. Third, there is no primary role for a key country or key fiat currency, yet *historically* it was well established before 1914 that the pound sterling dominated the 'classical' gold standard and post-1944 the US dollar dominated the BW US dollar–gold exchange standard. Indeed, 'the successful operation of a gold-centered monetary system is [based on] an unshakable confidence that the reserve currency of a dominant country will always be converted into gold on demand' (Schwartz 1986: 71). Finally, external balance has policy priority; domestic objectives were a by-product once monetary policy adjusted automatically to changes in foreign reserves.

Should the gold standard be voluntarily adopted through a spontaneous market process? Should gold be introduced or imposed by enlightened governments in an economically dominant nation? Gold standard doctrine

Table 8.1 Synthesis: a rule-based gold standard for the mid-twentieth century

Policy instrument	*Time horizon*	*Primary assignment*	*Secondary assignment*	*Rule*
Exchange rate policy	Short term	External balance	–	• Make discrete gold revaluation to ease transition from BW
	Medium–long term	External balance	–	• Fixed rate, set gold value of currency • Full currency convertibility into gold
Exchange controls	All	–	–	• Abolish
Official reserves	All	–	–	• Allow to fluctuate with current account balance • Link reserve movements directly and automatically to domestic money base
Monetary policy	All	External balance	Internal balance	• Accommodate free gold convertibility • Money supply adjusted to reflect gold reserve fluctuations (Heilperin, Rueff, Hayek) • 100% reserve banking (Mises, Hayek, Röpke) • Free banking allowed to evolve (Mises)
Fiscal policy	All	Internal balance	–	• Balanced budgets over normal business cycle
Trade policy	All	Not applicable	Not applicable	• Free trade in goods, services and gold
Investment policy	All	Not applicable	Not applicable	• No government role • Eschew reliance on World Bank

envisages an exceedingly small role for government in the major dimensions of economic policy listed in Table 8.1. There is an especially minor role for government in external policy of any description. Following hard-won effects during the BW era, it would be scarcely surprising if governments freely relinquished their control over macroeconomic policy to an impersonal gold standard mechanism. Certainly no marginal reforms of the BW architecture were going to be good enough for gold standard reformers. They leave no place for a highly formalized plan ensuring international monetary policy coordination. Ideally, countries could simultaneously choose to adopt a gold standard without reference to the plans and policies of other countries, though most writers on gold discussed in this chapter believed the United States as a major economic power – albeit a shaky pillar in the BW architecture – had to make the first move in any reconstruction process. According to Rueff and Heilperin, a United States' initiative in this connection could result in a near concerted intergovernmental European push to adopt a gold standard.

That European economists were in favour of constructing a gold standard for the international financial order variously finds its rationale in the personal experiences of the writers concerned, their nationality, their appreciation of regional events and the influence of doctrinal history. Foremost in the thinking of Mises and Röpke (both refugees from German National Socialism in the 1930s) was contempt for totalitarianism in political systems; they carried this attitude over to their international economic policy proposals. Both writers abhorred government interference in international trade and payments. A gold-based international financial architecture, on the other hand, would limit the place of government, and free gold convertibility would place severe bounds on national monetary policymakers. And French economists and policymakers, led by Rueff, did not want *international* monetary policy to be driven by IMF initiatives to increase world reserves by some means other than raising the price of gold. Rueff's scheme to reconstruct international finance outside the IMF was perhaps a reflection, at least in part, 'of the French view that the Fund was dominated by Anglo Saxons' (Solomon 1977: 76). But this would be trivializing the matter. Postwar reconstruction completed, Europe at the end of the 1950s was enjoying a wave of optimism and prosperity. By contrast, the United States was on the brink of becoming a world debtor nation. Dependence on United States' philanthropy, as Mises expressly stated the matter, was at the core of the BW Agreement and embedded in the BW 'twins' – the IMF and the World Bank. By the 1960s the United States was dependent on other countries giving it extended credit which it absorbed while protecting its gold reserves. It was the United States which now had to accept balance of payments discipline; it should accept the BW rule to devalue (against gold and hence other currencies), given its fundamental payments disequilibrium, while many other countries would voluntarily refrain from converting their dollar reserve balances into gold. Unfortunately, there was little prospect that a credible European fiat currency could immediately be transformed into a genuine international reserve and vehicle currency (like the US dollar and to a lesser extent sterling) without the assistance of highly developed financial centres in Asia or Western Europe (other than London).

Naturally, under these circumstances older gold standard doctrines were revisited. More liquidity in the form of US dollars or any other currency did not resolve the international financial problem. This also applied to international gold standard *practice* prior to 1914 which was regarded as a poor example of an otherwise exemplary architecture. Moreover, the gold exchange standard in the 1920s was an abject failure as assessed from the vantage point of a genuine full-blown gold standard. Admittedly, modifications to gold standard rules and practice had to be made. Existing contingencies in the world economy could not be ignored. Hayek even favourably considered a Graham-type commodity standard as a viable alternative in the 1940s. What bound gold standard architects together was their determination to reduce the place of politics and diplomacy in the international financial order and limit the role of governments both in macroeconomic policy and in regulating international trade and payments. As Röpke argued so forcefully, to sever financial reconstruction from international trade was incomprehensible; equally, it was nonsensical to conceive of a gold standard conjoined with highly restricted trade and payments schemes and government-regulated capital flows.

There was something paradoxical in a mid-twentieth-century gold standard doctrine which was strongly pro-market in orientation. Reviving a gold standard architecture for financial reform at the international level might not have proved successful in the years following the collapse of BW in 1971 had it not been deliberately imposed by a hegemonic power. It was not clear that gold could become completely dominant (let alone costless to employ) in all possible situations, for example as a vehicle for international trade and investment. National moneys may from time to time be accepted by the market as desirable and useful irrespective of the extent of any gold backing. Gold as pure international reserve units cannot be spent directly and the market may spontaneously produce a greater quantity and variety of 'currency' to serve a wide range of international economic interactions or transactions. Accordingly, strong incentives can develop to substitute fiat money for a commodity money, be it gold, silver or some composite commodity. With liberalization of international trade and capital markets that is precisely what occurred in the late twentieth century.

Monetary thought has often relied upon an invisible hand or market-led process to rationalize institutional orders apparently formed spontaneously and without deliberate governmental design (Selgin and White 1994). Here the role of the international financial architect would merely be to confirm a structure after the fact – that is, a choice of currency amid a set of international financial arrangements – decided by the market. Mises came closest to articulating international monetary *laissez-faire*: he was sure that the outcome would be a freely chosen gold standard supported by free, competitive national banking arrangements. Later in the 1970s Hayek's version of the same architecture dispensed with gold altogether and promoted the free banking idea across national borders, thereby envisaging a world of competitive currencies.[39] Work on the gold standard idea in the mid-twentieth century approached and reported the previous 150 years' international financial history in a particular way. There is one general finding: markets have seldom, if ever, been allowed full rein to determine the international architecture. Gold standard proponents pressed on with their architectural schemes without regard for the fact that the contemporary political environment was not congenial to their efforts.

Economic conditions in the 1960s gave rise to another group of reformers proposing fixed exchange rates and an officially managed, one-off increase in the price of gold so as to renovate the BW architecture. Further consideration will be given to a leading upholder of this doctrine in the following chapter. Related ideas on giving a deliberate boost to international liquidity will also be assessed. Another continuing theme is the fixed exchange rate, which was central to a more fundamental reconstruction of the international order proposed by Robert Mundell, turning on financial integration through regional monetary unions.

9 Salvaging the fixed exchange rate architecture

The ideas of Roy Harrod and Robert Mundell

> Fixed exchange rates are not an objective at all; they are a technical weapon, which may or may not be best suited to its purpose.
>
> (Harrod 1965: 34)

Roy Harrod's advocacy of a rise in the price of gold

Roy Harrod worked mainly at Oxford University from the late 1920s until his retirement in the early 1970s.[1] He became a specialist in international economics and policy well before BW. The core elements of his doctrine on the international financial architecture are indicated at an early date in *International Economics* (Harrod 1933) – a book commissioned by Keynes for the Cambridge Economic Handbook series. In a special section on 'World monetary reform' there are stated two requirements which he held tenaciously until his last work on the subject in the 1970s. First, world financial reform could be 'undertaken through international cooperation without it necessarily involving a common world money. The divergence of the interests of different countries could be recognized and allowed for.' Second, the international 'monetary system when left to itself seems to be subject to inherent instability'; therefore some deliberate, active policy was required to stabilize the system (1933: 172–3, 178).[2] For Harrod, the BW financial architecture had gone a long way towards satisfying these two requirements.

The US dollar had an overriding influence on international financial stability throughout the period from the 1930s to the 1970s. As Harrod explained in *The Dollar* (1953a), convertibility of the dollar into gold at an unvarying price in the post-Second World War years created a new environment in which countries linked their currencies to the dollar. This arrangement had a stabilizing effect. Monetary authorities, not individuals, were able to convert dollars into gold or vice versa at a fixed price. In addition, in the immediate postwar years the United States was a net creditor nation, offering credit facilities and thus enabling participating nations (and individuals) in the BW order the opportunity to supplement both their monetary reserves and operating balances to facilitate trade, by borrowing in the United States (or alternatively to earn interest on their US dollar credit balances). The United States played a unique, centre country role post-1944, supplying (or absorbing) dollar reserves by selling (or buying) gold in transactions with foreign monetary authorities. The United States was in a privileged position, financing its external imbalances, for example its current account deficit, mostly with its own currency. There was, however, a limit determined by the state of confidence in world financial markets.[3] The exchange rate between the US dollar and gold remained fixed at US$35 per ounce, though there was nothing in the IMF Articles of Agreement preventing the declaration of a new rate.[4]

Harrod fully supported the BW architecture; even as untoward events unfolded during the BW era he sought means to salvage the core 'technical weapon' of that architecture, namely the fixed, adjustable exchange rate rule.[5] In the face of opposition from leading financial architects including the Austrians, French economists Rueff and Rist, and Triffin, Harrod wished to retain a key (but not exclusive as per the Austrians) role for gold as a reserve 'currency' in the BW order. As a corollary, he had come to believe that the United States could cope with a fundamental external imbalance if there was a nonrepeatable increase in the value of the dollar in relation to gold. The dollar would not devalue against goods and services and would not be devalued against other currencies. With the consistent application of the IMF Article IV Section 7, allowing a 'uniform proportionate change in par values', Harrod expected that the price of gold could rise in terms of all currencies linked to the dollar, thereby creating a large, singular increase in liquidity. The volume of world reserves would increase immediately since in exchange for every unit of gold more currency (US dollars in particular) would be required.

Harrod's objective was to rescue the BW order from the threat of collapse inherent in the burgeoning United States' external payments imbalance.[6] He wanted to achieve for world liquidity what Triffin's plan promised except that instead of demonetizing gold and creating a new international credit money, gold was to be rehabilitated by substantially raising its official price.[7] Gold would not so much act as a currency standard as an official reserve. Unlike Rueff, Rist and Heilperin, Harrod did not propose to eliminate existing dollar (and sterling) balances from official monetary reserves – quite the contrary. For Harrod wanted to maintain the dollar–gold exchange standard and supplement international reserves by raising the dollar price of gold. Accounting for the inflation of the dollar price of commodities in general from 1944 to 1961, Harrod estimated that the price of gold should be doubled, thereby raising world reserves by US$40 billion.[8] BW member countries would then be able to expand domestic credit in pursuit of higher growth and full employment. While there are minor changes in emphasis to Harrod's advocacy of an increase in the price of gold as events and policies dictated, his case was made consistently throughout the BW era.

In the early 1950s Harrod was predicting the sort of crisis that befell the BW order some twenty years later. Gold supplies would not keep pace with the growth of world trade. The real value of gold was much lower than it was before 1940. Certainly, therefore, there was no avoiding the fact that money substitutes would have to play an ever greater role in the reserves of monetary authorities so long as the fixed exchange rate architecture remained in place and so long as unacceptable wage and price deflation could be avoided. Harrod (1953a: 138–9) bemoaned

> the present situation [which] is undoubtedly awkward and anomalous. Gold can hardly resume its traditional role as the main medium of reserve and settlement.... There is no doubt that, for its own convenience, the rest of the world [outside the US] would like the value of gold at a higher level so that the value of gold accessions might be raised to a more reasonable relation to the value of increases in world trade against which gold has to be held as a medium of reserve.

Having completed a study for the IMF demonstrating a slow rate of growth in world gold supplies and documenting its causes Harrod (1953b: 17–18) believed a 'radical cure' for the situation would have to be found. He was adamant that the BW order 'must be loosened up' by doubling the price of gold (1953a: 154). Otherwise the development of world trade would be impeded in due course by a shortage of international liquidity. Like Triffin, Harrod foresaw a liquidity crisis. Anxiety among policy-makers about their foreign exchange and gold reserve positions contributes to the maintenance of tighter, deflationary monetary policies, increasing the likelihood that such policies would be transmitted internationally. The United Kingdom in the late 1950s is regarded as a case in point:

> Anxiety about her reserve position has been a contributory cause of her maintenance of a tight monetary policy recently after the need for it, from a purely trade cycle point of view, had passed. Thus her industrial production has been stagnant for three years, during which, but for repressive measures, it would undoubtedly have expanded strongly, thereby entailing the need for higher imports. The failure of British imports to rise at a normal rate has, in its turn, been a contributory cause of the current world recession.
>
> (Harrod 1958b: 122)

Large industrialized countries had an obligation to maintain their growth rates not only for their own benefit; developing countries were also reliant on that growth to raise their populations' relatively low living standards.[9]

Would the sufficiency of world gold supplies be assured by an appropriate increase in its official price? Harrod was satisfied to assert that supplies would respond positively. If so, the world liquidity problem could be set aside. Key currencies, particularly the US dollar, would retain the backing of a gold pillar. Greater, overdue attention could then be accorded to balance of payments adjustment policies and a range of national policies to control inflation, thereby forestalling any need for further gold price changes. Harrod would have agreed with gold standard proponents insofar as economies would have to adapt to the available quantities of gold. A general rise in the rate and variability of inflation which acts as an indirect brake on the supply of gold (by increasing mining and production costs) should not be permitted.[10] In other words, the conditions which created the reason for a gold price increase must in the future be avoided. Indeed, Bordo (1993: 72) claimed that schemes such as Harrod's for boosting liquidity are 'time inconsistent. If the price of gold were doubled once what is to prevent it from being raised again?' Wouldn't speculators be encouraged by such a move?[11] The international financial architecture would certainly be tested by the large gold price increase Harrod suggested.[12] This might lead to the demonetization of gold as it became understood that gold was 'not intrinsically valuable but only a poker chip which can be revalued at will' (Kindleberger 1969: 103). Harrod would have replied to these concerns by pointing out that market participants would only count on future gold price changes if policies in the United States and other key currency countries were inflationary. Only then would they reduce their US dollar holdings in favour of non-interest-bearing gold hoards.

Harrod was not disconcerted by the obvious benefits accruing to certain individuals (gold hoarders), industries and countries (gold producers) when the official gold price was increased. There were also ideological objections relating to excessive windfalls accruing to major gold producers – the USSR and South Africa. Harrod dismissed these objections as petty since the 'free world' is presented with a major economic benefit. The boost to liquidity would facilitate more trade and growth (Harrod 1958b: 127, 1961c, 202). Were the honour and prestige of the United States damaged because the dollar was being 'devalued'? Not at all. As Harrod (1965: 63) explained, the dollar and all currencies linked to it were being reduced in value relative to gold; this should be regarded 'not as shaming, but as sensible'. The 'Americans would be applauded and honoured for being courageous and statesmanlike'. At other times he was more combative, charging that the international economy was being ruled by a 'dictatorship' of a few officials in the United States Treasury who had refused to discuss the eminently rational plan to increase the price of gold. There was also broader political opposition in the United States to Harrod's plan which he did not mention.[13] Yet Harrod urged Americans to remember that the price of gold was not exclusively their business; it was 'world business'. In this view the BW order had been constructed and maintained on a dollar–gold standard; gold was still *the* ultimate international money. It was sheer 'accidents of history' that placed the 'Americans into a strategic position in respect of [large postwar] gold holdings' (Harrod 1961b: 59–60). However, by the late 1960s the United States could not pay its growing debts with US$35 per ounce gold; US debt liquidation required a large gold price rise. Furthermore, to deny the rest of the world a quick means of increasing liquidity on a sufficient scale ran against the BW objective to facilitate the growth of international trade. With persistent liquidity shortages, policymakers were likely to respond by imposing more trade restrictions.

Harrod on IMF renovations: the case of SDRs

Gold, narrowly conceived as the pre-1914 bricks and mortar of the international financial architecture, was repudiated by Harrod and his mentor J.M. Keynes. Harrod was close to Keynes on matters of economic thought and policy. He was Keynes's official biographer. Nonetheless, Harrod (1967: 44) disapproved of Keynes's tendency to 'undermine the regard for gold as an international medium'. He once dramatized this disagreement:

> *Oh Maynard, Maynard, do be careful what you are saying.* You think that, if gold is displaced from its sovereign position, some person like yourself, or perhaps some of your disciples, will have the management of the world's monetary system. What you do not seem to realize is that it will not be those people at all who are in power. It will be the central bankers.
>
> (1967: 44, his emphasis)

Not only was Harrod deeply suspicious of US Treasury officials; he doubted the motives of central bankers and their international counterparts at the IMF not least because the former possessed a 'deflationary inclination' and the latter threatened national policy autonomy given their lack of direct accountability to any elected government (1965: 129).[14] By contrast, retaining gold as an international monetary pillar provided a 'sheet anchor of liberty'; indeed gold was 'a bulwark of human freedom' (Harrod 1965: 80, 172). For this reason also, Harrod opposed Triffin's plan for a world central bank and the eventual complete demonetization of gold. Again, Triffin's plan opened the way for the noxious conservatism of central bankers to rule on matters of economic policy; it would result in benign neglect of deflation and unemployment. Central bank control of fiat money replacements for gold at the national or international level ultimately ran against the broad policy objectives for the international financial order established at BW.

In a similar vein Harrod was unconvinced about IMF solutions to the problem of world liquidity formulated by legions of officials on international committees. In particular, he had much to say on the creation of special drawing rights (SDRs) for IMF member countries. By the mid-1960s all IMF member currencies were freely convertible; par currency values were fixed and adjustable under IMF rules established at BW. Reserve holdings of currency and gold varied in size and composition from country to country. Surplus countries would intervene in currency markets, buying foreign exchange in order to prevent their currencies from appreciating; deficit countries would intervene in currency markets, selling foreign exchange to prevent their currencies from depreciating. In both cases, exchange reserves functioned as exchange rate stabilizers. The IMF could augment members' reserves by activating exchange transactions with members or, in other words, by allowing members to draw their foreign currency requirements from the IMF's reserves (in the deficit case). With the growing US deficit in the 1960s international concern heightened about the accumulation of US dollars in other countries' reserves.[15] If the United States took immediate policy action to reduce its external deficit world foreign exchange reserves (or 'liquidity') might contract. Yet a dynamic, growth-oriented world economy housed in the BW architecture must have more liquidity to finance trade and international investment. In 1958 reserves amounted to 58 per cent of the value of world imports, but by 1967 this figure had fallen to 38 per cent (Gold 1970: 7). We turn next to the IMF solution.

At IMF meetings in 1963 and 1967 it was resolved that the BW order needed to reduce reliance on US deficits (or those of any other key currency), if not make them unnecessary. The growth of world reserves could be ensured by substantially amending original arrangements on IMF member drawing rights. The ultimate aim was to loosen dependence on gold in international reserves, perhaps even demonetize gold altogether (Johnson 1969c). A plan was formulated to create a new type of international credit money or reserve asset as a substitute for key currencies.[16] As discussed in Chapter 2 above, subscribing to 'quota' at the IMF gave members the opportunity to use a certain amount of the IMF's exchange reserves *conditional* on IMF approval of a country's policies. The amount in question was therefore considered conditional IMF liquidity. Raising the quota at the mandatory four yearly IMF reviews increased the amount of conditional liquidity available. However, Harrod (1965: 128–32) argued that these reviews allowed for too little an increase in IMF resources; annual reviews should be instituted, though he had little faith that such reviews would lead to increases sufficient to boost world liquidity.[17] After interminable delays and complex negotiations, the SDR scheme came into being. The SDR took the form of an *un*conditional credit line available through the IMF which would supplement the reserves of monetary authorities without at the same time reducing the reserves of any one authority. No additional quota, that is deposits of gold or currencies, was required beforehand.[18]

The essence of the SDR facility is explained below.[19] The SDR was an international reserve asset rather than money; it was not a transaction currency or vehicle currency for international trade. SDRs would act as a conduit to obtaining either vehicle currencies such as sterling or the dollar or other convertible currencies. SDRs

1 were officially allocated as a percentage of an IMF member's quota;
2 could be used to withdraw from a member's IMF account an equivalent amount of a specified convertible currency at an exchange rate detailed in (7) below, while the currency provider would receive SDRs;
3 could be used directly to settle debts with member countries without needing to meet conditions on national policies imposed by the IMF;
4 could be used for short-term, not persistent, balance of payments problems in the light of a country's reserve position but not simply to change the composition of its reserves;
5 could be used to purchase balances of own-country currency held by foreign monetary authorities;
6 attracted an interest payment (initially 1.5 per cent) on holdings, so that a country holding more SDRs than its original official allocation receives a net payment and those holding less make a net payment; and
7 possess a gold guaranteed obligation such that one SDR is equivalent to 0.888671 grams of gold which then equated to the gold content of one US dollar.

The first allocation of SDRs on 1 January 1970 provided for the creation of US$9.5 billion SDRs over a three-year period with the intention of bringing members' SDR holdings to about 25 per cent of their total gold reserves over that period (Gold 1970: 24–5). In short, the SDR was a credit instrument defined in terms of gold but not readily reimbursable in gold. It was later used exclusively to finance payments deficits in support of a country's fixed exchange rate. Once created, SDRs became an alternative rather than a complement to Harrod's scheme simply to raise the price of gold. For if the price of gold was raised as well at any time from 1970, SDR creditor nations stood to gain at the expense of debtors. Some nations might only use their SDR allocation as an emergency facility while others might ignore the low interest rate inducement to preserve SDRs and dispose of them eagerly – go on a spending binge – to attain real resources in exchange for an interest-bearing, gold-backed obligation (Humphrey 1973: 87; Kindleberger 1975: 73). None of this impressed Harrod. The SDR 'solved' the problem of liquidity by creating a cheap line of credit without applying any sensible discipline to adjust domestic economic policies to external payments imbalances. In fact, SDRs perpetuated external imbalances, contributing to the perception that they were a diversion from the real issue in the BW order, namely prompt exchange rate adjustment to persistent balance of payments disequilibria.

With a country's economic size determining IMF quota, large industrial countries in Europe, Japan and the United States would dominate in the allocation of SDRs. These large countries would therefore be in a position to control international liquidity created along these lines.[20] Harrod (1971: 39) remained sceptical because international supplies of SDRs would be limited relative to what was needed – 'US$40 billion' – hence his remark that the SDR facility in 1970 (US$9.5 billion) was 'very meagre'. Small open economies with deficits faced the same problem as before; they would still bear the burden of adjustment and deflationary policies would not be set aside, only postponed. The 'costive control of central bankers' in the major industrial nations never appealed to Harrod, and the SDR scheme was another example of that control at one remove, through the IMF (Phelps Brown 1980: 31).[21] To any observer, the SDR scheme seemed emasculated by complex rules and fine legal definitions on such things as the rules and practices of allocation, duration, use and liquidation of SDRs. All this gave enormous scope to international monetary officials to tinker with technicalities, revise definitions, and apply explicit or tacit conditions.[22] Credit of any kind did not seem possible without negotiations and conditions which inevitably crimped national policy variations. For Harrod, adequate official foreign exchange and gold reserves would not do this. Such reserves would rely on national policy self-discipline rather than international committees. That SDRs might not supersede the dollar or gold in international reserve holdings would not have surprised Harrod. In an article full of praise for Harrod's attempt to rescue BW arrangements, Humphrey (1973: 88) expressed the matter in Harrodian spirit:

> A reserve money that is entirely dependent on international agreements for its issue and acceptability is a fair-weather system. Since allocations are uncertain and the acceptability of SDRs may be limited in times of serious political conflict, one cannot imagine that a fiduciary asset which is necessarily political would be considered as safe and as dependable as gold.

Like all the great architects of international finance so far considered in this book, Harrod did not lose sight of the fact that the international order required not only imaginative schemes for liquidity management. The BW fixed exchange rate architecture also required supportive domestic policies consistent with the achievement of external balance. The decisive element in all architectural designs was not so much the mechanism proposed for liquidity expansion, but the quality and appropriateness of the other economic policies adopted by BW participants. In addition, raising the gold price was not considered by Harrod as a panacea; rather 'it should be regarded as a helpful first step'. However, 'if it is not done, the changes required to get a smoothly functioning international system will be much greater than they would otherwise need to be' (Harrod 1965: 59). Reforming IMF *conditional* liquidity arrangements also had a minor place on Harrod's agenda, complementing his advocacy of a rise in the gold price.

Harrod's principles for domestic policy in a reformed BW architecture

Harrod's reform plan relied heavily on national economic policy discipline and international harmonization of macroeconomic policies and policy goals. There would be no formal, binding agreement on harmonization, only a contrived consensus in the community of BW member countries founded on the very British notion of 'good neighbourliness' (Harrod 1958b: 122). Ensuring policy coordination and consistency in a world financial order is not dealt with very precisely in Harrod's work. He preferred to outline the broad principles governing domestic economic policy appropriate for a sustainable, fixed exchange rate architecture.[23]

Adjustment to external imbalances on the current account of the balance of payments must be considered ultimately on a case-by-case basis with a 'subtle intermixture' of major policy 'weapons' – monetary policy, fiscal policy, exchange rate policy and incomes policy. In the first place, achieving external balance on its own is not considered desirable or realistic. Internal balance, that is producing a combination of growth, high employment and price stability – ranked by Harrod in that order of importance – was also a crucial policy objective. Indeed, economic growth 'is the grand objective. It is the aim of economic policy as a whole' (Harrod 1965: 77, 164, 170, 1967: 70). Price stability for Harrod was a means of achieving sustainable economic growth rather than an objective in its own right.

Monetary and fiscal policy should be used for controlling and maintaining aggregate demand and for promoting growth in an open economy.[24] Along with most Keynesian economists, Harrod (1971: 37) set aside price level stability and distinguished two 'simple cases' faced by policymakers: (i) significant unemployment combined with an external surplus, when monetary and fiscal policy can be used to 'inflate' the economy and expand aggregate demand; and (ii) excess domestic aggregate demand combined with an external deficit, when monetary and fiscal policy can be used to 'deflate' the economy and reduce demand while not necessarily increasing unemployment. In both 'simple' cases, following these general prescriptions, an economy should approach external and internal balance simultaneously. Usually, however, real cases are more complex. Harrod therefore adds two more realistic 'conflict cases' which are more widely experienced and more problematic: (iii) excess aggregate demand combined with an external surplus; and (iv) high domestic unemployment combined with an external deficit. In both cases (iii) and (iv), possibly more so in the latter, the macroeconomic policy mix suggested in the simple cases might produce more short-term unemployment. Harrod (1971: 37) was implacably opposed to such an outcome:

> I regard the deliberate creation of unemployment as immoral. Unemployment is a very terrible thing. If it is objected that we sometimes have to do terrible things to achieve greater good, the answer is that in this case there are other ways of getting that greater good.

When considering monetary policy, Harrod did not want completely to divert that weapon from its role in keeping down interest rates, thereby maintaining investment and maximizing economic growth. Yet at the same time he wanted to use monetary policy primarily to look after foreign exchange reserves in order to protect the fixed exchange rate. It is therefore understandable why he viewed the immediate provision of sufficient international liquidity for all BW member countries as a means of averting an international crisis and as a support for domestic monetary policy. The latter functioned as a counterpart to an international response, protecting reserves and the exchange rate and maintaining national solvency. The primary task of monetary policy was to secure 'a continuing rise of each country in accordance with its maximum growth potential' (Harrod 1965: 60). Fiscal policy rested on an accommodative monetary policy. The full monetization of fiscal deficits was not problematic in case (i) above. Otherwise, methods of budget financing must carefully be crafted so as not to raise the rate and variability of domestic inflation. Nevertheless, policymakers should err on the side of allowing strong domestic demand rather than 'underfull demand' so that over a reasonable period of time demand did not lag behind an economy's growth potential (Harrod 1967: 53).

In the long run while exchange rate changes are desirable to correct a persistent, fundamental external disequilibrium, they would generally 'be an evil, but a lesser evil than deflation' (Harrod 1967: 39).[25] Exchange rate policy should be made in tandem with monetary policy with the immediate objective of exchange rate stability rather than changeability. There should be no such thing as a flexible exchange rate policy though regular, moderate variations may be permissible. However, the reserve requirements for a more flexible (not freely floating) exchange rate regime than originally intended at BW were not necessarily lower than under a fixed exchange rate regime. Foreign exchange market participants in a flexible exchange rate world would be less willing to take substantial positions in foreign currency because fluctuating rates would raise the perceived level of risk.[26] Continuing, successful foreign exchange market intervention may be a demanding task, all the more so for smaller open economies with a comparatively small stock of external reserves. Speculative activity would pose a greater threat to stability, given the heightened danger of capital movements as a precaution against the belief that a currency's value may be adjusted continuously over a short time period. Exchange controls might then have to be introduced as an ad hoc measure and Harrod always regarded these controls as an admission of exchange rate policy failure. It was not clear what Harrod would do about destabilizing capital movements.[27] Altogether, more flexible exchange rates along the lines of an 'adjustable peg' system were not a solution to inadequate world reserves (Harrod 1966: 142).

Free operation of the market price mechanism in the international realm could not be entertained. Contrary to Graham, Friedman and other free market-oriented economists, Harrod viewed currency exchange rates as fundamentally different from other prices. Other, day-to-day market prices did not always have long time horizons; they did not embody long-term growth potentialities, especially at the macroeconomic level. The disastrous experiment with flexible exchange rates in the 1930s and related competitive currency devaluations were only one reason for Harrod's support of the BW exchange rate rule. Since growth enjoyed priority over other policy objectives, in 'dynamic' economic conditions the long-term productive potential of an economy is not usually reflected in regular variations of a nation's currency exchange rate. This is the essence of Harrod's support for the fixed exchange rate architecture.[28]

The introduction of incomes policy into Harrod's armoury of 'policy weapons' differentiates his approach to reforming the BW architecture from that of most other great architects of international finance considered in this book. Wage, price and profit guideposts making up a complete incomes policy should be set to regulate average wages, specific prices and profits if a divergence is observed between the rate of growth of wages at the macrolevel and labour productivity, and the rate of growth of profits and productivity. Centralized, government-regulated wage setting, price controls and profit surtaxes should be used to control movements in the national wage and profit share in the interests of containing inflation and correcting a deficit on the current account of the balance of international payments. Harrod (1967: 54) went so far as to propose that 'incomes policy should be at the very centre of the picture in regard to policy making'. In a case where excess aggregate demand is exhibited in conjunction with a surplus on the current account, incomes policy could damp demand; if the surplus persisted for an extended period, then an exchange rate revaluation was recommended. In a case where high unemployment is observed in conjunction with a deficit on the current account, Harrod supposed that the unemployment could have two main causes: insufficient aggregate demand and endemic cost push inflation which rendered export industries less competitive, reduced employment and worsened the external deficit. Here, deflationary monetary and fiscal policies would be ineffective, as the inflation was caused mainly by supply-side forces rather than excess demand. Incomes policy, while slow to work relative to an immediate monetary, fiscal or exchange rate policy response, was more likely to protect employment and sustain growth; it would be far less likely by comparison with a currency devaluation to exacerbate inflation and create unemployment in some industries. Moreover, there is no certainty that an exchange rate change would render the right external balance outcome, at least immediately, because the short-term responsiveness ('elasticity') of import demand and export demand to an exchange rate change may not be very strong (Harrod 1966: 140).

Incomes policy and exchange rate changes are in Harrod's doctrine clear *alternatives* in the pursuit of long-term external balance.[29] Incomes policy is the preferred option in the menu of core policy weapons in Harrod's reformed BW order. When a fundamental disequilibrium is observed in the balance of external payments an incomes policy response dominates an exchange rate response:

> an incomes policy . . . is much to be preferred to exchange rate flexibility. In practice there is naturally a tendency to be favourably inclined to the latter on the grounds that it is simple to execute . . . while an incomes policy requires a most complicated plan . . . and a deep understanding of economies and social problems.
>
> (Harrod 1965: 40–1)

Harrod did not think policymakers and economists should shirk responsibility for unemployment and related social ills just because an incomes policy was difficult to plan and implement. That there may be trial, error and frustration in the process did not faze Harrod. Exchange rate changes on the other hand had unintended negative effects on employment and inflation. At this point he granted a supporting role for an active trade policy: import controls and export incentive schemes. When an external deficit was of sufficient magnitude and the unemployment rate historically high, an incomes policy on its own may be too slow in working. Selective import controls, saving foreign exchange, could then be instituted and guided by the rule that only certain categories of imports were required to achieve optimum domestic growth. Further, import controls should not be used to the detriment of poor trading partners in the less developed world. Overall, in the circumstances described above, import controls 'rightly condemned as unneighbourly, are far less unneighbourly than deflation'. In addition, carefully targeted export incentive schemes could be designed to assist the long-term objective of earning more foreign exchange and reducing the external deficit (Harrod 1967: 57, 67).

In specific conjunctures of macroeconomic conditions incomes policy gave more time to adjust the external balance – two or three years – without excessive reliance on immediate deflation, pressure on a nation's foreign reserves, exchange rate changes or extensive import and exchange controls. In Harrod's mind, under the BW fixed exchange rate rule it was not the absence of an adjustment mechanism as such which presented a problem; there was no tolerable method of *immediate* adjustment. External reserves offered some time for international adjustment, and incomes policy provided even more time while stabilizing prices and employment. In advocating incomes policy, Harrod ignored the negative influence of wage, price and profit regulation on the efficient allocation of resources in an economy. What long-term impact would the resulting inefficiencies have in retarding growth potential? Would not the price mechanism set in motion by an exchange rate adjustment engender various structural changes in an economy conducive to higher growth? For Harrod these questions were misleading and short-sighted; they were informed by the '"conventional wisdom" taught in most universities' to young economists and they emphasized market-driven, one-off resource allocative changes and efficiencies as preconditions for achieving an economy's full growth potential (Harrod 1972: 15). Harrod did not much care that his views might be deemed unfashionable or unwise by conventional standards.

Robert Mundell on the failing BW order, *circa* 1965–71

Robert Mundell, 1999 Nobel laureate in economic science, did not make his most influential contributions to the debate on international financial reform until the 1960s. A Canadian by birth, he completed his doctoral dissertation at the Massachusetts Institute of Technology (with supervisory input from James Meade at the London School of Economics in 1955–6) on the subject of international capital movements. From the late 1950s on, Mundell made some of the most original and innovative contributions to the study of international finance.[30] Among other positions, he served as a post-doctoral fellow in Political Economy at the University of Chicago (1956–7), worked in the Research Department at the IMF (1961–3), viewed the collapse of the BW architecture as a professor at the University of Chicago and spent a long period of his professional academic life at Columbia University in New York.[31]

Robert Mundell was concerned to salvage key pillars of the BW architecture, championing fixed exchange rates though for somewhat different reasons from those of Harrod. Unlike Harrod, he saw no central place for the deliberate, activist promotion of economic growth through *international* economic policy; gave no role to incomes policy; saw a one-off increase in the price of gold as a temporary expedient to relieve a liquidity problem but not a solution to the intimately related confidence problem; and he integrated capital movements into the policy framework supporting a redesigned BW-type architecture.

Mundell's historical overview of the BW architecture

As for the evolution of the BW financial order in the period from the 1940s to the late 1960s, we shall see that Mundell came to the same conclusions as

Harrod: BW was in a precarious state by the end of the 1960s. Following the First World War, sterling lost its dominant place in international finance. The problem of gold scarcity in the 1920s led to the gold exchange standard in which nations economized on gold, progressively substituting foreign currency for gold in their foreign reserves. Nations cooperated loosely, avoiding a return to 'a deflationary gold standard' and accepting the gold exchange approach 'because politics had made internal stability important'. Neither the classical, 'automatic' gold standard pre-1914 nor the gold exchange standard was established by full-scale, formal international agreement. In Mundell's estimation, the gold standard was well and truly buried by events in the 1920s – there was no prospect of restoring gold to its old role in the second half of the twentieth century.[32] And the gold exchange standard in the interwar years evolved haphazardly in a manner Mundell found unacceptable. Mundell favoured BW-type arrangements, that is legal blueprints. BW was unique in that it created a formal financial *order* around a set of rules.[33] By 1944, a pure national currency, the US dollar, had stepped into the breach left by the financial disorder of the interwar years; it replaced sterling, demoted gold and became *the* international standard at the centre of the BW order. The US dollar's dominance was complete by late 1971, filling the vacuum left by abandoning the gold link.

Mundell's review of the evolution of international financial arrangements in the twentieth century explicitly acknowledged Roy Harrod:

> The three decades 1914–44 represented a transition from a worldwide sterling area to an even more deeply rooted worldwide dollar area. The 'gold exchange standard' of the 1920s and the currency fluctuations of the 1930s were instruments of the transition manifested in political action, but the more enduring grip of the dollar as a rising vehicle currency was sharply limiting the power of any government to alter the outcome. The Bretton Woods system became a legal international system for running or sanctifying the global dollar area. As Sir Roy Harrod has put it, the 'establishment of the IMF is an episode in the history of the dollar'.
>
> (Mundell 1973c: 393)

In Mundell's many retrospectives and asides on the BW era, there is a common theme: the BW Agreement was an 'accommodation' to the economic size and dominance of the United States 'as a supereconomy', replacing the British Empire and its sterling area (Mundell 1977: 238).[34] The BW order evolved initially to harmonize 'the interests and rights of other members of the world community' with those of the United States. As Mundell's story goes, the original BW architects, in wishing to stabilize the world economy, abandoned the nationalistic policies of the interwar period, thereby avoiding a postwar depression. The BW Agreement ushered in a period of unparalleled prosperity though by the early 1970s it became clear that the 'opposite malaise' – high inflation and growing unemployment – had been tolerated, if not nurtured, by BW arrangements (Mundell 1972: 100).

Liquidity and confidence problems

As we observed in the chapter on Alvin Hansen who provided intellectual backing for Keynesian-style policymaking in the United States during the 1940s and 1950s, the US economy was first directed to attaining internal balance. At the same time, the United States became a key currency country in a vast US dollar area. Therefore, what happened in the US economy was vital to prosperity in other BW member countries. International economic interdependencies were brought into sharper focus when the US economy began to inflate more rapidly in the 1960s and early 1970s; an expansionary US monetary policy was transmitting inflation to the rest of the world. A US external deficit also developed, which entailed an excess supply of US dollars in the reserves of foreign monetary authorities. Cynically, it could have been argued that the United States was showering the world with more dollars so as to inflate away foreign external surpluses in the absence of a willingness in those countries to revalue currencies (for example the yen and deutschmark) in accordance with tacit BW protocol (Mundell 1971b: 6–9). A world of competitive inflation under fixed (nominal) exchange rates would, however, carry serious risks of world-wide recession. The stimulation of US export competitiveness by competitive inflation might give rise to more foreign trade restrictions – other countries could use non-monetary responses.

Writing in May 1971, some months before the dollar–gold link was severed, Mundell clearly perceived how the US dollar occupied a special place in the BW architecture, irrespective of its gold convertibility status.[35] First, increasingly through the 1950s and 1960s the United States supplied the rest of the world with financial assets, just as Depres *et al.* (1966) had maintained. In short, the United States supplied liquidity. This function accounted for about 20 per cent of the deposits of foreign banks, much of which took the form of US dollar-denominated bonds held as a store of value. Second, the US dollar was widely demanded to finance world trade; it was a key vehicle currency used for invoicing and settling trading deals across national borders. Market participants chose to use the US dollar extensively because it reduced the currency exchange costs – the transactions costs – of using a wide variety of currencies. Mundell (1972: 102) estimated that US dollar-denominated contracts accounted for over 50 per cent of all international settlements, a figure he thought would rise to 66 per cent within a short time. Third, the BW fixed exchange rate rule, coupled with an inadequate supply of gold to match official liquidity requirements, meant the US dollar was the major currency demanded for intervention purposes to defend exchange rates.

Expansionary monetary policy in the United States tended to increase the supply of world liquidity though it could also fuel inflation. An inflationary spiral promotes an increasing demand for US dollars as well, because foreign monetary authorities desire to 'maintain their customary conventional international-liquidity ratios ... which for most countries implies reserve holdings of about three to four months' imports' (Mundell 1971b: 8). As long as confidence in the US dollar holds – and this was a big proviso in the minds of our European gold standard proponents surveyed in Chapter 8 – the foreign use of US dollars will happily expand. The consequences may seem containable but international jealousies were always going to threaten the viability of this system. European policymakers complained vociferously; their complaints turned mostly on the real benefits accruing to the United States from issuing more dollars – sometimes referred to as seigniorage benefits. These benefits were enjoyed because the United States acquired European and other foreign goods in exchange for cheaply produced, printed, paper dollars. Viewed from another angle, seigniorage grew with ongoing inflation; the rising supply of US dollars was 'analogous to a tax on foreign dollar balances' (Mundell 1971b: 8, 1967: 131).[36] While some inflation was borne by United States' residents, part of the incidence of the inflation (or tax consequent upon an expansion in the supply of US dollars) fell on foreigners and eroded their real standards of living. For Mundell, the seigniorage issue was not crucial enough to justify complete redesign of the BW architecture, for the costs of such a change were incalculably higher.

In view of its supereconomy status, the disruption of the dollar–gold link in 1971 would not matter much for confidence in the US dollar as a vehicle currency or store of value.[37] The conduct of United States' monetary policy mattered most for confidence in Mundell's mind. The principle of dollar–gold convertibility was an indirect means by which foreign monetary authorities in particular had a say in United States' monetary policy since they could alter the composition of their reserves; they could demand gold or other currencies at any time as substitutes for the US dollar whenever they disapproved of the conduct of United States' monetary policy.

The BW architecture accommodated the pre-eminent position of the US dollar which was increasingly used in a wide range of international financial functions. In this process the IMF became a less potent force; it was replaced as a central BW pillar by United States' monetary policy:

> The dollar supplemented gold as a source of liquidity and U.S. monetary policy became a far more important determinant of the liquidity position of non-U.S. countries than any action that could be taken by the IMF.... And so it was that the IMF, created with the trappings of sovereignty, lost its assigned role as the center of the financial system to the United States.
>
> (Mundell 1969d: 482)

In a critical review of the IMF and its functions Mundell reported considerable inertia in its various provisions or rules which did not anticipate or respond to the growing dominance of the United States in the BW architecture. The IMF barely possessed sufficient resources to support the UK pound when it suffered difficulties in the 1960s. All currencies were patently not equal, yet the IMF was established on the basis of eventual currency equality. In fact, by the late 1960s 'a substantial fraction' of IMF reserves were constituted by small-country, inconvertible currencies; these were 'useless as assets upon which other countries can draw' (1969d: 488).

Attempts to reinstate the IMF in a central role by making it the chief administrator of the SDR would not be successful. Mundell agreed in general with Harrod on the SDR: the SDR scheme was 'positively harmful' and overcomplicated. Furthermore, 'it would distract attention from the more fundamental problems facing the world system' in the short term (1969e: 626, 646).[38] SDRs were an ad hoc reaction to a liquidity problem in the 1960s. He found no long-run potential in the SDR scheme for reforming the BW financial order on a fundamental basis. Certainly SDRs made growth in international reserves possible, taking immediate pressure off monetary policy in the United States to support the augmentation of other countries' reserves. Nevertheless, SDRs would not reduce the private demand for US dollars as an international vehicle currency. In general, giving an IMF member country a right to draw on the IMF with the resulting liabilities incurring a gold 'guarantee' did not obviously boost confidence in the international financial order. There was also the unresolved question of SDR adequacy: Mundell (1969c: 331) estimated that the world required US$50–80 billion of new reserves but IMF member countries would not be able to reach agreement on creating 'even half of that amount' through SDRs.

Why then did the BW architecture endure up to 1971? The structure of international liquidity was in tatters. Overall control of the BW order was vested in United States' monetary policymakers in tacit agreement with most other foreign monetary authorities. What seemed vital to Mundell and many other economists supporting the spirit of BW – notwithstanding divergent views on the liquidity problem – was retention of the BW exchange rate rule even though by the early 1970s it appeared unworkable and ineffective.

The BW exchange rate provisions and adjustment issues

The gold standard before 1914 was a fixed exchange rate system. As we saw in Chapter 4, John Williams preferred to describe the classical gold standard era as one based on a single dominant currency, namely sterling. Mundell fully concurred with this perspective. With the benefit of twenty years' experience of the BW order, Mundell went further, describing the 1960s as a period of the US dollar standard. The strong economic position of Great Britain as a centre country in the pre-1914 gold standard era meant that adjustment to external imbalances in that system was divided between surplus and deficit countries in proportion to the size of their economies measured in monetary terms (Mundell 1971a: 140).[39] To over-generalize, therefore, if a large reserve or centre country enjoyed a surplus, most of the adjustment would be borne by smaller economies. Applying this argument to circumstances in the 1960s, the United States as centre country was in a position to force the burden of adjustment on to other countries, given its central function as supplier of world liquidity. What protected the world economy from this stark form of international financial imperialism? For Mundell, flexible exchange rates should only reinforce this problem.[40] An international monetary order based on multi-lateral rules would be needed to 'protect the weak from the strong' just as in matters of international trade in goods and services.[41] The BW Agreement, especially its exchange rate provisions and IMF borrowing rules, was able to lessen the impact of international financial imperialism.

Some features of the IMF Articles of Agreement were nonetheless flawed, at least from the vantage point of the late 1960s. Experience had demonstrated six major defects:

1 Exchange rate adjustment could not be compelled.
2 The IMF had no great power over surplus countries: even though the scarce currency clause could be used as a threat it was never in fact implemented.
3 Short-term exchange rate fixity allowed balance of payments disequilibria to worsen when domestic policies were inappropriate – hot, speculative money would place pressure on the exchange rate once it became clear in which direction it would have to be adjusted.
4 In light of (1), (2) and (3), exchange rates remained far more rigid than originally intended by BW architects.
5 Economically large BW members (e.g. the United States, UK, Germany) were reluctant to alter their exchange rates downwards because of negative repercussions on the capital values of reserves denominated in their currency held in other countries – they did not want to prejudice the key currency status of their currencies.
6 Key currency revaluation or devaluation could instigate exchange rate changes throughout the world, thereby generating uncertainty and instability (Mundell 1969d: 482–4).

Now, simply to accede to the wishes of Milton Friedman and introduce freely flexible exchange rates would especially exacerbate the defect in (6). Flexible exchange rates would lead to an international financial system without any rules and on Mundell's (1969a) terms that would bring about financial crises and disorder. Mundell harboured long-standing objections to exchange rate flexibility advocated along the lines of Friedman and

Johnson. Abandoning the BW exchange rate rule would be costly. First, flexible rates are inflation promoting. Wage workers in particular bargain for real wage conditions, not money wages, and would quickly recognize a real wage cut embodied in an exchange rate devaluation. Workers would not suffer from money illusion for very long, if at all. Regular changes downward in exchange rates would lead to higher wage demands and then greater variability in the rate and level of inflation. Fixed rates on the other hand are a barrier against an inflationary wage–price spiral. Second, by abandoning fixed exchange rates countries would be relinquishing a viable adjustment system reliant on a time-honoured, inherently automatic mechanism.[42] Contrary to critics of the BW architecture, in a paper written while a researcher at the IMF, Mundell (1962) defended the existing system. He maintained that the BW fixed exchange rate rule contained an adjustment process normally at work in an open economy. It is assumed from the outset, quite realistically, that the hypothetical open economy welcomes free capital flows but has a fixed exchange rate. The short-run effects of monetary and fiscal policy are then analysed. Monetary policy in these circumstances is better used for targeting external balance and fiscal policy for targeting internal balance. More specifically, monetary policy should support the fixed exchange rate and fiscal policy should be used to promote investment and employment subject to a price stability rule. Mundell abstracts from the temporary use of central bank foreign reserves to support the exchange rate directly since these can only put off adjustment to an external imbalance. Later he expresses the view that reserves exist primarily to maintain confidence that a central bank could defend a fixed exchange rate; they were 'for display, not use' (Mundell 1973a: 115). Whether or not an economy is experiencing a surplus or a deficit, adjustment will proceed automatically under a fixed exchange rate if surpluses and deficits are allowed to reflect themselves fully in changes in the monetary base. For example, if a government chooses an expansionary monetary policy, using open market financial operations to purchase official securities in return for cash, domestic interest rates will decline, raising aggregate demand and employment. A current account deficit may eventually ensue, generating a loss of foreign exchange reserves. Capital outflows will also ensue in response to lower domestic interest rates. Aggregate domestic demand will then fall back and correct the current account deficit. Over time the price level adjusts and the real economic effects of the original monetary policy expansion will dissipate. In the limiting case monetary policy will have no effect on the quantity of money in the domestic economy or the domestic monetary base and would simply accommodate the fixed exchange rate – paralleling the way monetary policy operated under a pure international gold standard.

How would a Mundell-style fiscal policy be conducted in an open economy, with a fixed exchange rate and permitting free international capital flows? An expansionary tax and expenditure policy would not crowd out an equivalent amount of private expenditure. That is, if a country with an external deficit defending a fixed exchange rate has internal imbalances such as high unemployment, a higher government internal deficit will push up interest rates, thereby attracting capital inflows from abroad. The inflows will tend to offset the rise in interest rates. In such circumstances fiscal policy – lower taxes (or increased government expenditure provided it is not monetized) – will be effective. The speed of the adjustment process and the effectiveness of monetary and fiscal policy under fixed exchange rates depends crucially in this hypothetical case on international capital mobility (Mundell 1960). Given the major responsibility of fiscal policy exclusively to promote internal balance, Mundell insisted that it should not operate along simple Keynesian lines in the expectation that government deficit spending will be effective, come what may. The deficit should not be financed by creating money. In any event, monetary policy could not be conducted to support fiscal policy not only because it had a comparative advantage in being assigned to achieving external balance. Monetary acceleration could not be equated with high employment once '*inflationary expectations have become rooted in the psyche of the community*'. When the 'public anticipates fully the consequences of changes in the money supply', Mundell warned, it will not respond positively by making necessary changes in consumption and investment expenditure to raise output and employment (Mundell 1971b: 13, 26 his emphasis). Therefore, in all Mundell's deliberations over fiscal policy he takes a supply-side line: tax cuts are eminently more suited to an economy experiencing persistently low growth and high unemployment. Monetary policy is then left completely to support the fixed exchange rate, given the state of any external imbalance. Capital flows do the rest; there is no need for a restrictive, inefficiency-prone incomes policy *à la* Harrod.

The currency area option

The BW financial order did not appear to be incompatible with the establishment of what Mundell (1961) originally called 'currency areas' – an idea attracting widespread interest. The idea had important implications for policy formulation on major currency and monetary unions such as planning for a single European currency.[43] Instead of debating the issue of fixed versus flexible exchange rates, Mundell framed a different question: what is an optimum currency area? He defined such an area as a domain within which exchange rates are fixed and within which labour and capital are freely mobile. The area may have a common currency or many currencies tied to one another and freely convertible at fixed rates. All transactions between these currencies would be completely free, whether for goods and services or for capital. The currency area implies an overarching central banking authority responsible for supplying interregional means of payment.[44] Permanently fixed exchange rates are the essence of a currency area, with possibly adjustable exchange rates made in unison by currency area participants against other currency areas or single country currencies. Although there were several important analytical developments building on Mundell's original work, these need not detain our discussion.[45] The more important implications of the currency area literature in the 1960s and 1970s for international financial reform need to be considered here. How will the financial architecture change in a world of currency areas? What would be the advantages and disadvantages? These were issues canvassed by economists following Mundell's classic article.

In choosing exchange rate arrangements, Mundell believed that fixed rates were more likely to produce price stability in a given country and relative price stability between countries. The more integrated an economy or region operating on a common currency, the more likely prices would be stabilized. As well, an 'essential ingredient of a common currency, or a single currency area, is a high degree of factor mobility' (Mundell 1961: 661). Again, the greater the mobility of human, financial and physical capital within a region, the more economic integration is enhanced. Such a region will be suited to both a common, fixed currency among its constituent parts and a more flexible exchange rate between that currency and other regions into which factors of production such as labour and capital are relatively *im*mobile.

Small open economies were likely to benefit both from the fixed exchange rate in the BW order and, by extension, from fixing their currencies in a currency area. Some of the most frequently mentioned benefits enjoyed by currency areas and common currencies include: a chance for smaller economies to gain from lower inflation in the area; greater usefulness of fiat money owing to the simplification of calculation and accounting when markets are integrated by use of a single currency; reduction in costs of currency exchange; elimination of costs associated with issuing national money; and development of a coordinated monetary and fiscal policy in the currency area. Macroeconomic policy coordination, especially over monetary policy, will be easier in the currency area and more beneficial if economic shocks to parts of the area are uniform or symmetric in their impact.[46] Potentially, a large common currency area could develop a genuine *international* key currency to rival other key currencies such as the US dollar, thereby, among other things, earning seigniorage for the area.[47] Overall, the emergence of currency areas in different parts of the world would not be inconsistent with the BW architecture which easily accommodated multipolar arrangements within a fixed exchange rate structure. A multipolar world of currency areas amounted to a restoration rather than a fundamental reconstruction of BW. Unfortunately, many of the arguments for currency areas came too late to save the BW architecture. Nonetheless, they contained a grain of truth – that fixed exchange rates were not discredited or rendered unviable by the arguments of Chicagoans or by the events in 1971 which led to the severing of the dollar–gold link.

Mundell (1977: 13) remarked ruefully that during the BW era fixed exchange rates became 'confused by "pegged rates"'; they had become 'tarred with the same feather as "pegged rates" which usually, if not inevitably, leads to one-way speculation and currency crises'.

From an early date, Mundell (1961: 661) recognized that currency areas which preserved the fixed exchange rate system were viable only if national sovereignties over money were renounced, 'so that actual currency reorganization would be feasible only if it were accompanied by profound political changes'. Currency reorganization proceeds in tandem with political reorganization, perhaps including constitutional change and monetary reconstruction within full monetary unions. In 1973 Mundell was still championing the virtues of the BW-type fixed exchange rate rule. In respect of the ongoing planning for a single European currency he remarked:

> The expectations of exchange rate changes greatly unsettle the money markets, make planning difficult, and, in the long run, weaken the control a government has over economic policy.... Europe could reap appreciable gains from establishing a centralized financial market, not in the sense of a single location, but in the sense of unified rates on assets of different currencies.... The only way to establish a unified money market is to kill the sporadic and unsettling speculation over currency prices that ravaged the European markets between 1967 and 1969.
>
> (Mundell 1973b: 147)

Mundell fulminated against the Chicagoan view that the exchange rate was a price like any other commodity price; it was emphatically unlike 'the price of cabbage', for it 'provides a basis for expectation of future policy', linking the national currency as a unit of account to the world price level. In other words, the exchange rate and its long-term viability indicate the degree of commitment to a particular monetary policy (1973b: 149). From a reading of Mundell's work on a single European currency in the years immediately following the breakdown of BW it becomes clear that he was promoting a doctrine advancing far beyond one which was preoccupied with narrowly technical, architectural matters. Creating a common European currency which promised in due course to become an international currency to rival the US dollar had desirable socio-cultural implications. A common currency would assist in transforming attitudes and break down both competitive national interests and national suspicions in Europe – all of which had for so long contributed to the history of destruction in the region. A new, common money was socially transforming. Moreover, a common currency 'can unlock doors that are currently barriers to the flow of information and finance' between countries. Why cede to other currency areas, of which the United States is an exemplar, all such advantages (1973b: 170, 172)?

Reforming the BW financial architecture?

Roy Harrod definitely favoured reform of the BW financial order, as did Robert Mundell. Increasingly, Mundell's scepticism about international financial arrangements in the 1960s and early 1970s led him to design a new fixed exchange rate order founded on a new set of rules and structures possibly unrecognizable by original BW architects. However, the basic framework including the fixed exchange rate regime, the IMF and gold is retained.

Mundell and Harrod agreed on one core principle: the costs of salvaging and restoring the BW architecture were lower than the costs of completely demolishing and reconstructing it. Mundell added a caveat: we must start by assuming that BW could be restored. First, in anticipating the collapse of BW exchange rate agreements, Mundell (1971b: 11) set out several scenarios: United States' monetary isolationism, severing the gold–dollar link, a new international financial architecture created for many countries operating outside the orbit of the United States including *insular* monetary unions, and currency areas heralding more damaging trade restrictions. In a programmatic paper submitted to Hearings of the Joint Economic Committee of United States Congress (Subcommittee on International Trade and Payments) in 1968, Mundell was more optimistic about prospects for the restoration of the BW order. He set out a challenging reform blueprint to provoke greater debate on the subject before it was too late.[48] The plan was motivated by a desire to reinvigorate the old BW approach, namely multilateral (rather than strong, hegemonic) rule-making in international finance, which Harrod also endorsed. Thus, an

> international monetary system is easier to destroy than to rebuild. It was easy enough for a few amateurs in a few hours to wreck the international monetary system in August 1971. Compare that to the protracted negotiations that went into the Bretton Woods Articles of Agreement. It is not that this agreement created an international monetary system. Rather, it merely devised the set of rules and procedures for making other countries comfortable with the existing system, the anchored dollar standard. The great significance of the agreement lay in its *creation of a multilateral way of managing the international interdependence of exchange rates* in a forum in which the interests of the smaller countries could be taken into account.
>
> (Mundell 1997: 9, emphasis added)

The aim was to build reforms in the spirit and on the foundations of the BW architecture. Mundell had complete faith in the deliberate erection of institutions and rules to effect reform.

In Mundell's blueprint, the IMF gold reserve would be frozen at the point when the plan is implemented. As opposed to Harrod, Mundell asserted that countries would not agree to an increase in the official gold price to improve liquidity unless resulting profits did not arbitrarily accrue to countries fortunate enough to be holding large gold reserves. He saw too much room in Harrod's scheme for international recriminations, thereby reducing willingness to cooperate in the interests of creating lasting financial reforms. All official gold, then, should be vested in the IMF in return for gold certificates; the physical location of official gold holdings would not change. IMF governors would then negotiate annual gold revaluations. If the gold price was revalued upwards, more gold certificates would be issued by the IMF to member countries. In Mundell's plan it is the official valuation of gold, not its quantity, which is important for international liquidity. The resource costs involved in supplying more gold to back world liquidity would therefore be minimized. There is in fact no single, right or optimum price for gold, as implied in the reform proposals of Roy Harrod or Jacques Rueff. To increase the price of gold simply to pay off existing US dollar liabilities in the 1960s begged the question: would the price be increased again some time in the future in response to sterling or franc external liabilities? For Mundell (1973c: 391) gold revaluations must be used for international purposes.

Mundell's plan for IMF-led gold revaluations made gold certificates instruments of international liquidity. The need to rely on the US dollar as a reserve asset would be reduced, denying large seigniorage windfalls accruing to the United States' monetary authority. The US dollar still had a special place in the reform proposal – it would be allowed to operate at the apex of the international financial order – its value being fixed to the value of the gold certificates for a ten-year renewable term. Other countries could choose to fix their currencies to the US dollar or to the gold certificates. In the latter case, the IMF would effectively be an active manager of a currency's value, possibly altering it on an annual basis as gold is revalued. Mundell noted that under IMF Articles of Agreement (IV-4b), countries were in fact entitled to fix their currencies to gold directly. A free private market in gold must be permitted to buoy up the market price of gold, though private demand for gold would have no effect on the world money supply.

Mundell's plan, formulated in the 1960s, aimed to create a fully gold-backed international money with centralized international gold reserves (Mundell 1969c). He agreed with Harrod that gold was undervalued but departed from Harrod in retaining a central role for the IMF in the BW order. The plan not only granted the existing powers and functions of the US dollar in international finance; it aimed fully to internationalize the dollar by transforming it into a new world currency based on what Mundell dubbed the 'intor standard'. The 'intor' was the IMF-issued gold certificate, though a truly international unit in name only (Mundell 1969e: 648).

An alternative transitional arrangement proposed by Mundell involved acceptance of a pure US dollar international exchange standard with the US dollar fixed and all other currencies pegged to the US dollar and adjustable over time as individual country circumstances demanded. Such an arrangement carried inflationary risks because it relied heavily on the behaviour of monetary policymakers in the United States. The pure dollar standard could be workable. A variant of this standard has been successful and durable in the 1990s and early part of the twenty-first century with no obvious international restraints on United States' monetary policy. Indeed, if monetary policy in a key currency country such as the United States is conducted with a view to maintaining world financial stability, price stability and growth, it could recast the way economists think about the kind of formal international architecture required, if any. There is nothing sanguine in Mundell's writings on this score since the history of economic policy developments in the 1960s and 1970s in the United States gave him little confidence. In principle, if the whole world is viewed as a rather loose common currency area with free international capital flows and, historically, freer labour movements, the US dollar could be regarded as *the* common currency. Policymakers in the United States could develop a global conception of monetary management in which the production of dollars is linked to a stability index of world output and prices. If the United States represented, say, 50 per cent of the currency area output, then it would receive the same weighting in decision-making on the production of money or monetary policy. Monetary policy could be conducted by the United States' Federal Reserve in consultation with officials representing the IMF and central banks in other major industrial countries.[49] In practice, it may be more convenient to operate directly on a day-to-day basis with a vehicle currency than on a pure reserve unit or 'intor' standard. If the US dollar was that vehicle – as it in fact became in the last quarter of the twentieth century – it could be used by financial market participants without a need to convert it first.

It would clearly have been dangerous to proceed to a full dollar standard or other fiat money standard which was not founded on trust. Since the tradition and symbolism of gold mattered, especially in Europe and Asia, Mundell believed in a partial international gold-based money. Further, there was no escaping the creation of a world, gold-backed currency by *law*, the value of which was controlled by a special international monetary authority, probably a redesigned IMF. This new IMF would control international reserves and have a strong voice in the production of the world's key vehicle currency – the US dollar (Mundell 1972: 10, 1977: 244).

By contrast with Mundell, Harrod's ideas on international financial reform along with the associated national policy framework did not avidly accept international capital mobility. Mundell, by contrast, offered straightforward policy assignment rules embracing capital mobility. For both writers there was no such thing as a painless international adjustment to external imbalances. And a continuous process of adjustment was a fact of international trade and cross-border interdependence. While fixed exchange rates could be altered in the long term under BW rules, these should be made sparingly. The joint aim of the two great architects of international finance surveyed in this chapter was to find ways for economies to adjust without undue increases in unemployment or falls in the rate of economic growth. Harrod was more moralistic about the evils of unemployment; as shown in Table 9.1, his doctrine advises that countries not prepared to subordinate monetary policy to external balance (*à la* Mundell) need not opt for flexible exchange rates. Incomes policy can come to the policymaker's rescue. Mundell, on the other hand, eschews incomes policy, favouring strict assignment rules – monetary policy and the fixed exchange rate assigned to external balance, and fiscal policy assigned to internal balance in a world with internationally mobile capital. The degrees of freedom available for domestic monetary policy were minimized in Mundell's reform programme. Mundellian fiscal policy should use tax reductions where possible as key supply-side stimulants to sustain investment and therefore employment in the external adjustment process (see Table 9.1). Furthermore, Mundell did not believe international reserves should be relied upon to any significant extent merely to delay domestic economic adjustment to an external imbalance.

If any semblance of the BW architecture was to survive, the need for sufficient international liquidity or reserves to support fixed exchange rates should not be the sole responsibility of a key currency country. Both Harrod and Mundell concurred on this vital point. International financial cooperation on monetary policy in particular was paramount. A one-off increase in the price of gold (Harrod) or annual increases (Mundell) should be agreed upon. There was also complete concurrence between these two great thinkers in the 1960s that key currency countries such as the United States could not indefinitely finance their external deficits with their own currency. For both economists, confidence in fiat currencies is fragile and quickly extinguishable. Gold must be retained as a central pillar of the international financial structure.

In the final analysis, Mundell's proposals were more expansive, original and sophisticated than Harrod's. Mundell offered the currency area option, founded on a sound theoretical framework, as a check on, and eventual competitor for, US dollar hegemony. Greater international currency competitiveness, perhaps initiated by creating a common European currency, was a desirable development; it would potentially divide the international currency reserve function between two major currencies – the US dollar and a common European currency. In this, Mundell was perhaps more active than Harrod in promoting the interests of small open economies. Harrod's concentration on the liquidity issue had broader, more general international implications; his policy framework could be viewed as Anglocentric, and his whole architectural approach exuded a liberal, socialist outlook.

Table 9.1 Restoring BW: Harrod's and Mundell's rules and policy reforms

Policy instrument	*Time horizon*	*Primary assignment*	*Secondary assignment*	*Policy rules and reforms*
Exchange rate				
i) All countries	Short term	External balance	–	• Fixed rate
	Medium–long term	External balance	–	• Fixed, adjustable rate
ii) Currency areas (Mundell)	All	External balance	–	• Perpetually fixed in currency area • Fixed, adjustable against non area currencies
Exchange controls	All	–	–	• Eliminate
Official reserves	All	External balance	–	• Retain gold, raise official price • Use key currencies (Harrod) • Use US dollar as prime reserve currency *OR* • 'Intor' standard: IMF controls gold price and reserve creation (Mundell)
Monetary policy	All	External balance	Internal balance (Harrod)	• Accommodate reserve position • Support exchange rate • Support low interest rates for domestic investment (Harrod)
Fiscal policy	All	Internal balance	–	• Activist management of domestic aggregate demand (Harrod) • Use to manage domestic aggregate supply (Mundell)
Incomes policy (Harrod)	Long term	External balance	Internal balance	• Use as first option to correct external disequilibrium • Promote as domestic price and employment stabilizer
Trade policy	All	–	–	• Liberalize (Mundell)
	Short term	External balance	–	• Activist policy: import controls and export incentive schemes (Harrod)
Investment policy	All	–	–	• Accept capital mobility (Mundell) • Support central role for world development bank (Harrod)

So what did Mundell make of the 1971 breakdown of BW triggered by severing the dollar–gold link? He complained that the dollar–gold link was 'stripped away – too impetuously' in 1971 by a 'few amateurs'. He was unperturbed. The 1971 'crisis' was 'psychological rather than economic' (Mundell 1973c: 393). Nothing had changed inasmuch as the US dollar was still the main world vehicle currency. The 1971 events carried the likelihood that a world of floating exchange rates, obviously in prospect, would only lead to greater use of dominant key currencies in international finance, simply because markets in key currencies such as the US dollar were deep and liquid. Pressure would also build to create currency areas or unions.

As a Nobel prize background essay in honour of Mundell noted, Mundell possessed 'uncommon foresight about the future development of international monetary arrangements' (Persson 2001: xi). While some of the great architects of international finance presented in this book had remarkable prescience, Mundell's understanding of the full evolution of the BW order from its inception in 1944 until 1971 gave him some advantage in the competition to predict future architectural developments. He was right to emphasize the enduring hold of the US dollar in international finance despite the break in the dollar–gold link. Like Harrod, Mundell remained curiously sentimental about gold-linked international money, reflecting joint scepticism about the supposed political independence of central bankers in their control over the production of fiat currencies (though Mundell had more faith in international monetary officials at the IMF). Yet Mundell's BW restoration proposals also relied rather wishfully on successful international negotiations, financial diplomacy and formal legislative arrangements in international finance. For both Harrod and Mundell, the way forward was emphatically not in the direction of allowing market processes free rein to conjure up a desired architecture.

10 The plurality of international financial architectures in the BW era

> It would be unreasonable to expect that anyone could devise an international monetary system serving all purposes optimally. Since people's aims are different, and to some extent incompatible with one another, *no* system can be 'objectively' called the best.
>
> (Machlup 1966b: 1, his emphasis)

Implications arising from the architecture metaphor

The purpose of this book has been to present a procession of 'great architects of international finance'. We have provided a retrospective account of the doctrines of each economist, not a mere description of their schemes. The foregoing chapters have attempted a reconstruction of ideas, consciously applying a metaphor likening economists to architects. What lessons can be drawn from our use of the metaphor of the architect to describe the intellectual efforts of economists endeavouring either to design a completely new international financial order or redesign some part of an existing system? Can the use of the architecture analogy shed light on what it is that makes a 'great' architectural scheme in international finance as opposed to a mediocre one? What gives the various architectures surveyed in this book acknowledged merit or 'greatness'?

Like architects, economists working on international financial arrangements and policy wish to see their schemes realized in the world. At the very least they would want to see elements of their schemes assimilated into the existing financial system. The intellectual reconstructions in this book amount to providing a story about a cascade of different styles, just as a history of architecture might offer a procession of styles promoted for new buildings. In architectural history proper, there is always a link created between 'the tangible and intellectual worlds.... Discussion ... may involve analysis of the physical form of buildings and their construction, or may gravitate toward a discussion of the mental operations' used by architects to deal with their surroundings (Ballantyne 2004: 30). Our task has been to reconstruct the *purely mental operations* of financial architects since, perhaps excepting BW architects, not all were able to produce tangible, archetypal, built forms corresponding closely to their mental operations, at least during the period in which they created their designs. To borrow Keynes's (1933: v) description, such techniques of thinking, as he called them, did not always 'furnish a body of settled conclusions immediately applicable to policy', that is to policy in a real international financial system. The history of architecture can demonstrate how different stylistic traditions evolve, how architects experimented with new possibilities, some of which may have been construed as advances on others that had come before (Ballantyne 2002a: 4). Similarly, our study of international financial architectures in the BW era reveals how several traditions grew out of the experiences of financial orders existing before BW and emerged from the BW order itself. Though not always compatible in overall structure, and usually for completely different reasons, some identifiable traditions emerged. For example, there were approaches which wished to dispense altogether with the gold pillar (Hansen, Williams, Friedman); those which used gold as a subsidiary support (Triffin, Harrod, Mundell); a line of thinking favouring a broader-based commodity reserve pillar (Graham, Kaldor, Tinbergen and even Hayek), and of course those who wished to construct an international financial order exclusively upon a gold base (Mises, Heilperin, Röpke, Rueff).

The architecture metaphor has important implications for the way we appreciate normative aspects in any scheme. Formally, architecture has been defined concisely by Andrew Ballantyne (2004: xiii) as 'the cultural aspect of buildings'. As demonstrated in foregoing chapters, the range of possible ways of conceiving the international financial architecture is quite wide. Indeed, architecture proper 'can range from something very personal and idiosyncratic to something that everyone seems to agree upon' (Ballantyne 2002a: 19). From time to time we have seen this very phenomenon emerge in the way economists have conceived of the international financial architecture. Initially, the BW architecture was held in high esteem by the majority of economists. Architectures held up as significant or worthy of merit are shaped by the culture in which architects participate. During the BW era, the realm of international finance came into contact with economists' mental apparatus and was configured in different ways. The BW architecture was steeped in the Keynesian policy culture rapidly becoming received wisdom in economics during the 1940s and it produced a distinctive architectural style for international financial policy. That style manifested itself very clearly in a cultural framework underscoring the priority which must be given to removing currency disorder, creating exchange rate stability and promoting the full employment and growth objectives in national economic policy. None of these matters could be delegated to free market processes – they had to be managed both internationally through the IMF and World Bank and nationally by government policymakers. Anything that did not make currency stability, full employment and growth central and immediate objectives was ignored by most economists. With a touch of sarcasm, Lionel Robbins (1951: 27) characterized the culture: 'It is in any case somewhat alien to our post-war way of thinking that internal policy should pay heed to the international position – why should the realization of our dreams be broken by outside realities?'

In the light of what we have claimed so far in this chapter, it is scarcely surprising that the schemes proposed by Frank Graham, John Williams and Milton Friedman were set aside by BW adherents as peculiar and idiosyncratic while gold standard schemes were dismissed as downright fanciful. Some concrete implications of these schemes were variously seen as inviting deflation, importing inflation and creating mass unemployment. There were also broader political ramifications embodied in various schemes. For example, Williams's key currency architecture supplied a hegemonic role to the United States and the US dollar (and perhaps later to the United Kingdom and UK pound), and it was styled on a close examination of existing institutions and realities in which the United States possessed economic size advantages and superior financial organization. Williams's architecture offers a clear example of a scheme resisted and shunned because American leadership was equated by many – including some economists, financial experts and diplomats – with financial imperialism.[1]

The BW architecture had monumental presence in world financial affairs by the 1950s. The BW doctrine supporting the architecture developed a greatness or canonical status reinforced by fervent practitioners such as Ragnar Nurkse and Alvin Hansen. Like many of the schemes that were proposed in the 1940s and 1950s, the BW doctrine embodied a particular interpretation of economic experience in the interwar years. Like any great building, BW at some point crossed the threshold and became an imposing entity. To press our architectural metaphor further, if economists were not impressed or moved by the BW architecture then they had better learn to be impressed, just as budding and rival architects would have to learn to respect Egyptian pyramids.[2] Triffin and Harrod were full of admiration for key elements in the BW architecture. Triffin's plan for a credit-creating world bank and Harrod's plan for revaluing gold were ultimately motivated to protect the fixed exchange rate aspect of BW and the national full employment objective. Both Triffin's and Harrod's architecture were configured to fit neatly into the Keynesian policy culture and they became 'great' and widely acknowledged because of their Keynesian doctrinal lineage. Both economists sought to salvage the key pillars of BW while offering renovations to suit a changing international economic environment.

Chicagoans and European gold standard supporters were unimpressed by BW and subsequent renovation proposals. Furthermore, gold standard writers always represented a consistent dissenting view throughout the BW era. They were perhaps not as inventive as other architects, preferring instead to hark back to an earlier era in which all principal economic variables – wages, prices and interest rates – were fully flexible. Gold standard proponents saw gold as an effective, natural deterrent to government-led international financial architectures which inevitably, in their view, portended reckless inflationary expansion of the world money supply. With flexibility in wages and other costs, adjustment to external payments imbalances was regarded as quick and relatively painless under a smoothly operating gold standard, thereby rendering irrelevant fear of deflation and periodic, magnified reductions in output and employment. National economic policy would be subordinated to gold movements consequent upon persistent external imbalances. Monetary policy in particular would be rule based and slavishly accommodative of gold movements. Perceptive gold standard critics – Williams, Triffin and Mundell – took pleasure in showing that gold standard adherents generally ignored the fact that the successful, genuine international gold standard pre-1914 relied on the hegemonic power, even the nationalistic control, of the United Kingdom and its (mostly) well-behaved monetary policymakers.

By contrast with gold standard architects, all other schemes chosen in this book were selected because of their innovativeness and inventiveness. Some proposed to refurbish aspects of the BW architecture (Harrod, Triffin, Mundell), others wished completely to replace BW (Graham, Williams, the Chicagoans). All except Graham's commodity reserve standard accepted that money should be produced independently of the laws of gold or commodity production; they gave central place to human agency – governments and banking institutions – in the production of money. Andrew Ballantyne (2004: 1) reminds us from the perspective of architectural history that certain features of buildings such as special adornments were an integral part of some architectural styles. In fact, he continues, '[e]xtravagance is the piety of architecture, and its defining feature'. What is the purpose of such extravagance? In short, glory, prestige and even fame for the architect. In our sketch of various international financial architectures there are two schemes that are brought to mind in this respect. Triffin's plan for a world central bank seemed overly optimistic and based on some quite dramatic predictions about the fate of the US dollar and a world liquidity crisis which never materialized. Ludwig von Mises proposed an inflexible, automatic gold standard notable for its complete denial of the immediate, essentially utilitarian benefits derived from a BW architecture supported by Keynesian full employment policies widely endorsed by democratically elected governments in the BW era. Likewise, for somewhat different reasons, Charles Rist and Jacques Rueff called for a rehabilitation of a gold standard but they offered an extravagant scheme motivated by France's strong gold reserve position. Rist and Rueff were influenced by a political element which we might characterize as envy of the central international financial position of the US dollar and its promised free gold convertibility. In addition, the special position of the US dollar in the BW era conferred on the United States the special privilege of expanding its dollar liabilities to the rest of the world. Rist and Rueff produced an architecture which sought to negate the power of the US dollar and it brought them much European support and recognition. By comparison, Wilhelm Röpke and Michael Heilperin, while proposing similar gold-based architectures to those of Rist and Rueff, occupied a strong internationalist position in Geneva. Being strongly internationalist and viewing gold as the pillar of economic liberalism in international financial affairs, they could not see beyond the gold standard architecture; it was *the* only viable framework acceptable to decent, civilized participants in a harmonious, well-ordered international economy. Where else could one think like this except in the isolated, cocoon-like intellectual milieu prevailing in Geneva during the BW era?

Principal beliefs embodied in various architectures

The plurality of architectures proposed for international financial arrangements in the BW era should not be a source of incomprehension and the architects should not be thought of as confused. For each tradition of international political economy produced distinctive intellectual constructs with particular implications and recommendations for policy. As we argued in Chapter 1, it is these policy aspects which turn a seemingly scientific proposition on organizing a world financial structure into a unified doctrine. Harry Johnson (1972c: 408) was clearly referring to the difference between purely positive, scientific analysis of a set of propositions about the international financial architecture and a full-blown doctrine when he declared that the 'scientific-theoretical approach to international monetary relations' had become favoured among economists. However, he proceeded to warn us: 'trained economists are usually clever enough at concealing their emotions with the trappings of scientific analysis to pass as dispassionate experts.'

Table 10.1 sets out some of the main beliefs held by various architects of international finance presented in this book. Their principal beliefs had consequences for the way each architecture was framed and projected in the BW era. Some of their beliefs might be tested empirically though not easily proved or disproved once and for all. For example, do world capital markets fail significantly? Are IFIs needed to correct such failures? Both questions may be settled through extensive 'scientific' work, to use Johnson's term. Nonetheless, the performance of IFIs such as the IMF and World Bank is still vigorously disputed although we have long experience, extensive formal empirical research, more rigorous analytical techniques and vastly more data than ever to assess the performance of these institutions (Krueger 1998). Answering questions about the efficiency of world capital markets and the usefulness or otherwise of IFIs is not a one-time event. History can yield evidence for a range of generalizations quite contrary to one another, depending on the time period or country chosen.

Architect(s)	*Are there stabilizing market processes in the international economy?*	*International capital markets**	*Desirable scope of international cooperation*	*Method of international cooperation: preferred basis*	*Are IFIs essential?†*	*Do IFIs fail?‡*
BW	No	Fail significantly	Global	Strong management and policy coordination	Yes	Unrecognized
Hansen	No	Fail significantly	Global	Strong management and policy coordination	Yes	Unrecognized
Williams	Mistrusted	Fail sometimes	Regional: key currency countries	Strong management and policy coordination between key currency countries, ad hoc coordination elsewhere	No	Unrecognized
Graham	Yes	Work tolerably well	Minimal	Automatic self-disciplining system	No	Yes, significantly
Triffin	No	Fail sometimes	Regional, then global	Strong management	Yes	Yes, *in*significantly
Simons, Friedman/ Johnson	Yes	Work well	Minimal	Automatic self-disciplining system	No	Yes, significantly
Mises/Rueff/ Heilperin, Hayek, Röpke	Yes	Work well	Minimal	Automatic self-disciplining system	No	Yes, significantly
Harrod	No	Fail significantly	Global	Limited management; some cross-border policy consultation	No, except for world development bank	Yes, significantly
Mundell	Mistrusted	Fail significantly	Regional (or global)	Strong policy coordination if in currency area (or through IMF leadership, if global)	Yes	Yes, *in*significantly

Notes

* Where 'failure' *requires* policy interventions at the international level: some interventions more significant and long term than others.

† International financial institutions – the IMF and World Bank.

‡ Where 'failure' is believed to be 'significant': the existence of the IMF, for example, is brought into question since the perceived costs of its operation are greater than its perceived benefits.

Certainly there are normative judgements embodied in some architectures surveyed in this book which favour a strong role for IFIs. In particular, several architects saw a prominent role for the IMF, plainly for utilitarian reasons, in easing a country's burden of adjustment to external payments imbalances, thereby reducing the impact on employment and output. Similarly the World Bank is regarded as essential by some architects to provide development capital not otherwise readily available from imperfect, failing private capital markets.

The age-old question concerning the degree of inherent stability in national and world market processes is not answered definitively in the BW era. The bias in our architects' belief systems was clearly against the idea that markets, if left alone, are inherently stable. If stability is broadly understood as a natural equilibrating tendency in financial markets, then the prevailing belief referred to above seems to be founded on long-held beliefs impervious to evidence or not easily corroborated by scientific analysis. Extraordinary events in financial markets during the interwar years may have had a disproportionate effect on beliefs in this connection. Notable here is the contrast between Nurkse, BW architects and Chicagoans over the extent of destabilizing speculation in international financial markets. Modern research is replete with references to international financial 'instability', 'volatility' and 'contagion' and the accompanying discourse usually carries negative connotations (Endres 2000: 955). It is still not clear, however, that flexible exchange rates and free capital movements are violently unstable. Furthermore, in contrast to the beliefs of Nurkse, Hansen, Williams and Triffin, the evolution of the international financial system since the collapse of the BW order has not required strong management and strict international policy coordination; it has not been an anarchic international financial system since 1971 though some may argue that it has been occasionally imperialistic. The search for enduring blueprints and overall international monetary constitutions seems to have been abandoned. Rules or codes for capital allocation and policy surveillance by IFIs have been watered down in an ad hoc manner as events, policies and politics demanded.

The 'strong management' belief also extended to endorsing trade restrictions and controls on capital movements in the cause of maintaining fixed exchange rates. Several financial architects exhibited reluctance to allow regular exchange rate changes, let alone complete flexibility. Incidentally, it was not obvious that the BW Agreement, while favouring central management of international finance through the IMF, associated the fixed, adjustable exchange rate rule with *increasing* restrictions on international trade, payments and capital movements. The original BW archetype was in fact more open-ended and the 'fundamental disequilibrium' idea (as Triffin noticed) had to be understood on a country-specific basis. Frank Graham and the Chicagoans designed alternative architectures in which flexible exchange rates were perceived to be fundamentally stable so long as monetary policy was transparent, rule-based and predictable. In this way, leading industrial nations would set an example; others would follow. There would be no need for an enforceable international blueprint and no special arrangements for less developed countries. In addition, flexible exchange rate proponents believed that flexibility complemented trade liberalization, whereas for them BW fixed rates were only temporarily stable because trade restrictions and capital controls kept them in that state.

Strong macroeconomic management and international policy coordination tended to be favoured by Keynesians or those sympathetic to the Keynesian doctrine that fiscal and monetary policies should be applied in a mutually supportive manner *quickly* to secure full employment and high growth. Nurkse and the BW architects, along with Hansen, Williams, Triffin and Harrod (also Mundell to a lesser extent), took for granted that national economies in the BW order were generally characterized by inflexible wages and prices. As a result, they were sceptical of so-called automatic, market-driven adjustments to external payments imbalances for if they worked at all they would be intolerably slow and therefore costly in terms of lost output and higher unemployment. A foreign reserve fund or 'international liquidity', as it was often called, was therefore a prime policy instrument easing the pace of adjustment under the BW exchange rate rule. IMF finance also supported this instrument, as did capital controls, incomes policies and trade restrictions.

Those favouring an automatic, minimal approach to economic management including Graham, Simons, Friedman, Johnson, Mises, Rueff, Hayek, Heilperin and Röpke saw little need for international financial agreements and IFIs. Gold standard writers minimized international liquidity management problems, attributing them to excessive national money creation while blithely assuming highly flexible wages, prices and interest rates; they also took a leap of faith when asserting that the supply of gold would solve liquidity requirements. Others thought a one-off gold revaluation supported by highly disciplined national monetary policies would suffice (including Harrod, Rueff and Mundell). The flexible exchange rate writers – Graham, Friedman and Johnson – dismissed the international liquidity management issue altogether, relying instead on fully flexible exchange rates which they thought were compatible with capital mobility. In their architectures the allocation of world capital would presumably be based on creditworthiness rather than on the conditions set by IFIs. Flexible exchange rates were considered the best means of protecting low inflation countries against the transmission of inflation across national borders. As well, flexible exchange rate architects were looking ahead to a world economy somewhat like that of the 1990s in which prices, wages and interest rates were significantly more flexible (up and down) than they were in the 1950s and 1960s. It is interesting that most of the great architects surveyed in this book clearly understood that the behaviour of policymakers, especially monetary policymakers in the United States, was crucial to the BW order, and that as long as monetary policy was non-inflationary it would generally have a stabilizing influence on exchange rates and the world economy as a whole – irrespective of the nature of exchange rate regimes.

On occasion we noticed concern to design an international financial architecture, and use IFIs, for the purpose of assisting less developed countries and not simply to manage international liquidity for the purpose of easing adjustment to external imbalances. While Hansen's architecture was founded on American economic leadership, he considered the threat of secular stagnation in developed economies as well as the problem of underdevelopment which would be dealt with by international development banks such as the IBRD in a world capital market that lacked depth and foresight. In Williams's key currency system, less developed countries seem to be treated as an afterthought. Flexible exchange rate writers and gold standard adherents accorded no special place to less developed countries. Triffin came closest to building an inclusive architecture as far as smaller, less developed countries were concerned. His reconstituted IMF – the credit-creating SCB – was structured so as to link reserve creation to development assistance. For Triffin, the problems of international financial reform and the transfer of capital to less developed countries were intimately related.[3] The creation of SDRs did not impress Harrod or Mundell, neither of whom saw lasting benefits in the scheme for less developed countries; they did not link their assessments of SDRs to development aid issues or World Bank capital. As a new international reserve asset, SDRs had to develop credibility, that is central bank preference for holding SDRs reserves over (say) US dollars or, more to the point, World Bank bonds as reserve assets. The latter would have had more direct, beneficial implications for developing countries than SDRs.[4]

A plurality of financial architectures: some lessons from our survey

The selected doctrines surveyed in this book all aimed to achieve an international financial architecture delivering order and stability, without defining these terms very well, if at all. A common aim of all the architectures surveyed was to stabilize the financial interactions and interdependencies between nation-states. In reconstructing the BW architecture in Chapter 2, we translated the desire for 'stabilization' into two closely related policy objectives – internal balance and external balance. These objectives were held in common, at least implicitly, by all our great architects, though of course they offered different schemes for achieving them.

In many cases, the architects surveyed in this book attempted to design schemes inducing national governments to surrender at least some sovereignty over monetary policy to an international institution under a constitution or binding agreement. It was a false hope of some great architects that a genuinely full-fledged international money could be produced by formal blueprints, international law or decrees arising from solemn intergovernmental agreements secured after much international diplomacy. In the aftermath of the collapse of BW, Robert Triffin (1972: 400) pleaded for the restoration of 'a viable international monetary order, fair and acceptable to all'. More recently, Stanley Fischer (1999: F557) exhorted: 'we need a new international financial architecture'.[5] In response to these statements in the light of our survey, we can now say: 'Perhaps so.' Nevertheless, we cannot presume that only one design, one architectural scheme, will fit all regions of the international economy or all countries. Furthermore, we cannot presume that only one architecture is optimal, possible or desirable. There is greater likelihood that economists will not know what architectures will in fact evolve.

The issues which our procession of architectural schemes have raised for the organization of international finance all have real, practical ramifications. They also alert us to quite different ways in which perceived financial problems in the international economy might be resolved. But we should hesitate before leaping into believing that any plan, any one mental construct, could prevail in practice. Many of the schemes surveyed in this book have never been implemented. Some looked too good, too neatly coherent, to be feasible or applicable. The BW order reinforced by Hansen's Keynesian interpretation and bolstered to some extent by Triffin's plan, elements of Mundell's schemes, and gold revaluation proposals were all ultimately command and control based. There was also a sense in which some of the gold standard writers, especially Rueff and Heilperin, inadvertently espoused a command and control doctrine. They were all tainted with the idea that governments, not markets, determine what constitutes international money. As Kindleberger (1967: 10) put it, many doctrines on international financial organization wish to bring into being 'a synthetic, deliberately created international medium of exchange'. He concluded with a farsighted observation that too many economists have designed futile schemes for international money which 'share a basic weakness that they do not grow out of the day-to-day life of markets, as the dollar standard based on New York has done'.[6] Precisely. Kindleberger's argument lives on, for it could still be made in cautionary response to Stanley Fischer's call for a new international financial architecture at the end of the twentieth century.

All too often in the BW era, the great architects of international finance sought to distil a single, optimal design for international money. There were a few exceptions. Williams rejected formal plans on practical grounds, preferring to accept existing key currency hegemony. Graham offered a commodity reserve standard as an alternative to fully flexible exchange rates and Mundell wanted, on the one hand, to reinstate gold while seeing the rationale for currency areas on the other. Most other schemes aimed to balance a group of sometimes conflicting national and international objectives – growth of national income and employment, efficient international resource allocation, stable prices, stable and convertible currencies, sufficient international finance to support freer world trade and, in a few instances, improved distribution of world income. BW architects offered an exchange rate rule and broad policy guidelines for national economic policy. Other great architects who followed saw the need for national economic policy frameworks complementing the recommended international architecture. Each architect assigned various policy instruments to a range of objectives consistent with international financial commitments and agreements with other countries.

The architects who condoned or advocated free market processes as a way of delivering an appropriate outcome in international finance included Frank Graham, the Chicagoans, the Austrians – Mises and Hayek – and the Geneva-based economists Röpke and Heilperin. Their commonly held view was that individual countries must find their own way first: they must adopt monetary, fiscal and trade policies that stabilize their economies, *before* entering into any major agreements on policy coordination with other countries, if needed to engineer international stability. Some schemes required persistent implementation of a rule-based national policy framework to contain financial uncertainty and provide policy predictability and credibility (Simons and Friedman come to mind here). Gold standard rules established fixed parities of national currencies in terms of gold; they required monetary authorities to conduct monetary policy in a manner that did not neutralize or counterbalance gold movements. Mundell also designed a rule-based national macroeconomic policy framework for currency areas in a world with capital mobility.

That the real international financial system has evolved organically since the collapse of BW did not usher in a form of global financial anarchy. The present system combines elements of the different architectures proposed in this book. Different architectures can coexist in a multipolar system, for example managed exchange rates, floating exchange rates and fixed rates can be widely observed in conjunction with a *de facto* US dollar standard and a European currency union.[7] International financial arrangements are freer now than they were in 1944 or 1971. International capital markets have extended their reach; the stock of mobile capital has grown vastly since the 1940s. Not one of our great architects fully predicted or designed the existing system. There is an overarching international *order* though it is one which has issued largely from the interaction of a whole host of financial market participants, including bankers, governments, financial managers and so-called financial gurus, most of whom are not well trained in the discipline of economics and not apt to take a position on the desirable financial architecture for the world as a whole.

As mentioned in Chapter 8, gold standard architects wanted to protect money, including international money, from day-to-day politics. However imperfectly, modern international currency competition between various key vehicle currencies seems to be achieving that task without one government or economist planning for it. We might therefore be driven to the conclusion that international money should be protected from certain overzealous economists with grand schemes for the international architecture. To be sure, elements in Williams's, Graham's, Friedman's and Mundell's financial architectures are evident in the existing system. Nonetheless, too few of the great architects whose work has been discussed in this book allowed for the spontaneous, organic development of the international financial order perhaps because they could not accept the idea that markets operating across national borders create what Hayek called a 'spontaneous order'. In the 'Theory of complex phenomena', Hayek (1967) described the very type of problem faced by our great architects. Real international financial markets are changing and changeable by individual decisions, events and government policies; they are an example of Hayekian 'organized complexity' and are not controllable by one great designer. From this perspective, the international financial order cannot be built according to the dictates of one mind for it is not possible to capture events, individual decisions in financial markets and changeable policies in a single architecture. To know what is *possible* in the realm of international financial organization is a significant intellectual challenge in its own right; believing that the whole organizational order could be amenable to deliberate design in practice is to neglect what Kindleberger called the 'day-to-day life of markets'.

International financial architects would do well to take heed of the central message contained in Friedrich Hayek's Nobel Memorial Lecture:

> If man is not to do more harm than good in his efforts to improve the social order, he will have to learn that in this, as in all other fields where essential complexity of an organized kind prevails, he cannot acquire the full knowledge which would make mastery of the events possible. He will therefore have to use what knowledge he can achieve, not to shape the results as the craftsman shapes his handiwork, but rather to cultivate a growth by providing the appropriate environment, in the manner in which the gardener does this for his plants.
>
> (Hayek 1974: 7)

There is indeed a parallel danger inherent in many of the great doctrines on international finance in the foregoing chapters. For there is an impression given by these doctrines that economists knew what architectures were optimal and they proceeded to provide much more than 'the appropriate environment' for organic development in the international order; they also promoted policies to control and 'stabilize' international financial relations. To a large extent, since the collapse of the BW order the international financial system has been a Hayekian, self-organizing complex structure in which market processes and individual market participants have been pre-eminent. Most of our great architects recognized the pre-1914 international gold standard as a splendid example of an essentially complex, ordered financial arrangement which evolved spontaneously. Only a small minority, however, accepted the possibility that BW would break down completely, and be followed by a new order in which government direction was comparatively minimal. The desire to bolster, restore and renovate the BW order was motivated by doctrinal beliefs. While a spontaneously generated market order might have been possible, it was considered inferior to a 'scientifically' designed order which would replace the putative instability of market processes. Would the reactions and proposed architectures have been different if the writers surveyed in this book had been given the opportunity to observe the international economic events unfolding in the 1980s and 1990s? Undoubtedly they would have altered their designs in detail, not necessarily in substance. Doctrinal roots run deep.

In a subsequent volume we shall review the ideas and policies of a new generation of international financial architects. Quite new approaches and designs became evident in the last quarter of the twentieth century in an era of rapidly globalizing resource allocation and increasing international economic integration.

Notes

1 Essential elements of a doctrinal approach

1 Nurkse (1944) represents the best example of a thorough historical study of the international financial system in the interwar years. Nurkse brought to the fore the benefits of studying international financial 'experience' as opposed to idealistic plans for reforming international financial arrangements. He damned the latter with faint praise, noting that they 'may have certain attractions in theory' (1944: 20). For a modern counterpart of Nurkse with the necessary changes for late twentieth century-experience see Obstfeld (1995).

2 In a parallel field Richard Irwin (1996) contributed a widely applauded doctrinal study of international trade doctrine.

3 For a stinging rebuke of economists and a compelling case for rehabilitating the history of economic ideas in the education of economists see Mark Blaug (2001).

4 By contrast Solomon (1977: 5) conflates 'system' and 'order' in his definition of the international monetary system. 'We may', he writes, 'define the international monetary system as the set of arrangements, rules, practices and institutions under which payments are made and received for transactions carried across national boundaries.'

5 Scammell (1975: 17) therefore considers the notion of an international monetary *order* unhelpful since it 'implies a mechanism of interrelated parts functioning for some clearly defined end, according to known laws. It implies knowledge, certainty and predictability.' To be sure, the ideal order will never be found in reality, though the general constructs of the architects will identify functions, arrangements and practices common to many factual states of affairs.

6 We will, however, make reference to Meade's work at various points in the following chapters. The same comment applies to pioneering work at the IMF on balance of payments difficulties and adjustment problems in the 1950s and 1960s by Jacques Polak, Sidney Alexander and J. Marcus Fleming. On these achievements see Endres and Fleming (2002b).

7 By 'coordination' we mean the management and occasionally significant modification of national policies in recognition of economic interdependencies among nations. See Frenkel *et al.* (1994).

8 Bryant (1995: 13–14) offers a useful taxonomy which describes a range of economic interactions among nations along a continuum from mutual recognition to weak cooperation to strong coordination in the context of an international financial order embodying shared principles, rules and codes of conduct.

9 Fritz Machlup (1963) attempted with some success to reduce the confusion among economists about key financial terms.

10 Companion trade doctrines will not feature in this book. Readers will find sections of Irwin (1996: 180–206) useful in this connection.
11 On these principles as employed in late twentieth-century research on international financial reform, see Frenkel *et al.* (1994).
12 A quick perusal of the most popular journal in the field, the *Journal of International Money and Finance*, published by Butterworths, will confirm this impression.
13 See also Paul De Grauwe (1989: 14) who viewed the BW system as 'probably the most ambitious international monetary agreement between sovereign states in history'.

2 The Bretton Woods financial order – a distinctive economic doctrine

1 The following account of the principal conclusions in Nurkse (1944) draws heavily on his final chapter (pp. 210–32). For a modern assessment of Nurkse's contribution to international monetary economics and policy, see Endres and Fleming (2002a: 167–96).
2 Later in the twentieth century in the context of more developed, sophisticated foreign currency markets, economists could still observe warily how 'some participants in the exchange market rely on a "follow-the-leader" approach; changes in the exchange rate thus reflect a bandwagon effect. Hence there may be "speculative bubbles" in the exchange rate' (Aliber 1987: 212).
3 Without entering into the technicalities, a single nominal exchange rate is the nominal price of two national moneys; this rate (or price) ought perfectly to parallel, over a *long period* of time, the real purchasing power over goods and services of those moneys in each of the national economies (i.e. the nominal and real exchange rates should coincide over the long run).
4 Formally, in a fixed exchange rate environment, sterilization amounted to using monetary authorities such as a domestic central bank; authorities would intervene by purchasing or selling 'foreign-currency bonds that are matched by equivalent sales or purchases of domestic currency bonds, leaving the monetary base unchanged' (Obstfeld 1995: 176). That is, a change in the central bank's net foreign currency reserves is offset by a corresponding change in its net domestic assets so that monetary liabilities (the monetary base) remains unchanged.
5 The quoted material in the foregoing two paragraphs is drawn from Nurkse (1944: 220–1, 223, 224).
6 There was a consensus among economists in 1944, especially on the eastern side of the Atlantic and in Australia, that 'a serious depression' was likely when the war ended (Cooper 1993: 105).
7 Some of the best commentaries are Gardner (1969), Horsefield (1969a, 1969b, 1969c), De Grauwe (1989), Bordo and Eichengreen (1993) and James (1996). Kahn (1976) has shed light on its historical origins.
8 After 1945, as Harold James (1996: 30) so lucidly demonstrated in his Chapters 3 and 4, BW was 'a very different sort of system to that which did in fact emerge.... For a long time it might well have appeared that Bretton Woods was more of an unrealized idea.' And Michael Bordo (1993: 73) similarly finds that by '1968, the international monetary system had evolved very far indeed from the model of the architects of the Articles of Agreement'.
9 This reconstruction is assisted by original documents contained in Horsefield (1969c), as well as the United States Department of State *Proceedings and Documents of the United Nations Monetary and Financial Conference* (1948). Secondary contemporary readings on the BW Agreement were also helpful: Crowther (1948: 325–35); Goldenweiser and Bourneuf (1944); Haberler (1944);

Halm (1944, 1945); Harris (1944); Lachmann (1944); Lutz (1943); and Mikesell (1947, 1949).

10 Convertibility meant the ability for individuals (and governments) to complete current account transactions – paying or receiving amounts for trade in goods and services and also for foreign investments (and receipts or spending by governments from (or in) foreign jurisdictions). The ability to effect such transactions must not be subject to exchange controls, otherwise convertibility is compromised.

11 As it happened, from 1945 (and certainly the process was completed by 1950), the United States was the only country with a direct gold peg, valued at US$35 per ounce. The United States held about 70 per cent of the gold possessed by world monetary authorities at this time (De Grauwe 1989: 15). McKinnon (1996: 44–9) later dubbed the actual system which formed around the BW order 'the fixed-rate dollar standard' because other currencies were fixed against the US$ which was in turn pegged to gold at a fixed rate. The US$ was not mentioned in the Articles of the Agreement even though it became a key currency.

12 See Bernstein (1945) for a careful dissection of the BW Articles of Agreement on the scarce currency question.

13 The IBRD subsequently became part of the World Bank group. For a concise history see Krueger (1998).

14 What is one to make, therefore, of the following contemporary remark? 'The concept of international equilibrium as the product of freely competitive forces operating in world markets for commodities and services is basic to the policies and operations of the Monetary Fund *as it was conceived by its authors*' (Mikesell 1947: 501, emphasis added). This is a highly idiosyncratic interpretation and certainly not consistent with the manner in which the BW order evolved.

15 See De Vries (1969: 19–21).

16 Gottfried Haberler (1944) complained, quite correctly from an academic point of view, that the term 'fundamental disequilibrium' was opaque and ambiguous. Perhaps so, but the BW Agreement was not designed for purists.

17 Nurkse distinguished in principle between equilibrating and disequilibrating capital movements; he provides examples of the meaning of 'hot' money (disequilibrating movements) and its treatment by policymakers during the interwar period (Nurkse 1944: 16, 72 notes 1 and 102).

18 On this issue see especially Gardner (1969, 1971: 27).

19 Cf. Halm (1944: 174) in whose view the architects 'who drafted the Agreement know that they cannot hope to integrate policies of the members to the degree required for perfect exchange stability'.

20 See Scammell (1975: 110).

21 As already discussed, this belief was also forged on the minds of League of Nations' economists, represented by Nurkse (1944). Barry Eichengreen (1996: 52) demonstrated that Nurkse's critics (and by extension BW critics) 'contended that policy instability was a given and exchange rate instability its consequence. In their view the exchange rate responded to policy whereas Nurkse saw causality running also in the other direction.'

22 This reconstruction is assisted by John Williamson's prolific work on the BW system which he believes embodied a series of assignment rules for various macropolicy instruments. See Williamson (1977, 1985). Giovannini (1993) is also helpful.

23 McKinnon (1996: 41) includes in his 'spirit' of the BW architecture 'rules' whereby member countries must 'sterilize' the domestic monetary impact of exchange market interventions. See also De Grauwe (1989: 17–18), which

includes in the BW 'rules of the game' an imperative that, in the case of excess demand for foreign exchange, domestic central banks must automatically conduct restrictive monetary and fiscal policy. We concur with both reconstructions though nowhere in the BW Agreement are these sterilizing procedures expressly mentioned.

24 Many specialists on international financial problems and monetary history since BW have used the terms 'rules', 'rule-based' and 'rule-bound' to describe the BW system. See, for example, Solomon (1977: 13); Bordo and Eichengreen (1993: 84, 107, 117–20; 152–3) and McKinnon (1996: 40).

25 No plans or blueprints were required in the latter case, just as in the years when the international gold standard was in operation.

26 Contemporary British economists were in the vanguard of this intellectual movement, underscoring the need to frame a grand 'plan for the monetary governance of the world' (Robertson 1943: 357). See also Joan Robinson (1943).

27 See for example Moggridge (1986) and Meltzer (1989). David Vines (2003) offers a more sobering view of Keynes's intentions in this regard. In Vines's estimation, Keynes did not seek to design a rigidly coherent, optimal financial order which would create the greatest good of the greatest number of countries.

28 This chapter has therefore reinforced the main finding in Cohen (1982: 35): 'Implicit in the original charter of the IMF was a remarkable optimism regarding prospects for monetary stability in the post-war era.'

3 Alvin Hansen's Keynesian interpretation of Bretton Woods

1 See Williams (1976), Haberler (1976: 11) and Tobin (1976: 32).

2 For Hansen's version of Keynes's economics and its application to the United States see Hansen (1947, 1949, 1953).

3 See Hansen (1944a).

4 By price elasticity of demand we mean the degree of responsiveness of demand to price changes. Foreign demand for exports may not be very favourable (responsive) to falling prices (denominated in the exporter's currency) when the currency is devalued; domestic demand for imports may not be very unfavourable (responsive) to rising import prices (denominated in local currency) as the currency is devalued. Both factors would militate against balance of payments adjustments to a current account deficit.

5 See Hansen (1965: 172–3) for elaboration. For example: 'Imagine our meeting the competition of the Volkswagen by bolstering our automobile industry with a devalued dollar' (p. 173).

6 Kenyan Poole (1947: 374 note 5) referred to the 'important school of thought in the United States [which] emphasizes the role that must be played by high levels of employment in bringing about exchange stability'. Poole identifies Hansen as the propagator of this school of thought, though he disagrees with its key proposition: 'It should be noted that with full employment there is no reason to believe that stable exchanges *must* result from full employment' (his emphasis). Hansen did not, in fact, make this strong claim.

7 In his immediate postwar treatment of exchange rate policy, Hansen (1945b: 261) ruled out frequent revisions of exchange rates from par values established by the BW Agreement.

8 See Fellner (1966: 111).

9 The original BW rule specified up to 10 per cent variation against the originally announced par values in 1945–6, a reference point that had become 'hopelessly

out-of-date': Joint Statement of Twenty Seven Economists reprinted in Fellner (1966: 113).

10 At the time, two-thirds of world foreign exchange reserves were held in the form of gold (Hansen 1965: 60).

11 That is, Hansen's 'International Reserve System' would not be free to engage in open market purchases and sales of government securities in Group of Ten countries and would not be permitted to use the issue of international units or dollars as a monetary base to make loans to member countries (Hansen 1965: 114–15).

12 See IMF Articles VI Section 3, VII and XIV Section 2; also in Horsefield (1969c: 195).

13 For example, Hansen (1944b: 248): 'High levels of employment and a high degree of economic stability are basic for the success of all other programs of international relations.'

14 Full employment is defined in Hansen (1945d: 408, 1945e: 102) as a condition in which a 4–5 per cent unemployment rate was tolerable; such unemployment was seen to be the result of 'transitional' and frictional factors.

15 The following four paragraphs draw heavily on Hansen (1949: 173–5). By 'liquidity preference' Hansen (1953: 126, 134) meant the public's desire to hold money as inactive balances or 'the propensity to hoard'. This is identical with Keynes's (1936: 168, 205) original idea.

16 In response to scepticism emanating from University of Chicago economists – Simons and Mints – Hansen (1946: 69) argued forcefully: 'I should want to vary public outlays contracyclically and also to vary taxes with the cycle. I would use both expenditures and taxes in a stabilization program.' But as one commentator in the subsequent Hansen–Mints debate perceived, the real issue for Chicagoans as against Hansen was that fiscal activism can be destabilizing to national income and employment because it raised questions concerning the consistency of government expenditures. Private market participants could not therefore always form 'seasoned judgements' on the precise role of government in the macro-economy. At the very least Chicagoans wanted monetary and fiscal policy to 'settle down [on] a coherent and stable basis' (Ellis 1946: 74).

17 He later announced: 'At long last we have achieved management of our domestic monetary system. We must [now] achieve international monetary management' (Hansen 1964b: 686).

18 Hansen (1945a: 164, 1965) did not make substantial changes to his trade policy views during his lifetime. In a remark exaggerating the matter, Poole (1947: 347 note 5) refers to a Hansen 'school of thought' [which] points out that imports are generally regarded as desirable *only when there is full employment*' (emphasis added). See also Haberler (1943: 333) who refers to the 'Hansen group' which, in the case of postwar Britain, saw 'no other way out' except through retention of 'trade control' at prewar levels.

19 Hansen expressed this matter in another way: 'major structural change presents a threat to international stability' (1938: 214).

20 The source of these insights probably hailed from Hansen's familiarity with European economics. According to Samuelson (1976a: 27), Hansen 'was attracted to the Continental view that the great swings in economic activity have been of *quasi-exogenous* origin, being associated with intermittent waves of innovational activity, of population and of over- and undershoots in the process of capital formation' (his emphasis). See also Rosenof (1997: 44–52).

21 See Hansen (1944b: 249, 251).

22 In the 1960s Hansen (1965: 136 note 26) recalled 'a statement by Keynes made in the course of casual conversation to the effect that he hoped ... the World

Bank would boldly assume risks. This statement I subscribe to, the World Bank bonds are backed by strong governments.'
23 Moral hazard generally involves any situation where a perceived reduction in risk leads a party to take riskier actions or neglect precautionary actions.
24 Again, Hansen expresses deep distrust of market forces in allocating capital: 'the effect of foreign lending may well be disastrous if we rely upon automatic forces' (1945a: 159).

4 John Williams's 'key currency' alternative for the international financial order

1 Williams was Nathaniel Ropes Professor of Political Economy at Harvard from 1933 to 1957. For a brief autobiographical sketch see Williams's testimony to the Senate Committee on Banking and Currency, 21 June 1945 (Williams 1945b: 331–2). See also Salant (1976: 20) and Clarke (1987).
2 Williams (1932a: 280) cited a remarkable figure: the US four-year export surplus over the 1914–18 period was $11,150 million – an amount that roughly equalled the total US export surplus for the entire thirty-one-year preceding period, 1873–1914.
3 In a subsequent article he explained how the French price level proved insensitive to gold inflow; how gold inflows did not result in a proportionate increase in bank credit owing to the dearth of investment outlets and a banking convention dictating that lending would not be pursued up to the limits of a constant ratio of reserves. In 1932 France had nearly 100 per cent gold coverage for banknotes on issue (Williams 1932b: 291).
4 For this he was criticized by Hawtrey (1946: 41): 'Professor Williams is not quite free from the present-day tendency to over-estimate their [movements of capital] causal efficacy.'
5 An immediate objective of the Tripartite Agreement was to prevent further exchange rate instability as a result of the contemplated devaluation of the franc. As well, Belgium, the Netherlands and Switzerland became signatories to the Agreement (Bernstein 1944: 780).
6 Australia and Argentina are given as 'small country' examples: 'Since these countries are a minor part of the world economy, currency variation by them would probably not hurt others so much as it might help them' (Williams 1937: 166).
7 Only a *small* step because the Agreement required official exchange market intervention according to specific guidelines but it lacked robust provision for collaboration over external economic policy in general (e.g. trade policy) and it did not establish provisions for inter-country cooperation on internal policies such as monetary or fiscal rules (Williams 1943: 154).
8 According to Gardner (1980: 132) Williams provided 'the only constructive alternative' to the BW Agreement. Bordo (1993: 33 note 24) noted that Williams's plan 'was never seriously considered'.
9 In one place he wrote: 'I have doubted whether in the present divided state of national attitudes and circumstances the world was ready for such a [BW-type] plan, or that it would really have teeth even if it were adopted' (1944c: 183).
10 This and the two preceding quotations in this paragraph are sourced from Williams (1943: 151).
11 See Williams (1945a: 126).
12 He explained further: 'I believe in evolution not revolution. I don't see any reason why we ought to give up gold as an international money if we can find

effective ways of using it. The thing is to make the system work. The difficulty isn't with gold' (1945b: 351–2).

13 See also (1944a: 118, 1945a: 127).

14 The complete set of corrective measures to ensure key currency exchange rate stability will be discussed in the following section.

15 There is nothing here to suggest that Williams had changed his view from an observation made in 1936: 'There will always be diversity of change and of pace and character of development. There will always be business-cycles, leads and lags as between countries. There will be crises here and there' (1936: 327).

16 Immediately postwar, Williams (1945b: 360) expected there would be a 'sterling area currency' used in bilateral arrangements but he was highly dubious about sterling quickly returning to the status of a key international currency *without* assistance from the United States.

17 Eventually an Anglo-American loan of US$3.75 billion was negotiated in December 1945. This loan was not part of the BW Agreement. It was used especially to develop Great Britain's productive capacity and not especially for exchange rate management (Bordo 1993: 34).

18 Noted in Williams (1944a: 115 note 1) and reported from a remark made at BW in the *New York Times* of 7 July 1944. Later Williams (1945b: 349) suggested this comment was made by 'the leading British delegate' and was motivated by 'pride' rather than logic. Incidentally, other prominent British economists preferred a full international plan rather than the key currency approach. See Robinson (1943) and Robertson (1943).

19 See also Bernstein (1944: 783) and Brown (1945).

20 See Halm (1945: 164–9) which reported some of the main criticisms of the key currency approach up to that date.

21 In being preoccupied with the key US–Great Britain relationship, Williams offers no discussion of lender-of-last-resort facilities for small countries faced with balance of payments crises and intractable liquidity problems. Under the BW financial order temporary finance from the IMF would help stave off crises in advance; if problems persisted orderly exchange rate adjustments were permitted.

22 Late twentieth-century research found that 'once a currency emerges as a vehicle, economies of scale enter into play, further decreasing transaction costs and enhancing the currency's position as a vehicle' (Tavlas 1991: 6).

23 Thus 'key currency approach is likely to lead to the establishment and perpetuation of closed trading systems with trade between these systems conducted on a bilateral rather than multilateral basis' (Mikesell 1945: 575).

24 The implications deriving from this conflict will be elaborated upon in Chapter 6.

25 Convertibility restrictions may be necessary for a time because a large portion of world demand for US dollars to buy US goods is facilitated by free convertibility of the pound, and a dollar shortage would then be exacerbated. Trade restrictions should be granted on grounds of consistency since the 'British complain, too, that non-discrimination works one-sidedly; we feel free to resort to "tied loans" but object to "tied trade", the matching of exports and imports between pairs of countries' (Williams 1947a: 62).

26 The following summary is drawn from Williams (1941, 1942, 1945c, 1947a and 1948b) and Machlup (1945).

27 One leading British economist, Ralph Hawtrey (1946: 45), argued for integrated monetary policies as an indispensable pillar in the key currency architecture: 'it is the internal credit policies of the key countries that determine the wealth-value not only of their own monetary units but of the monetary units

linked to them'. Further support for this view by contemporaries is noted in Halm (1945: 164–9). See also in later literature similar expressions of support from Johnson (1972a: 7–9), Depres (1973: xvi) and Scammell (1987: 7).

28 Reporting on a final discussion with Keynes just before his death, Williams recalls how Keynes 'complained that the easy money policy was being pushed too far, both in England and here [USA]' in the early postwar years (1948a: 20 note 1).

29 On this issue see Kindleberger (1983) and Tavlas (1991). Perhaps Williams refrained from discussing these questions because the process in question was potentially destabilizing to the international economy?

30 Specifically, British and American officials at BW believed that 'as victors in war to save democracy, they had an obligation to create a stable postwar international monetary order that would help secure peace' (Bordo 1993: 34).

5 Frank Graham on international money and exchange rates

1 Without being more precise, Graham (1940a: 19, 21) refers in an understated fashion to 'unquiet times' and 'disturbed conditions' rather than cycles or shocks as such.

2 Much later in the twentieth century Grubel (1984: 28) still found it necessary to remind readers that a currency 'exchange rate is a price, just like that of bread and steel'.

3 Graham (1940a: 19) includes shrewdly managed foreign banks in that 'powerful class of speculators'.

4 Thus we have Keynes on two occasions in the 1940s drawing back from reliance on impersonal, international gold standards: 'The fundamental reason for thus limiting the objectives of an international currency scheme is the impossibility, or at any rate the undesirability of imposing stable price-levels from without' (Keynes 1943b: 187); and 'I doubt the political wisdom of appearing, more than is inevitable in any orderly system, to impose an external pressure on national standards' (Keynes 1944: 430).

5 For Graham (1943b: 334), overcoming 'economic evil' seemed often associated with the economist's independence from day-to-day politics: 'Let us not', he urged, 'mix the political situation and economic considerations'.

6 The Keynes Plan and White Plan submitted at BW had 'not precisely defined' what they meant by exchange rate 'stabilization'. Graham was left to draw the conclusion, quite correctly in my view, that Keynes and White meant fixed rates (Graham 1943a: 10–11, 15 note 9).

7 George Halm (1945: 125) disagrees. The architects

> who drafted the Agreement do not want to combine stable exchanges with diverging price developments. They propose rather that we should try to do our best in integrating the domestic monetary policies of the member countries and that we should change the parities only when national employment policies lead to divergent price developments; furthermore, that these changes should not be made by unilateral action.

8 See also Graham (1949: 8).

9 'The "new" system . . . would then . . . be not much else than a reversion to the traditional international gold standard' (Graham 1949: 19 note 12).

10 See Graham (1930).

11 Other writers, including Benjamin Graham (1937), did not regard the CRS as a monetary reform; they saw it as a method of financing and promoting multi-commodity buffer stocks for the purpose of stabilizing the income of raw

materials producers and primary product producers. In this he was supported by Goudriaan (1932) and Keynes (1938).

12 See Graham (1936, 1940b: 13, 1942: 103–5). Fisher had proposed a backing of 100 per cent cash reserves against demand deposits in commercial banks; Graham wanted to extend that idea.

13 Under a gold standard, the gold industry alone is stimulated during a depression; under a CRS the scale of stimulation is much larger and at least acts to retard deflationary impulses.

14 Under a pure CRS regime, governments cannot run active fiscal policies by expanding currency issuance. Governments must balance their budgets continuously and finance temporary deficits by borrowing from the private money market or obtain funds from accumulated hoards of currency. See Friedman (1951: 206). Otherwise, as Graham allowed, ad hoc government action would be required to manage money and adjust official reserve requirements.

15 Kaldor *et al.* (1964) made their submission to the UN Conference on Trade and Development; they considered the CRS a meaningful approach to international financial reform in a period when liquidity problems were becoming acute (see Chapters 6 and 8 below). Reminiscent of Graham in the 1940s, they claimed that the CRS 'would create an international reserve medium which is far more responsive to the needs of an expanding world economy than gold, and the rules of operation of which would exert a powerful stabilizing effect on the world economy' (Kaldor *et al.* 1964: 168–9). Kaldor (1973) was still pressing the case for a CRS a decade later when BW collapsed.

16 In opposition to Keynes, Kaldor *et al.* (1964: 144) supported Graham's view on potential policy independence under a CRS in the context of a parallel debate in the 1960s. The following passage is perfectly consistent with what Graham had written some twenty years earlier (and there is no acknowledgement to Graham):

> It should also be emphasised that the advocacy of a commodity-*reserve* is not the same thing as the advocacy of commodity-*money*: any more than the gold reserve is the same thing as gold currency. There is no suggestion that individual currencies should have a fixed and unalterable par value in terms of commodities: on the contrary, the proposal is advanced in order to make changes in par value (i.e. adjustments in exchange rates) easier to introduce than it is under the so-called 'gold-exchange standard' at present.

17 See Graham (1943a: 23, 1944: 428).

18 See Friedman (1951), Grubel (1965), Hart (1966) and Williamson (1973: 721–6).

19 Estimates range from 3 per cent to 6 per cent per annum of the value of the commodity stock, though such a cost could be covered by the difference between the stock's buying and selling price spread. In Williamson's (1973: 724) estimation a CRS would cost US$6–$8 billion *per annum* if adopted in 1973.

20 As early as 1940 Graham (1940a: 28–9) fully anticipated Friedman's (1953) case for flexible exchange rates though this is not recognized in prominent literature on the subject. See, for example, the priority given to Friedman on this matter in Isard (1995: 189–91), Krueger (1998: 1986 note 12) and Cooper (1999: 102).

21 Graham in a letter to Randall Hindshaw, dated March 1949, reprinted in Graham (1971: 249), bracketed insert added.

22 Since fixed costs are not covered by the FRC there will always be risk of business losses.

6 Robert Triffin's supranational central bank: a plan to stabilize liquidity

1 A brief biographical sketch is contained in Roosa (1978). See also Kervyn (1987). For a short intellectual autobiography describing his early work, see Triffin (1966a: 141–2). Triffin (1957: v) acknowledges the influence of Williams and Hansen, at least so far as instruction on money and banking is concerned.

2 He only cites Williams once on the bilateral payments discrimination issue created by the BW scarce currency clause. See Triffin (1954: 210 note 13). Later he mentions in passing and without discussion Williams's creation of the key currency scheme (Triffin 1957: 138).

3 Flanders (1989: 23) labels Triffin a 'revisionist' thinker who understood 'the apparent smoothness with which the international payments system worked in the pre-World War I period' as having little to do with central banks following the textbook 'rules of the gold standard game'. The accepted textbook version of the rules which we shall outline below was not, as it turned out, consistent with a pure gold standard order after all (Triffin 1947a: 53).

4 On Hume's doctrine see Fausten (1979: 664–5).

5 See Triffin (1964a: 3).

6 See Triffin (1964a: 3) for supporting data.

7 See Triffin (1964a: 9).

8 See Triffin (1947a: 53) and (1964a: 4–5).

9 Gresham's Law states that 'bad money drives out good'. It is attributed to Sir Thomas Gresham, an adviser to Queen Elizabeth I. Gresham found that when a currency was debased and new ones used as substitutes, the substitutes were perceived as more valuable and tended to be hoarded and removed from circulation. The old currency would be akin to a hot potato – to be dispensed with as quickly as possible.

10 In this connection see Eichengreen (1989: 282) for a modern discussion of various episodes involving the 'dynamics of hegemonic decline' in the international economy since the nineteenth century. Triffin anticipated Eichengreen's conclusion: 'since hegemony is transitory, so must be any international monetary system that takes hegemony as its basis. Given the costs of international monetary reform, it would seem unwise to predicate a new system on such a transient basis' (Eichengreen 1989: 287).

11 The following list draws heavily on Triffin (1947a: 47, 63–4, 66, 68, 71–2, 77, 78).

12 This is a variation on the 'multiple currency' practice authorized by the IMF Articles of Agreement VIII, 3, implementable only after prior IMF approval. See Horsefield (1969c: 195).

13 Prébisch became notorious in the 1950s for advocating exchange controls and protectionist import substitution policies for less developed countries so that they could begin a process of industrialization by producing high income elastic goods which would otherwise have to be imported. On Prébisch see Palma (1987).

14 The quotations in this paragraph have been sourced from Triffin (1966a: 72, 73, 75–6). Triffin refers to monetary and exchange control legislation in Guatemala and Paraguay as already embodying these ideas, though they did not include allowance for international responsibilities that might go with IMF membership (p. 76).

15 Harrod (1947: 96) condemned Triffin's flirtation with exchange controls and the multiple currency idea: they amounted to an 'admission of failure', in effect introducing other trade barriers.

16 See also Triffin (1957: 25–6).

17 See also Triffin (1956: 382).

18 Unlike his silence on the matter of inflation in earlier articles, now Triffin was

criticizing the BW order and the IMF for not being 'in a position to impose quickly and effectively an adequate anti-inflationary policy upon a recalcitrant member' (1949: 185).

19 See Triffin (1960: 25). Upon fully reviewing the operational meaning of convertibility concepts embodied in various IMF Articles of Agreement, Joseph Gold (1971a: 58) concluded that 'the convertibility of a currency is a relative concept'.

20 See Salant (1956: 407).

21 See Triffin (1957: 113).

22 See Triffin (1954: 207–8, 1956: 381).

23 *Gold and the Dollar Crisis* (1960) includes nineteen tables and three charts. See also Triffin (1963) for additional statistical support.

24 The BW order anointed US dollar gold convertibility from the mid-1940s. Later, sterling and general European convertibility into US dollars in the 1950s opened an 'indirect channel from sterling into gold' (Triffin 1965b: 349). See also James (1996: 155–7).

25 See Triffin (1961b: 248) where he argues that 'the world cannot tolerate much longer an international monetary system [supporting] ... [t]he perpetuation of our balance-of-payments deficit and the continued acceptance of dollar IOUs as monetary reserves by other countries ... without undermining confidence in the dollar and its acceptability as a reserve currency'. See also Triffin (1961a).

26 There are clear hints of the Triffin 'dilemma' as early as Triffin (1954) and (1957: 296) where he warns of the BW dependence on the gold exchange standard. In the preface to *Gold and the Dollar Crisis* (1960: ix) he summarized the problem thus:

> the basic themes of this book will remain valid for policy-makers for a long time to come. Gold production is unlikely to increase sufficiently in the foreseeable future to provide an adequate supply of liquidity to an expanding world economy; and the haphazard use of national currency holdings as supplementary form of reserve accumulation cannot but undermine, more and more dangerously as time goes on, the key currencies used for this purpose and, by way of consequence, the world monetary superstructure erected upon them.

27 See Triffin (1960: 96–101).

28 See also Triffin (1960: 145, 1964a: 21).

29 See Triffin (1960: 70–1, 1963: 112).

30 The following synopsis of Triffin's proposal draws heavily on Triffin (1960: 102–20, 1961a, 1961b, 1964b, 1965b). Accessible contemporary literature on Triffin's plan is extensive. See especially Machlup (1962: 30–3), Altman (1961) and Machlup and Malkiel (1964).

31 Triffin (1964a: 31) was keen to dispense altogether with gold in principle as part of the reserves of both central banks and the IMF. In practice, he realized that popular attitudes did not make such a scenario possible.

32 He did not, however, propose a 'rigid mechanical' rule connecting world economic growth rates to growth in IMF reserves. He suggested an 'anti-inflationary safeguard' by setting a ceiling on the annual increase in IMF loans and investments (Triffin 1965b: 357; see also Triffin 1964a: 32).

33 See Triffin (1965b: 360–2, 371, 1961b: 428).

34 See also Triffin (1969b: 486–7).

35 See Depres *et al.* (1966: 268); also Grubel (1984: 137–8) and James (1996: 157–8).

36 See Furth (1961: 420), Angell (1961: 693, 696) and Yeager (1961: 290).

37 Roy Harrod (1963: 222) reported sceptically that Triffin 'hopes that nations would not in effect want to convert' their IMF balances into gold. And

> [i]nternational liquidity would be increased only to the extent that they did not insist on doing so. It might be thought that this was the path of wisdom. Make the balances in principle convertible and hope that no one will wish to convert them.

38 Unless there was an unlikely joint-member pact renouncing gold conversion rights (Williamson 1973: 719).
39 Main criticisms along these lines are maintained by Kaldor (1964: 138–9), Yeager (1966: 476) and Williamson (1973: 715).
40 See Altman (1961: 149), Yeager (1961: 194–5) and Rueff (1961b: 267).
41 See Triffin (1957: 303, 1965, 1966b: 98–101).
42 Nicolas Kaldor (1964: 40) pointed to the lack of stringent rules for setting the aggregate amount of IMF credit creation and unclear IMF loan conditions. For more favourable opinions, with qualifications, to Triffin's approach see MacDougall (1960), Balogh (1960) and Hirsch (1964).
43 Alvin Hansen (1960: 132) was quick to judge that 'the Triffin proposals appear currently to be outside the pale of practical politics'.
44 See Triffin (1957: 284–6, 1961a: 435–8, 1960: 121–44, 147, 1964a: 30).
45 All this was due to 'our absurd and immoral venture in Vietnam [which] perpetuates deficits of several billion dollars a year on our balance of payments' (Triffin 1969c: 9).
46 Though later he admitted being 'totally wrong in underestimating the duration and size of the U.S. deficits that foreign central bankers would be willing to absorb at the cost of an inflationary explosion of world monetary reserves' (Triffin 1978: 4).
47 See De Grauwe (1989: 28).
48 On these events see Solomon (1977: 175–212).
49 Triffin argued trenchantly against giving up control over exchange rates: 'No responsible, or even irresponsible, government or monetary authorities will accept tying their hands behind their backs . . . and leaving a policy instrument as powerful as their country's exchange-rate at the tender mercy of accidental forces and/or currency speculators' (Triffin 1969a: 55). As we saw earlier, Triffin (1947a) believed that external payments problems may be due to different causes not all of which could be overcome by a high degree of exchange rate flexibility. He was still repeating this message near the end of the BW era. See Triffin (1971).

7 A Chicagoan international financial order

1 Two examples should suffice here. First, Jacob Viner left Chicago in 1946 *after* making some telling criticisms of the BW Agreement in several important articles. He later commented that he was 'at no time . . . consciously a member' of the Chicago School. Moreover he was adamant that 'if there was such a school it did not regard me as a member, or at least a loyal and qualified member' (Viner to Patinkin quoted in Reder 1982: 7 note 19). Second, there were fundamental differences in principle between Harry Johnson and Robert Mundell (who also spent time in Chicago) on international financial reform during the 1960s and early 1970s – so much so that Johnson (1972b: 133) was moved to state: 'Mundell and I exist to demonstrate that there is no such thing as a Chicago School – because we come out at the opposite ends of several major issues in this field'. Mundell's work will be considered in Chapter 9 below.

2 See Bronfenbrenner (1962: 75) and Reder (1982: 25).
3 See Stigler (1962: 70).
4 Friedman (1967b: 84–6) offers a clear explanation of Simons's interpretation of the causes of the great depression in the 1930s.
5 Friedman (1967b: 92) demurred, reproaching Simons for misperceiving the facts: 'There is no evidence to support Simons's fear that a fixed quantity of money might involve "the danger of sharp changes on the velocity side". On the contrary, the evidence is precisely the reverse – that it would lessen the danger of sharp changes in velocity.' As a result, Simons 'was led to compromise the short run and propose radical reform for the long run'.
6 By contrast he quietly condemned the primacy given by Alvin Hansen to an 'infinitely flexible scheme of discretionary action' for fiscal policymaking without reference to binding rules (Simons 1942: 205). He probably had Hansen in mind when later referring to 'finance-be damned schemes for domestic full employment' (1945b: 295).
7 History was instructive in this connection: 'Acquiring financial hegemony after the last war. We [in the United States] administered it abominably in spite of our abundant power' (Simons 1944a: 273).
8 See also Simons (1944a: 276). The title of Simons's (1944c) article in *Fortune* magazine made the matter clear: 'The U.S. holds the cards'.
9 In their 'scrupulous observance of a tacit injunction against meddling' in trade policy, BW conference participants had missed an opportunity to deal with a chief cause of international economic instability. For Simons, monetary policy and trade policy were aspects of the same thing. After all, currency devaluations were like tariff increases; inappropriate tariff increases can make currencies 'violently unstable' and may even debase whole monetary systems (Simons 1944a: 261, 262).
10 See also Simons (1942: 205 note 14).
11 In a retrospective appreciation of BW, Viner expressed satisfaction that it provided a scheme akin to 'regulated quasi gold standard' (Viner 1947a: 295).
12 Viner's plea did not escape a sympathetic contemporary commentator. See Fellner (1945: 262–3).
13 See also Viner (1944: 239, 1947a: 296–8).
14 While Viner did not use the term 'moral hazard' he clearly understood its meaning in his remarks on the IBRD. In the late twentieth century in international finance the idea was widely applied to circumstances where a considerable reduction in risk faced by any party leads that party to take *riskier* actions, or to neglect precautionary risk management measures.
15 His paper was later published in Friedman (1953: 157–203). He acknowledged the comments of James Meade – one of only a few contemporaries who held a similar view. Unlike Friedman, Meade wanted flexible exchange rates so as to free up monetary and fiscal policy for domestic objectives such as the maintenance of high employment. Friedman was more concerned about removing exchange controls and free trade. See Meade (1955) and also Lutz (1954). In an earlier article, Friedman (1948: 142) clearly foreshadowed a preference for flexible exchange rates. As we saw in Chapter 4, Frank Graham completely anticipated this school of thought on exchange rates.
16 Accordingly, it 'is a sorry reflection on the scientific basis for generally held economic beliefs, that Nurkse's analysis is so often cited as "the" basis of "proof" of the belief in destabilizing speculation' (Friedman 1953: 176 note 9). Nurkse's work is discussed in Chapter 2.
17 This question is addressed in Friedman (1960).
18 In 1966, this recognition prompted twenty-seven economists including

Friedman to propose wider margins for allowable exchange rate variation in the BW architecture. While Friedman was a signatory to the proposal he did not believe that it would provide sufficient flexibility if implemented (Fellner 1966: 112–14).

19 See also Friedman (1968a: 208).

20 See for example his statement to the Congressional Subcommittee on International Exchange and Payments (Friedman 1966), and also Friedman (1969b).

21 In one exaggerated remark Friedman concluded that 'central banks are a necessary – and today almost sufficient – condition for a balance-of-payments problem' (1967a: 11).

22 See Friedman (1968d: 275, 1967a: 11, 1968c: 13).

23 Realistically, Friedman took as given a world divided into separate political or economic units with separate fiat currencies. It was therefore utopian to focus unduly on a first best, ideal solution for international finance which for Friedman (1969b: 117) meant 'a world money with*out* a world monetary authority' (his emphasis). It is difficult to sustain Isard's (1995: 19) comment on Friedman, that he 'committed the common error of comparing the perceived shortcomings of the [BW] exchange rate regime with an idealization of an alternative'.

24 Culminating in Friedman and Schwartz (1963).

25 See also Friedman (1951: 227, 1948: 154).

26 By contrast Simons (1936) and Mints (1950: 134–8) chose, for practical reasons, a price level stabilization rule for monetary policy. We should recall from Chapter 4 above that Frank Graham chose a price level target as well.

27 The parallel between gold and old soldiers is drawn in Friedman and Schwartz (1963: 60).

28 See Friedman (1959: 83–5, 1967a: 18).

29 See Friedman (1968c: 9–10).

30 See Johnson (1962). Johnson (1972a) offered highly critical retrospective assessment of the BW order at the point of its collapse in 1971.

31 Johnson (1969a: 214) was sure that 'the historical record provides no convincing supporting evidence' for the claim that flexible exchange rates allow scope for destabilizing speculation. In the same year Friedman (1969b: 114–15) chimed in: 'Destabilizing speculation is a theoretical possibility, but I know of no empirical evidence that it has occurred even as a special case, let alone a generic rule.'

32 That is, if world bank liabilities were freely convertible into gold, 'the bank would have to manage its asset portfolios so as to maintain the confidence of its (national) customers in its liquidity. This would in all likelihood prevent it from giving grants to less developed countries . . . and restrict its freedom to purchase the securities of less developed country governments' (Johnson 1969a: 309).

33 See also Machlup and Malkiel (1964).

8 Reconstructing the international gold standard: European perspectives

1 Kirzner (2001) studies Mises – the man and his contribution to economics – but does not mention his reactions to BW or the Mises's alternative.

2 Bordo and Kydland (1996: 65–8) date the full 'classical' period as 1717 to 1914; the sterling price was fixed at £3.85 per ounce for most of that time.

3 See, for example, Yeager (1966: 482).

4 Modern research has confirmed his suspicion. In fact under the flexible 'classical' gold standard pre-1914 the rules were flouted. The rules were highly conditional on circumstances and during some episodes government commitment

to gold in Great Britain and the United States was severely weakened. See Bayoumi *et al.* (1996).

5 On this point much has been written about Mises's position and its implications. The most accessible treatments are McCulloch (1986), Selgin (1999) and Herbener (2002).

6 Mises (1949: 780) expressly acknowledged that he initially overlooked dangers lurking in the interwar gold exchange standard.

7 Mises (1928: 71) expressed disquiet over the aims and methods of what was regarded as 'cyclical policy' in the 1920s which turned on 'the fallacy that prosperity can be produced by using banking procedures to make credit cheap'.

8 For elaboration on this point see Mises (1949: 780–4, 1953: 472–4).

9 As Kindleberger (1989: 54) reported: 'When the deflationary troubles came in the United States in 1933, the run on banks made it necessary to call in gold at the [old] official price, and forbid further private possession.'

10 See Mises (1949: 794, 1953: 475).

11 For a full discussion of the nature of interest in Mises's work see Mises (1949: 786–7).

12 He went further: 'Keynes did not add any new idea to the body of inflationist fallacies, a thousand times refuted by economists' (Mises 1946).

13 On the Tripartite Agreement see Chapter 4.

14 De Gaulle quoted in Rueff and Hirsch (1965: Preface).

15 See especially Rist (1954: 222–3) and Rueff (1966: 107–10).

16 See Rist (1950: 99, 1952a: 187).

17 For an excellent treatment of the 1968 gold rush see Solomon (1977: 115–27).

18 Much later, Rueff (1967a: 181) committed to an approximate twofold increase in the US dollar price of gold, thus doubling the value of the United States' gold reserve.

19 International monetary experts in the United States were especially critical of this outcome. For example, Kenen (1973: 195 note 8) opposed Rueff's plan because it 'would redistribute world assets arbitrarily.... Those who favor a gold standard would not object to this redistribution; it would merely reward those who have abstained virtuously from accumulating dollars. But the United States and its present creditors would oppose it as unfair.'

20 On these matters see Rueff (1961a: 328, 1967a: 185, 1969: 177–8).

21 Heilperin was born in Poland, receiving his education in economics at the University of Geneva. He participated in the BW Conference. For a biographical sketch see Salerno (1985: 107).

22 Salerno (1985: 99) rightly maintains that Heilperin accurately predicted the inflationary outcomes accompanying immediate post-BW era experiments with floating exchange rates.

23 Heilperin (1939) gives a full explanation of the classical gold standard. See also Salerno (1985: 102) on the importance of managed money in Heilperin's work.

24 On this possible IMF role see Heilperin (1964: 116, 1961).

25 Röpke was a colleague of both Mises and Heilperin. He actively defended Jacques Rueff's ideas 'from [being] the butt of so many attacks' (Röpke 1961: 228). Zmirak (2001) offers a superb intellectual biography of Röpke.

26 Röpke was calling for the revival of a gold standard in the early 1950s. Röpke (1960) is an English translation of his book first published in 1954.

27 Röpke (1942a, 1942b) gave evidence for a long period of economic integration from about 1700 to 1914, followed by economic disintegration still ongoing in the 1950s under the impact of Keynesianism (Röpke 1963).

28 In a highly accurate portrayal of Röpke's complete international political economy Sally (1998: 131) maintains: 'of the few Germans neoliberals who

tackle the question of international economic order, it is Röpke alone who develops a comprehensive [doctrine]'. In Sally's account, Röpke is portrayed as a classical liberal economist who rejects the idea of world government and is sceptical of the role of international organizations such as the IMF, IBRD and the General Agreement on Tariffs and Trade. Röpke preferred 'example setting' in international economic policy (Sally 1998: 141). This conclusion applies with equal force to Röpke's ideas on the international financial architecture.

29 These three foundational concepts are discussed at length in Röpke (1960: 252–5). The present paragraph is a brief exposition of that material.

30 Röpke was impressed with the move towards integration in the European community by the enactment of currency convertibility on current account transactions facilitated by the European Payments Union in December 1958. Otherwise he rarely favoured such collective, cooperative arrangements in the world economy. See Sally (1998: 141, 144).

31 Röpke (1960: 212–14) provides an updated critique of the full employment movement in Keynesian economic thought.

32 Hayek abandoned any possibility of reviving a gold standard by the 1970s: 'There is just not enough gold to go about. An international gold standard today means only that a few countries maintained a real gold standard while the others hung on to them through a gold exchange standard' (Hayek 1976a: 83). See also Hayek (1976b, 1979).

33 Originally publication no. 18 of the Graduate Institute of International Studies, reprinted in Kresge (1999: 37–99). All citations below refer to the reprint. Röpke (1942a) gave high praise to Hayek's lectures in Geneva.

34 On these attributes of a gold standard see Hayek (1937: 99–100, 1943: 176–7).

35 See Hayek (1943) and Kresge (1999: 20–2).

36 This suggestion is made by Eric Helleiner (1999: 148).

37 On these events in respect of gold demand in the 1960s see Gilbert (1968: 38–9) and Solomon (1977: 27–32).

38 Humphrey (1973: 96) warned that raising the US dollar price of gold 'in order to monetize newly mined gold is a simple means of restoring Bretton Woods – a satisfactory system that is known to work when given a chance, but which was made unworkable by the shortage of gold'. We shall see in the next chapter how Roy Harrod proposed raising the price of gold for precisely this reason.

39 See Hayek (1976a). Hayek's idea stood in sharp contrast to the BW philosophy which ultimately aimed to create a world of equal national currencies.

9 Salvaging the fixed exchange rate architecture: the ideas of Roy Harrod and Robert Mundell

1 For a short period in the early 1950s he served as an economic adviser to the IMF, producing an important report (Harrod 1953b). Harrod was a prolific writer, publishing hundreds of journalistic pieces on international financial issues. For a list of his articles up to 1960, see Harrod (1961c: 251–65). For a comprehensive obituary of Harrod see Phelps Brown (1980). See also Hinshaw (1978).

2 Both propositions are tantamount to a rejection of a pure commodity or gold standard architecture. In a review of Heilperin's work on international money, Harrod (1939: 834) criticized the gold standard: it was the outgrowth of a 'primitive way of thinking' and Heilperin is taken to task for the 'unobtrusive dogmatism latent in his advocacy' of a gold standard.

3 On 15 August 1971, foreign official US dollar holdings amounted to approximately four times United States' currency plus gold reserves. The US dollar

indebtedness led to a crisis of confidence and the dollar–gold guarantee had to be withdrawn. See Solomon (1977: 177, 186).

4 See Article IV Section 7, Horsefield (1969c: 190).

5 Right through to the end of his career and after the breakdown of the BW order, Harrod rejected flexible exchange rates, asserting that they 'would produce intolerable oscillations' (Harrod 1972: 38, 93).

6 In this task he was supported by Peter Oppenheimer (1969), an Oxford colleague who made a sounder, technical case for a one-off increase in the official price of gold.

7 Harrod (1963: 222–3) objected to Triffin's doctrine on the grounds that it relied on a weak gold convertibility link. Creating a vast international credit money on a very precarious, restricted gold base was inviting distrust since the new money was not obviously 'as good as gold' (as we observed in Chapter 6). Moreover, to make the new money 'in principle convertible in the hope that no one will wish to convert' clearly amounted to a 'ruse' which Harrod believed market participants and monetary authorities would be unwilling to accept.

8 This proposal compared with raising IMF quotas for lending by 50 per cent, increasing reserves by only US$5 billion. See Harrod (1961b: 58, 1953b: 154,1971: 38).

9 For the impact of a liquidity crisis in the world economy on poor countries see Harrod (1964a).

10 Johnson (1990: 291) expressed scepticism over Harrod's belief that a one-off gold price increase would make gold supplies elastic. Rapid world economic growth and uncontained general price inflation could attenuate 'new monetary gold supplies to vanishing point'.

11 For an explanation of the speculative frenzy that may be associated with discrete changes in official gold prices see Johnson (1969c: 345–6). See also Machlup (1962: 48–9).

12 James Meade (1964: 7) definitely thought the test was uncalled for. He opposed Harrod's scheme, instead preferring 'a more rational control' over international finance. Finance was a matter for 'bookkeepers and not mining engineers'.

13 Alvin Hansen (1960: 132) suggested that Harrod was not fully informed about the political feasibilities pertaining to a gold price increase.

14 For bureaucrats in general Harrod (1964b: 177) reserved the following unflattering generalization: 'it appears to be very difficult for the official mind to recognize the existence of a new problem' in the realm of international finance.

15 By mid-August 1971 official foreign US dollar holdings (liabilities from the United States' standpoint), were approximately four times the value of US currency reserve assets (Emminger 1971: 242).

16 For early IMF planning and deliberation on the new reserve asset (to be called the SDR), see Meier (1974: 218–97), Gold (1970: 9–10) and Solomon (1977: 128–50).

17 James Meade had more faith in IMF officials and practices. He thought more regular reviews of quota would do the trick and solve the liquidity problem in a gradual and more orderly manner than a one-off gold price increase. See Meade (1964: 18–24).

18 This is not the place to recount the convoluted legalese and negotiating procedures associated with the creation of this new SDR reserve asset. On this see Gold (1970, 1971b) and Polak (1971).

19 The following explanation is drawn from Horsefield (1969c: 525–41), Gold (1970) and Grubel (1984: 152–8).

20 See Harrod (1965: 177). Triffin (1971: 134) agreed though he went further, charging that the United States as a leading deficit country would be a chief beneficiary of SDRs; that SDRs would largely be 'an outright gift with no strings attached'.

21 According to Johnson (1970: 289), Harrod was 'averse to having international agencies take over control'; they 'would subordinate growth policies to monetary policies . . . whereas national growth problems differ widely'.

22 One revision suggested by Jacques Rueff (1969: 172) turned on the high likelihood of major capital outflows suddenly and adversely affecting a large industrial country. This event, he predicted, would place pressure on the IMF to expand the issue of SDRs. The result would be highly inflationary, with inflation being transmitted from creditor countries to the rest of the world.

23 Harrod wrote extensively on the principles of macroeconomic policy. See especially Harrod (1947, 1958a, 1966, 1967).

24 Harrod took this general position along with fellow English Keynesian economist James Meade (1964: 24) who neatly summarized the doctrine: 'It is essential for the health and well being of the world that the main developed countries ... should use their domestic budgetary and monetary policies for domestic economic expansion – for full employment and steady growth.'

25 Freely floating exchange rates favoured by fellow British economist James Meade for the British pound in the 1950s were acceptable to Harrod only in principle. That principle was founded on an 'ideal system' wherein the structure of trade was balanced, trade cycles contained and confidence stable. Harrod found no evidence that these conditions obtained the 1950s (1961a: 63).

26 See Harrod (1964a: 114, 1965: 37). The supposed reduction in monetary policy credibility accompanying flexible rates would have to be countered by holding more reserves. Reserve holdings and exchange rates would, in the event, become even more volatile. See Black (1985: 1168).

27 Harrod's intense dislike of exchange controls is foreshadowed in a commentary on the early functioning of BW arrangements (Harrod 1947: 96). See also Harrod (1967: 56). For Harrod, exchange controls were a barrier to trade and growth; their impact on investment in poor countries was clearly pernicious. World capital was especially scarce in the postwar world and the IMF and IBRD had played a crucial role in allocating much of that capital over the short and long term respectively (Harrod 1972: 19).

28 See Harrod (1967: 70). According to Hinshaw (1978: 369), Harrod never wavered on this subject; he 'remained firmly in the fixed exchange rate camp' throughout his career.

29 By contrast, we saw in Chapter 6 how Robert Triffin assigned incomes policy to *internal balance* – the maintenance of price stability in particular.

30 That he came late to the field by comparison with other great architects of international finance studied in this book is no better illustrated than in Machlup's *International Monetary Economics* (1966a) which makes no mention of his work.

31 A truly mobile scholar, Mundell spent his immediate post-doctoral years at the University of Chicago (1956–7), University of British Columbia (1957–8), Stanford University (1958–9) and Johns Hopkins University (1959–61); after working at the IMF he spent longer periods at the University of Chicago, University of Waterloo and Columbia University. See Mundell (1997) and Persson (2001).

32 Mundell (1973c: 386). He added wryly: 'was it Charles Rist who said that universal suffrage killed the gold standard?'

33 The nineteenth-century classical gold standard was a 'system' rather than an

'order' bound by the rule of law as such. Similarly, in the Roman–Byzantine era from the time of Julius Caesar (100 BC) until the fall of Constantinople (1203), gold coinage was accepted as an international reserve asset and means of payment; an international financial 'system' was imposed by Roman and Byzantine imperialism and not the rule of international law. See Mundell (1972: 91–8).

34 See also Mundell (1969d: 459–60, 1972: 92).

35 See for example Mundell (1971b, 1969d: 479–81).

36 See Mundell (1969b: 37) for a more technical definition of seigniorage.

37 Mundell (1971a: 91) produced the following data: the US economy had a GNP of about US$900 billion; the next four major industrial countries – Germany, France, Japan and the United Kingdom – had a combined GNP of $120 billion. He concluded: 'In that system, you can't speak of any kind of symmetry, because it is a world in which the U.S. economy dominates.'

38 This view on SDRs he reinforced some years later. See Mundell (1977: 242).

39 Mundell (1964, 1965) showed in more technical articles that there was asymmetry in the adjustment of small and large countries such that the burden varied inversely with economic size.

40 In explaining Keynes's support for flexible exchange rates in the 1920s, Mundell (1971a: 109) was aware of the importance of context: 'Keynes . . . was supporting flexible exchange rates [in] . . . a world . . . of middle-sized states. There was no great superpower. That situation has changed.'

41 See Mundell (1997: 8). He continued: since BW, 'the rest of the world need[ed] an international monetary system much more than the USA'.

42 'It is sometimes argued that a fixed exchange rate regime cannot work because there is no adjustment mechanism. . . . The argument is sheer nonsense' (Mundell 1969e: 634).

43 A vast literature has since developed and extended the currency area idea originally propounded in Mundell's now classic 1961 article. See Mundell (1973a, 1973b, 1997), Tower and Willett (1976) which offers an excellent survey of the issues, Kawai (1987) and Cohen (1992).

44 See Mundell (1961: 657–8).

45 It is important to record two notable contributions – McKinnon (1963) and Kenen (1969) – both extending the currency area idea and both endorsing the BW exchange rate regime.

46 The above-mentioned benefits are drawn from Mundell (1969b: 31–2, 1969e: 637–41, 1972: 103, 1997: 19–20).

47 This last factor may act as a vital support factor against the dominant role of the US dollar in the BW order.

48 See Mundell (1969e). Here we should be mindful of Dornbusch's (2000: 8) warning: Mundell 'always had an undeniable streak of the *enfant terrible*'.

49 Mundell (1969e: 641–5) had nagging doubts about such an arrangement. Smaller economies and larger, less developed countries would not easily be taken into account.

10 The plurality of international financial architectures in the BW era

1 On this attitude in retrospect see Johnson (1972c: 407–8).

2 For the phraseology here and the pyramid analogy we are indebted to Andrew Ballantyne (2002a: 44–5).

3 In Triffin's case, as we observed in Chapter 6, he was influenced by early research and experience in which he concentrated on monetary problems in the Latin American region. Moreover, the early influence of Raul Prébisch on

Triffin should not be underestimated. On the importance of international financial reform for less developed countries, see Prébisch (1969).

4 On this suggestion see Johnson (1969d: 230). Johnson admitted that World Bank bonds would probably be less liquid than SDRs but produce a higher return.

5 In this endeavour, Fischer was supported by the IMF which at the same time reported on progress it was making in strengthening the international architecture. See IMF (1999).

6 For similar sentiments expressed after the collapse of BW see Kindleberger (1972: 426).

7 On these developments see Kenen *et al.* (1994).

Bibliography

AEA (1969) 'Ludwig von Mises: distinguished fellow 1969', *American Economic Review*, 59, 4.

Aliber, R.Z. (1987) 'Exchange rates', in J. Eatwell and J. Chipman (eds) *The New Palgrave: a dictionary of economics*, Vol. I, 210–12, London: Macmillan.

Altman, O.L. (1961) 'Professor Triffin on international liquidity and the role of the Fund', in H. Grubel (ed.) *World Monetary Reform* (1963), 120–49, Stanford, Calif.: Stanford University Press.

Angell, J.W. (1961) 'The reorganization of the international monetary system: an alternative proposal', *Economic Journal*, 71: 691–708.

Ballantyne, A. (2002a) *Architecture: a very short introduction*, Oxford: Oxford University Press.

—— (2002b) 'Introduction', in A. Ballantyne (ed.) *What Is Architecture?*, 1–6, London: Routledge.

—— (2004) 'Introduction: architectures in the plural', in A. Ballantyne (ed.) *Architectures. Modernism and after*, 1–32, Oxford: Blackwell.

Balogh, T. (1960) 'International reserves and liquidity', *Economic Journal*, 70: 357–77.

Bank for International Settlements (1998) *Reports on Strengthening the International Financial Architecture*, Basle: BIS.

Bayoumi, T., Eichengreen, B. and Taylor, M. (1996) 'Money perspectives in the gold standard: introduction', in T. Bayoumi, B. Eichengreen and M. Taylor (eds) *Modern Perspectives on the Gold Standard*, 3–16, Cambridge: Cambridge University Press.

Bernstein, E.M. (1944) 'A practical international monetary policy', *American Economic Review*, 34: 771–84.

—— (1945) 'Scarce currencies and the International Monetary Fund', *Journal of Political Economy*, 53: 1–14.

Black, S.W. (1985) 'International money and international monetary arrangements', in P.B. Kenen and R.W. Jones (eds) *Handbook of International Economics*, Vol. II, 1154–193, Amsterdam: North Holland.

Blaug, M. (1996) *Economic Theory in Retrospect*, fifth edn, Cambridge: Cambridge University Press.

—— (2001) 'What price the history of economic thought?', *Journal of Economic Perspectives*, 15: 145–64.

Bordo, M.D. (1993) 'The Bretton Woods international monetary system: a historical overview', in M.D. Bordo and B. Eichengreen (eds) *A Retrospective on the Bretton Woods System*, 3–89, Chicago: University of Chicago Press.

Bordo, M.D. and Eichengreen, B. (eds) (1993) *A Retrospective on the Bretton Woods System*, Chicago: University of Chicago Press.

Bordo, M. and Kydland, F. (1996) 'The gold standard as a commitment mechanism', in T. Bayoumi, B. Eichengreen and M. Taylor (eds) *Modern Perspectives on the Gold Standard*, 55–100, Cambridge: Cambridge University Press.

Bourneuf, A. (1944) 'Professor Williams and the Fund', *American Economic Review*, 34: 840–7.

—— (1946) 'Leading operations of the International Monetary Fund', *Review of Economics and Statistics*, 28: 237–47.

Bronfenbrenner, M. (1962) 'Observations on the "Chicago School(s)"', *Journal of Political Economy*, 70: 72–5.

—— (1966) 'Trends, cycles and fads in economic writing', *American Economic Review*, 56: 538–52.

Brown, W.A. (1945) 'The repurchase provisions of the proposed International Monetary Fund', *American Economic Review*, 35: 111–20.

Bryant, R.C. (1995) *International Coordination of National Stabilization Policies*, Washington, DC: Brookings Institution.

Chamberlain, N.W. (1945) 'Professor Hansen's fiscal policy and the debt', *American Economic Review*, 35: 400–7.

Clarke, S.V.O. (1987) 'Williams, John Henry', in J. Eatwell, M. Milgate and J.S. Chipman (eds) *The New Palgrave: a dictionary of economics*, Vol. IV, 922, London: Macmillan.

Cohen, B. (1992) 'Currency areas', in P. Newman, J. Eatwell and M. Milgate (eds) *The New Palgrave Dictionary of Money and Finance*, 556–7, London: Macmillan.

Cohen, B.J. (1982) 'Balance-of-payments financing: evolution of a regime', *International Organization*, 36: 315–36.

Cohen, S.D. (1970) *International Monetary Reform 1964–69: the political dimension*, New York: Praeger.

Cooper, R.N. (1993) 'Comment', in M. Bordo and B. Eichengreen (eds) *A Retrospective of the Bretton Woods System*, 104–7, Chicago: University of Chicago Press.

—— (1999) 'Exchange rate choices', in J.S. Little and G.P. Olivei (eds) *Rethinking the International Monetary System*, 99–123, Boston, Mass.: Federal Reserve Bank of Boston.

Crotty, J.R. (1983) 'On Keynes and capital flight', *Journal of Economic Literature*, 21: 59–65.

Crowther, G. (1948) *An Outline of Money*, revised edn, London: Thomas Nelson.

De Grauwe, P. (1989) *International Money: post-war trends and theories*, Oxford: Clarendon Press.

De Vries, M.G. (1969) 'Exchange restrictions: the setting', in J.K. Horsefield (ed.) *The International Monetary Fund 1945–1965*, Vol. II: *Analysis*, 217–28, Washington, DC: International Monetary Fund.

—— (1976) *The International Monetary Fund 1966–71: the system under stress*, 2 volumes, Washington, DC: International Monetary Fund.

Depres, E. (1973) *International Economic Reform Collected Papers of Emile Depres*, ed. G.M. Meier, New York: Oxford University Press.

Depres, E., Kindleberger, C. and Salant, W. (1966) 'The dollar and world liquidity: a minority view', reprinted in G. Meier (ed.) *International Economic Reform Collected Papers of Emile Depres* (1973), 266–79, New York: Oxford University Press.

Dietze, G. (1969) 'Foreword', in W. Röpke, *Against the Tide*, v–xii, Chicago: Henry Regnery.

Dornbusch, R. (2000) 'Nobel Laureate Robert A. Mundell', unpublished mimeograph, 10pp.

Ebeling, R. (1985) 'Ludwig von Mises and the gold standard', in L.H. Rockwell and L.B. Yeager (eds) *The Gold Standard: an Austrian perspective*, 35–59, Lexington, Mass.: D.C. Heath.

Ebenstein, A. (2001) *Friedrich Hayek: a biography*, New York: Palgrave.

Eichengreen, B. (1989) 'Hegemonic stability theories of the international monetary system', in R.N. Cooper (ed.) *Can Nations Agree?*, 255–98, Washington, DC: Brookings Institution.

—— (1990) *Elusive Stability: essays in the history of international finance 1919–1939*, New York: Cambridge University Press.

—— (1994) *International Monetary Arrangements for the 21st Century*, Washington, DC: Brookings Institution.

—— (1996) *Globalizing Capital: a history of the international monetary system*, Princeton, NJ: Princeton University Press.

—— (1999) *Toward a New International Financial Architecture: a practical post-Asia agenda*, Washington, DC: Institute for International Economics.

Ellis, H.S. (1946) 'Comments on the Mints and Hansen papers', *Review of Economics and Statistics*, 28: 74–7.

Emminger, O. (1971) 'The dollar and the international monetary system', in W. Schmitz (ed.) *Convertibility, Multilateralism and Freedom: world economic policy in the seventies, essays in honour of Reinhard Kamitz*, 241–51, Vienna: Springer-Verlag.

Endres, A.M. (2000) 'Rethinking the international monetary system' (review), *Journal of Economic Literature*, 38: 954–6.

Endres, A.M. and Fleming, G. (1999) 'The ILO and League of Nations: a distinctive perspective on macroeconomic stabilization policy in the 1920s', in L. Pasinetti and B. Schefold (eds) *The Impact of Keynes on Economics in the 20th Century*, 202–20, Cheltenham: Edward Elgar.

—— (2002a) *International Organizations and the Analysis of Economic Policy, 1919–1950*, New York: Cambridge University Press.

—— (2002b) 'The shaping of research agendas in international organisations: illustrations from the World Bank, IMF and OECD', University of Auckland, Department of Economics Working Paper Series No. 233, June: 41pp.

Faustean, D.K. (1979) 'The Humean origin of the contemporary monetary approach to the balance of payments', *Quarterly Journal of Economics*, 93: 655–73.

Fellner, W. (1945) 'The commercial policy implications of the Fund and Bank', *American Economic Review*, 35: 262–71.

—— (1966) 'On limited exchange rate flexibility', in W. Fellner (ed.) *Maintaining and Restoring the Balance of Payments*, 111–27, Princeton, NJ: Princeton University Press.

Fischer, S. (1999) 'Reforming the international financial system', *Economic Journal*, 109: F557–F576.

Fisher, I. (1935) *100% Money*, New York: Adelphi Company.

Flanders, M.J. (1989) *International Monetary Economics, 1870–1960: between classical and the new classical*, New York: Cambridge University Press.

Frenkel, J.A. and Johnson, H.G. (1976) 'Introductory essay', in J.A. Frenkel and H.G. Johnson (eds) *The Monetary Approach to the Balance of Payments*, 21–45, London: George Allen & Unwin.

Frenkel, J.A., Goldstein, M. and Masson, P.R. (1994) 'International coordination of economic policies', in J. Frenkel and M. Goldstein (eds) *Functioning of the International Monetary System*, 17–59, Washington, DC: International Monetary Fund.

Friedman, M. (1948) 'A monetary and fiscal framework for economic stability', reprinted in M. Friedman, *Essays in Positive Economics* (1953), 133–56, Chicago: Chicago University Press.

—— (1951) 'Commodity-reserve currency', *Journal of Political Economy*, 59: 203–32.

—— (1953) 'The case for flexible exchange rates', in M. Friedman, *Essays in Positive Economics*, 157–203, Chicago: Chicago University Press.
—— (1959) *A Program for Monetary Stability*, New York: Fordham University Press.
—— (1960) 'In defense of destabilizing speculation', in M. Friedman, *The Optimum Quantity of Money and Other Essays*, 285–91, Chicago: Aldine Publishing Company.
—— (1966) 'The free market determination of exchange rates', in L. Officer and D. Willett (eds) *The International Monetary System* (1969), 191–200, Englewood Cliffs, NY: Prentice-Hall.
—— (1967a) 'First lecture', in M. Friedman and D. Roosa, *The Balance of Payments: free versus fixed exchange rates*, 1–24, Washington, DC: American Enterprise Institute.
—— (1967b) 'The monetary theory of Henry Simons', reprinted in *The Optimum Quantity of Money and Other Essays* (1969), 81–93, Chicago: Aldine Publishing Company.
—— (1968a) *Dollars and Deficits*, Englewood Cliffs, NY: Prentice Hall.
—— (1968b) 'Gold and the dollar', reprinted in M. Friedman, *Dollars and Deficits*, 235–46, Englewood Cliffs, NY: Prentice Hall.
—— (1968c) 'The role of monetary policy', *American Economic Review*, 58: 1–17.
—— (1968d) 'The political economy of international monetary arrangements', reprinted in M. Friedman, *Dollars and Deficits*, 266–79, Englewood Cliffs, NY: Prentice Hall.
—— (1969a) 'Roundtable on monetary policy', *American Economic Review*, 59: 364–66.
—— (1969b) 'Panel', in M. Friedman, *The International Adjustment Mechanism*, 15–21, Boston, Mass.: Federal Reserve Bank of Boston.
Friedman, M. and Schwartz, A. (1963) 'Has government any role in money?', *Journal of Monetary Economics*, 17: 37–62.
Furth, J.H. (1961) 'Professor Triffin on the problem of international monetary reform', *Zeitschrift für Nationalökonomie*, 22: 415–25.
Gardner, R.N. (1969) *Sterling–Dollar Diplomacy*, 2nd edn, New York: Macmillan.
—— (1971) 'Dialogue on the issues', in R. Hinshaw (ed.) *The Economics of International Adjustment*, 27–9, Baltimore, Md.: Johns Hopkins Press.
—— (1980) *Sterling–Dollar Diplomacy*, 3rd edn, New York: Columbia University Press.
Gilbert, M. (1968) *The Gold–Dollar System: conditions of equilibrium and the price of gold*, Essays in International Finance No. 70, Princeton, NJ: International Finance Section, Princeton University.
Giovannini, A. (1993) 'Bretton Woods and its precursors: rules versus discretion in the history of international monetary regimes', in M. Bordo and B. Eichengreen (eds) *A Retrospective on the Bretton Woods System*, 109–47, Chicago: University of Chicago Press.
Gold, J. (1970) *Special Drawing Rights: character and use*, Washington, DC: IMF.
—— (1971a) *The Fund's Concepts of Convertibility*, Washington, DC: International Monetary Fund.
—— (1971b) *Special Drawing Rights: the role of language*, Washington, DC: IMF.
Goldenweiser, E.A. and Bourneuf, A. (1944) 'A review of the Bretton Woods Agreements', in M. Shields (ed.) *International Financial Stabilization*, 105–42, New York: Irving Trust Company.
Gordon, K. (1971) 'Foreword', in L.B. Krause (ed.) *Sequel to Bretton Woods*, vii–viii, Washington, DC: Brookings Institution.
Goudriaan, J. (1932) *How to Stop Deflation*, London: Search Publishing Company.

Graham, B. (1937) *Storage and Stability*, New York: McGraw-Hill.

Graham, F.D. (1930) *Exchange, Prices and Production in Hyperinflation: Germany 1920–1923*, Princeton, NJ: Princeton University Press.

—— (1936) 'Partial reserve money and the 100 per cent proposal', *American Economic Review*, 26: 428–40.

—— (1940a) 'Achilles' heels of monetary standards', *American Economic Review*, 30: 16–32.

—— (1940b) 'The primary functions of money and their consummation in monetary policy', *American Economic Review*, 30: 1–16.

—— (1941) 'Transition to a commodity reserve currency', *American Economic Review*, 31: 520–5.

—— (1942) *Social Goals and Economic Institutions*, Princeton, NJ: Princeton University Press.

—— (1943a) *Fundamentals of International Monetary Policy*, Essays in International Finance No. 3, Princeton, NJ: International Finance Section, Princeton University.

—— (1943b) 'Discussion', *American Economic Review*, 33: 334–5.

—— (1944) 'Keynes *vs.* Hayek on a commodity reserve currency', *Economic Journal*, 54: 422–9.

—— (1946) 'Full employment without public debt, without taxation, without public works, and without inflation', in A.P. Lerner and F. Graham (eds) *Planning and Paying for Full Employment*, 40–66, Princeton, NJ: Princeton University Press.

—— (1949) *The Cause and Cure of 'Dollar Shortage'*, Essays in International Finance No. 10, Princeton, NJ: International Finance Section, Princeton University.

—— (1971) 'Miscellany', letter to Randall Hinshaw, 7 March 1949, *Journal of International Economics*, 1: 249.

Grubel, H.G. (1963) 'Introduction: plans and issues', in H.G. Grubel (ed.) *World Monetary Reform. Plans and issues,* 1–11, Stanford, Calif.: Stanford University Press.

—— (1965) 'The case against an international commodity reserve currency', *Oxford Economic Papers*, 17: 130–5.

—— (1984) *The International Monetary System*, 3rd edn, Harmondsworth: Penguin Books.

Haberler, G. (1943) 'Discussion', *American Economic Review*, 33: 333–4.

—— (1944) 'Currency depreciation and the International Monetary Fund', *Review of Economics and Statistics*, 26: 178–81.

—— (1945) 'The choice of exchange rates after the war', *American Economic Review*, 35: 308–18.

—— (1976) '[Alvin H. Hansen:] Some reminiscences', *Quarterly Journal of Economics*, 90: 9–13.

Halm, G.N. (1944) 'The International Monetary Fund', *Review of Economic Statistics*, 26: 170–5.

—— (1945) *International Monetary Cooperation*, Chapel Hill: University of North Carolina Press.

Hansen, A.H. (1938) *Full Recovery or Stagnation?*, London: A. & C. Black.

—— (1943) 'The postwar economy', in S.E. Harris (ed.) *Postwar Economic Problems*, 9–26, New York: McGraw-Hill.

—— (1944a) 'A brief note on "fundamental disequilibrium"', *Review of Economics and Statistics*, 26: 182–4.

—— (1944b) 'World institutions for stability and expansion', *Foreign Affairs*, 22: 248–55.

—— (1944c) 'The views of Alvin H. Hansen', in M. Shields (ed.) *International Financial Stabilization*, 18–35, New York: Irving Trust Company.

—— (1945a) *America's Role in the World Economy*, New York: Norton.

—— (1945b) 'Stability and expansion', in P.T. Homan and F. Machlup (eds) *Financing American Prosperity*, New York: Twentieth Century Fund.

—— (1945c) 'Three methods of expansion through fiscal policy', *American Economic Review*, 35: 382–7.

—— (1945d) 'A note on fiscal policy: a clarification', *American Economic Review*, 35: 408–10.

—— (1945e) 'A new goal: full employment', *Review of Economics and Statistics*, 27: 102–3.

—— (1945f) 'The new crusade against planning', *New Republic*, 112: 9–12.

—— (1946) 'Notes on Mints's paper on monetary policy', *Review of Economics and Statistics*, 28: 69–74.

—— (1947) 'Keynes on economic policy', in S.E. Harris (ed.) *The New Economics*, 197–207, New York: A.A. Knopf.

—— (1949) *Monetary Theory and Fiscal Policy*, New York: McGraw-Hill.

—— (1953) *A Guide to Keynes*, New York: McGraw-Hill.

—— (1960) *Economic Issues of the 1960s*, New York: McGraw-Hill.

—— (1964a) *The Postwar American Economy. Performance and Problems*, New York: W.W. Norton.

—— (1964b) *Business Cycles and National Income*, expanded edition, London: George Allen & Unwin.

—— (1965) *The Dollar and the International Monetary System*, New York: McGraw-Hill.

—— (1971) 'Dialogue on the issues', in R. Hinshaw (ed.) *The Economics of International Adjustment*, 50–1, 60–1, Baltimore, Md.: Johns Hopkins Press.

Hansen, A.H. and Kindleberger, C.P. (1942) 'The economic tasks of the postwar world', *Foreign Affairs*, 20: 468–76.

Hansen, A.H. and Perloff, R. (1944) *State and Local Finance in the National Economy*, New York: W.W. Norton.

Harris, S.E. (1944) 'The contributions of Bretton Woods and some unsolved problems', *Review of Economic Statistics*, 26: 175–7.

Harrod, R.F. (1933) *International Economics*, London: Nisbet and Company.

—— (1939) 'International monetary economics [review]', *International Affairs*, 4: 834.

—— (1947) 'A comment', *Review of Economics and Statistics*, 14: 95–7.

—— (1953a) *The Dollar*, London: Macmillan.

—— (1953b) 'Imbalance of international payments', reprinted in R.F. Harrod, *Topical Comment: essays in dynamic economics* (1961), 16–56, London: Macmillan.

—— (1958a) *Policy Against Inflation*, London: Macmillan.

—— (1958b) 'Why the dollar price of gold must rise', *Optima*, 8: 120–30.

—— (1961a) 'The convertibility of sterling', reprinted in R.F. Harrod, *Topical Comment: essays in dynamic economics*, 61–85, London: Macmillan.

—— (1961b) 'Postscript on gold', reprinted in R.F. Harrod, *Topical Comment: essays in dynamic economics*, 56–60, London: Macmillan.

—— (1961c) *Topical Comment: essays in dynamic economics*, London: Macmillan.

—— (1963) 'Liquidity', in H. Grubel (ed.) *World Monetary Reform*, 203–26, Stanford, Calif.: Stanford University Press.

—— (1964a) 'Statement by Sir Roy Harrod', in F. Machlup and B. Malkiel (eds) *International Monetary Arrangements: the problem of choice*, 113–16, Princeton, NJ: International Finance Section, Princeton University.

—— (1964b) 'New thinking on international liquidity', *Optima*, 14: 176–82.

—— (1965) *Reforming the World's Money*, London: Macmillan.

—— (1966) 'The speed of adjustment', in W. Fellner (ed.) *Maintaining and Restoring Balance in International Payments*, 137–43, Princeton, NJ: Princeton University Press.

—— (1967) *Towards a New Economic Policy*, Manchester: Manchester University Press.

—— (1971) 'Dialogue on the issues', in R. Hinshaw (ed.) *The Economics of International Adjustment*, 37–9, 93–4, Baltimore, Md.: Johns Hopkins Press.

—— (1972) 'Problems perceived in the international financial system', in A.L.K. Acheson, J.F. Chant and M.F.J. Prachowny (eds) *Bretton Woods Revisited*, 5–19, London: Macmillan.

Hart, A.G. (1966) 'The case for and against an international commodity reserve currency', *Oxford Economic Papers*, 18: 237–41.

Hartmann, P. (1999) *Currency Competition and Foreign Exchange Markets*, Cambridge: Cambridge University Press.

Hawtrey, R.G. (1946) 'Postwar monetary plans and other essays [review], *Review of Economics and Statistics*, 28: 40–1.

Hayek, F.A. (1937) *Monetary Nationalism and International Stability*, London: Longmans, Green and Co., reprinted in S. Kresge (ed.) *The Collected Works of F.A. Hayek*, Vol. IV (1999), 37–100, Chicago: University of Chicago Press.

—— (1943) 'A commodity reserve currency', *Economic Journal*, 53: 176–84.

—— (1944) *The Road to Serfdom*, Chicago: University of Chicago Press.

—— (1945) 'Social goals and economic institutions [review]', *Journal of Political Economy*, 53: 177–9.

—— (1967) 'Theory of complex phenomenon', in F.A. Hayek, *Studies in Philosophy, Politics and Economics*, 22–42, Chicago: University of Chicago Press.

—— (1969) 'Addendum: tribute to Röpke', in P.G. Klein (ed.) *The Collected Works of F.A. Hayek*, Vol. IV (1992), 195–7, Chicago: University of Chicago Press.

—— (1974) 'The pretence of knowledge', Nobel Memorial Lecture, 11 December, reprinted in *American Economic Review*, 79: 3–7.

—— (1976a) *Denationalisation of Money*, London: Institute of Economic Affairs.

—— (1976b) *Choice in Currency*, London: Institute of Economic Affairs.

—— (1979) 'Toward a free market monetary system', reprinted in S. Kresge (ed.) *The Collected Works of F.A. Hayek*, Vol. VI (1999), 230–7, Chicago: University of Chicago Press.

Heilperin, M. (1939) *International Monetary Economics*, London: Longmans, Green.

—— (1945) *International Monetary Reconstructions: the Bretton Woods Agreements*, New York: American Enterprise Association.

—— (1952) 'The international aspects of inflation', reprinted in M. Heilperin, *Aspects of the Pathology of Money* (1968), 163–78, Geneva: M. Joseph for the Graduate Institute of International Studies.

—— (1955) 'Fixed parties and international order', reprinted in M. Heilperin, *Aspects of the Pathology of Money* (1968), 222–30, Geneva: M. Joseph for the Graduate Institute of International Studies.

—— (1961) 'Plans reforming the I.M.F.: some basic criticisms', reprinted in M. Heilperin, *Aspects of the Pathology of Money* (1968), 259–68, Geneva: M. Joseph for the Graduate Institute of International Studies.

—— (1962) 'The case for going back to gold', *Fortune*, 108–10, 146–54, reprinted in M. Heilperin, *Aspects of the Pathology of Money* (1968), 269–80, Geneva: M. Joseph for the Graduate Institute of International Studies.

—— (1964) 'The present monetary crisis of the West: the first phase', reprinted in M. Heilperin, *Aspects of the Pathology of Money* (1968), 281–95, Geneva: M. Joseph for the Graduate Institute of International Studies.

—— (1971) 'Other choices', in R. Hinshaw (ed.) *The Economics of International Adjustment*, 118–19, Baltimore, Md.: Johns Hopkins Press.

Helleiner, E. (1999) 'Economic liberalism and the "national question" in currency affairs', in E. Gilbert and E. Helleiner (eds) *Nation-States and Money: past, present and future of national currencies*, 139–58, London: Routledge.

—— (2001) 'The southern side of embedded liberalism: the politics of postwar monetary policy', International Political Economy Centre, Working Paper, 01/05, 26pp.

Herbener, J.M. (2002) 'Ludwig von Mises on the gold standard', *Quarterly Journal of Austrian Economics*, 5: 67–91.

Hinshaw, R. (1978) 'Sir Roy Harrod', *Journal of International Economics*, 8: 363–72.

Hirsch, F. (1964) 'Statement by Fred Hirsch', in F. Machlup and B. Malkiel (eds) *International Monetary Arrangement: the problem of choice*, 116–18, Princeton, NJ: International Finance Section, Princeton University.

Horsefield, J.K. (ed.) (1969a) *The International Monetary Fund 1945–1965*, Vol. I: *Chronicle*, Washington, DC: IMF.

—— (ed.) (1969b) *The International Monetary Fund 1945–1965*, Vol. II: *Analysis*, Washington, DC: IMF.

—— (ed.) (1969c) *The International Monetary Fund 1945–1965*, Vol. III: *Documents*, Washington, DC: IMF.

Humphrey, D.D. (1973) 'The case for gold', in C.F. Bergsten and W.G. Tyler (eds) *Leading Issues in International Economic Policy*, 81–98, Lexington, Mass.: D.C. Heath.

IMF (1999) *A Guide to Progress in Strengthening the Architecture of the International Financial System*, (http://www.imf.org/external/np/exr/facts/arch.htm).

Irwin, R.D. (1996) *Against the Tide: an intellectual history of free trade*, Princeton, NJ: Princeton University Press.

Isard, P. (1995) *Exchange Rate Economics*, Cambridge: Cambridge University Press.

James, H. (1996) *International Monetary Cooperation Since Bretton Woods*, New York: Oxford University Press.

Johnson, H.G. (1962) 'International liquidity – problems and plans', reprinted in H. Grubel (ed.) *World Monetary Reform* (1963), 367–91, Stanford, Calif.: Stanford University Press.

—— (1963) 'Objectives, monetary standards, and potentialities', *Review of Economics and Statistics*, 45: 137–44.

—— (1966) 'International monetary reform and the less developed countries', reprinted in H.G. Johnson, *Essays in Monetary Economics* (1967), 293–320, London: George Allen & Unwin.

—— (1967) 'Theoretical problems of the international monetary system', *Pakistan Development Review*, 7: 1–28.

—— (1969a) 'The case for flexible exchange rates', reprinted in H.G. Johnson, *Further Essays in Monetary Economics* (1972), 198–222, London: George Allen & Unwin.

—— (1969b) 'The international monetary crisis, 1969', reprinted in H.G. Johnson, *Further Essays in Monetary Economics* (1972), 295–352, London: George Allen & Unwin.

—— (1969c) 'The gold rush of 1968 in retrospect and prospect', *American Economic Review*, 59: 344–8.

—— (1969d) 'Statement of Harry G. Johnson' (to Joint Economic Committee, Subcommittee on International Exchange and Payments, 91st Congress, 1st Session), reprinted in G. Meier, *Problems of a World Monetary Order*, 227–30, New York: Oxford University Press.

—— (1970) 'Roy Harrod on the price of gold', in W. Eltis, M. Scott and J. Wolfe (eds) *Induction, Growth and Trade*, 266–93, Oxford: Clarendon Press.
—— (1972a) 'The Bretton Woods system, key currencies, and the "dollar crisis" of 1971', *Three Banks Review*, 94: 3–23.
—— (1972b) 'A general commentary', in A.L.K. Acheson, J.F. Chant and M.F.J. Prachowny (eds) *Bretton Woods Revisited*, 129–38, London: Macmillan.
—— (1972c) 'Political economy aspects of international monetary reform', *Journal of International Economics*, 2: 401–23.
Jones, B.L. (1972) 'The role of Keynesians in wartime policy and postwar planning 1940–46', *American Economic Review*, 62: 125–30.
Kahn, A.H. (1976) 'Discussion', in A.P. Thirlwall (ed.) *Keynes and International Monetary Relations*, 60–1, London: Macmillan.
Kahn, R. (1973) 'The international monetary system', *American Economic Review*, 63: 181–8.
Kaldor, N. (1964) 'The problem of international liquidity', in N. Kaldor, *Further Essays in Applied Economics* (1978), 28–46, London: Duckworth.
—— (1973) 'International monetary reform: the need for a new approach', reprinted in N. Kaldor, *Further Essays in Applied Economics* (1978), 90–8, London: Duckworth.
Kaldor, N., Hart, A.G. and Tinbergen, J. (1964) 'The case for international commodity reserve currency', reprinted in N. Kaldor, *Further Essays in Applied Economics* (1978), 131–71, London: Duckworth.
Kawai, M. (1987) 'Optimum currency areas', in J. Chipman, J. Eatwell and M. Milgate (eds) *The New Palgrave: a dictionary of economics*, 740–3, London: Macmillan.
Kenen, P.B. (1969) 'The theory of optimum currency areas: an eclectic view', in R. Mundell and K. Swoboda (eds) *Monetary Problems of the International Economy*, 41–60, Chicago: University of Chicago Press.
—— (1973) 'Convertibility and consolidation: a survey of options for reform', *American Economic Review*, 63: 189–98.
Kenen, P.B., Papadia, F. and Saccomanni, F. (1994) 'Introduction', in P.B. Kenen, F. Papadia and F. Saccomanni (eds) *The International Monetary System*, 1–15, Cambridge: Cambridge University Press.
Kervyn, A. (1987) 'Triffin, Robert', in J. Eatwell, M. Milgate and J. Chipman (eds) *The New Palgrave: a dictionary of economics*, Vol. IV, 701–2, London: Macmillan.
Keynes, J.M. (1933) 'Preface', in R. Harrod, *International Economics*, 1st edition, iv–v, London: Nisbett & Company.
—— (1936) *General Theory of Employment, Interest and Money*, London: Macmillan.
—— (1938) 'The policy of government storage of food-stuffs and raw materials', *Economic Journal*, 48: 449–60.
—— (1943a) 'Proposals for an international clearing union', in J.K. Horsefield (ed.) (1969) *The International Monetary Fund 1945–1965*, Vol. III: *Documents*, 19–36, Washington, DC: IMF.
—— (1943b) 'The objective of international price stability', *Economic Journal*, 53: 185–7.
—— (1944) 'Note by Lord Keynes', *Economic Journal*, 54: 429–30.
—— (1946) 'The balance of payments of the United States', *Economic Journal*, 56: 172–87.
Kindleberger, C. (1967) *The Politics of International Money and World Language*, Essays in International Finance No. 61, Princeton, NJ: International Finance Section, Princeton University.
—— (1969) 'The eurodollar and the internationalization of United States'

monetary policy', reprinted in C. Kindleberger, *International Money* (1981), 100–10, London: George Allen & Unwin.

—— (1972) 'The benefits of international money', *Journal of International Economics*, 2: 425–42.

—— (1975) 'The SDR as international money', reprinted in C. Kindleberger, *International Money* (1981), 63–75, London: George Allen & Unwin.

—— (1983) 'Key currencies and financial centres', in F. Machlup, G. Fels and H. Müller-Groeling (eds) *Reflections on a Troubled World Economy*, 75–90, New York: St Martin's Press.

—— (1989) *Economic Laws and Economic History*, New York: Cambridge University Press.

Kirshner, J. (2003) 'The inescapable politics of money', in J. Kirshner (ed.) *Monetary Orders. Ambiguous Economics, Ubiquitous Politics*, 3–24, Ithaca, NY: Cornell University Press.

Kirzner, I. (2001) *Ludwig von Mises: the man and his economics*, Wilmington, Del.: ISI Books.

Krause, L.B. (1971) *Sequel to Bretton Woods*, Washington, DC: Brookings Institution.

Kresge, S. (1999) 'Introduction', in *The Collected Works of F.A. Hayek*, Vol. VI, 1–36, Chicago: University of Chicago Press.

Krueger, A.O. (1998) 'Whither the IMF and the World Bank?', *Journal of Economic Literature*, 36: 1983–2020.

Lachmann, L.M. (1944) 'Notes on the proposals for international currency stabilization', *Review of Economics and Statistics*, 26: 184–91.

Laidler, D. (1999) 'The Chicago monetarist tradition', *Journal of Economic Perspectives*, 13: 240–1.

Lutz, F.A. (1943) *International Monetary Mechanisms: the Keynes and White Proposals*, Princeton, NJ: International Finance Section, Princeton University.

—— (1954) 'The case for flexible exchange rates', *Banca Nazionale del Lavoro Quarterly Review*, 7: 175–85.

McCulloch, J.H. (1986) 'Beyond the historical standard', in C.D. Campbell and W.R. Dougan (eds) *Alternative Monetary Regimes*, 73–81, Baltimore, Md.: Johns Hopkins University Press.

MacDougall, D. (1960) *The Dollar Problem: a reappraisal*, Essays in International Finance No. 35, Princeton, NJ: International Finance Section, Princeton University.

Machlup, F. (1945) 'Summary and analysis', in P.T. Homan and F. Machlup (eds) *Financing American Prosperity*, 394–496, New York: Twentieth Century Fund.

—— (1962) *Plans For the Reform of the International Monetary System*, Special Paper in International Economics No. 3, Princeton, NJ: International Finance Section Princeton University.

—— (1963) *Essays on Economic Semantics*, Englewood Cliffs, NY: Prentice Hall.

—— (1966a) *International Monetary Economics*, London: Allen and Unwin.

—— (1966b) *International Monetary Systems and the Free Market Economy*, Reprints in International Finance No. 3, Princeton, NJ: International Finance Section: Princeton University.

—— (1978) *Methodology of Economics and Other Social Sciences*, New York: Academic Press.

Machlup, F. and Malkiel, B.G. (1964) *International Monetary Arrangements: the problem of choice*, Princeton, NJ: International Finance Section, Princeton University.

McKinnon, R.I. (1963) 'Optimum currency areas', *American Economic Review*, 53: 717–25.

—— (1996) *The Rules of the Game: international money and exchange rates*, Cambridge, Mass.: MIT Press.

Meade, J.E. (1955) 'The case for variable exchange rates', *Three Banks Review*, 27: 3–27.

—— (1964) 'The international monetary mechanism', *Three Banks Review*, 63: 3–25.

Meier, G.M. (1974) *Problem of World Monetary Order*, New York: Oxford University Press.

Meltzer, A.H. (1989) 'Keynes on monetary reform and the international economic order', in F. Capie and G. Wood (eds) *Monetary Economics in the 1980s*, 101–39, London: Macmillan.

Mikesell, R.F. (1945) 'The key currency proposal', *Quarterly Journal of Economics*, 59: 563–76.

—— (1947) 'The role of the international monetary agreements in a world of planned economies', *Journal of Political Economy*, 55: 497–512.

—— (1949) 'The International Monetary Fund', *Journal of Political Economy*, 57: 395–412.

—— (1994) *The Bretton Woods Debates: a memoir*, Princeton Essays in International Finance No. 192, Princeton, NJ: International Finance Section, Princeton University.

Miller, H.L. (1962) 'On the "Chicago School of Economics"', *Journal of Political Economy*, 70: 64–9.

Mints, L.W. (1950) *Monetary Policy for a Competitive Society*, New York: McGraw-Hill.

Mises, L. von (1923) 'The return to gold', reprinted in L. von Mises, *On the Manipulation of Money and Credit* (1978), 22–56, New York: Free Market Books.

—— (1928) 'Monetary stabilization cyclical policy', reprinted in L. von Mises, *On the Manipulation of Money and Credit* (1978), 57–171, New York: Free Market Books.

—— (1934) *The Theory of Money and Credit*, reprinted 1981, Indianapolis: Liberty Classics.

—— (1946) 'The trade cycle and credit expansion: the economic consequences of cheap money', reprinted in L. von Mises, *On the Manipulation of Money and Credit* (1978), 215–26, New York: Free Market Books.

—— (1949) *Human Action: a treatise on economics*, London: William Hodge.

—— (1953) 'Monetary reconstruction', in L. von Mises, *The Theory of Money and Credit*, New Haven, Conn.: Yale University Press, reprinted 1981, 453–501, Indianapolis: Liberty Classics.

Moggridge, D.E. (1986) 'Keynes and the international monetary system 1909–46', in J.S. Cohen and G.C. Harcourt (eds) *International Monetary Problems and Supply-Side Economics*, 56–83, New York: St Martin's Press.

Mundell, R. (1960) 'The monetary dynamics of international adjustment under fixed exchange rates', *Quarterly Journal of Economics*, 74: 227–57.

—— (1961) 'A theory of optimum currency areas', *American Economic Review*, 51: 657–65.

—— (1962) 'The appropriate use of monetary and fiscal policy under fixed exchange rates', *IMF Staff Papers*, 70–9; reprinted in R. Mundell, *International Economics* (1968), New York: Collier-Macmillan.

—— (1964) 'Capital mobility and size', *Canadian Journal of Economics and Political Science*, 30: 421–31.

—— (1965) 'The proper division of the burden of international adjustment', *National Banking Review*, 3: 81–7.

—— (1967) 'Robert A. Mundell' (discussion), in R. Hinshaw (ed.) *Monetary Reform and the Price of Gold*, 129–33, Baltimore, Md.: Johns Hopkins Press.

—— (1969a) 'The crisis problem', in R.A. Mundell and A.K. Swoboda (eds)

Monetary Problems of the International Economy, 343–9, Chicago: University of Chicago Press.

—— (1969b) 'Problems of the international monetary system', in R.A. Mundell and A.K. Swoboda (eds) *Monetary Problems of the International Economy*, 21–38, Chicago: University of Chicago Press.

—— (1969c) 'Real gold, dollars and paper gold', *American Economic Review*, 59: 324–31.

—— (1969d) 'The International Monetary Fund', *Journal of World Trade Law*, 3: 455–97.

—— (1969e) 'Toward a better international monetary system', *Journal of Money, Credit and Banking*, 1: 625–48.

—— (1971a) 'Mundell' (discussion), in R. Hinshaw (ed.) *The Economics of International Adjustment*, 91–3, 108–10, 141–2, Baltimore, Md.: Johns Hopkins Press.

—— (1971b) *The Dollar and the Policy Mix: 1971*, Essays in International Finance No. 85, Princeton, NJ: International Finance Section, Princeton University.

—— (1972) 'The future of the international financial system', in A.L.K. Acheson, J.F. Chant and M.F.J. Prachowny (eds) *Bretton Woods Revisited*, 91–104, London: Macmillan.

—— (1973a) 'Uncommon arguments for common currencies', in H. Johnson and A.K. Swoboda (eds) *The Economics of Common Currencies*, 114–32, London: George Allen & Unwin.

—— (1973b) 'A plan for a European currency', in H. Johnson and A.K. Swoboda (eds) *The Economics of Common Currencies*, 143–72, London: George Allen & Unwin.

—— (1973c) 'The monetary consequences of Jacques Rueff: review article', *Journal of Business*, 46: 384–95.

—— (1977) 'Concluding remarks', in R.A. Mundell and J.J. Polak (eds) *The New International Monetary System*, 237–44, New York: Columbia University Press.

—— (1997) 'Optimum currency areas', online, available: http://www.columbia.edu/~ramIS/eOCATAviv4.html (accessed 7 May 2003).

Musgrave, R.A. (1987) 'Hansen, Alvin', in J. Eatwell, M. Milgate and J.S. Chipman (eds) *The New Palgrave: a dictionary of economics*, Vol. II, 591–2, London: Macmillan.

Nurkse, R. (1944) *International Currency Experience*, Geneva: League of Nations.

Obstfeld, M. (1995) 'International currency experience: new lessons learned on relearned', *Brookings Papers on Economic Activity*, 1: 119–220.

Officer, L. and Willett, D. (1969) 'Conclusion: a further look at the alternatives', in L. Officer and T. Willet (eds) *The International Monetary System*, 216–31, Englewood Cliffs, NY: Prentice-Hall.

Oppenheimer, P.M. (1969) 'The case for raising the price of gold', *Journal of Money, Credit and Banking*, 1: 649–65.

Palma, J.G. (1987) 'Prébisch, Raul', in J. Eatwell, M. Milgate and J. Chipman (eds) *The New Palgrave: a dictionary of economics*, Vol. III, 934–6, London: Macmillan.

Patinkin, D. (1969) 'The Chicago tradition, the quantity theory, and Friedman', *Journal of Money, Credit and Banking*, 1: 46–70.

Persson, T. (2001) 'Nobel Prize background survey', in G.A. Calvo, R. Dornbusch and M. Obstfeld (eds) *Money, Capital Mobility and Trade: essays in honor of Robert A. Mundell*, xi–xxii, Cambridge, Mass.: MIT Press.

Phelps Brown, H. (1980) 'Sir Roy Harrod: a biographical memoir', *Economic Journal*, 90: 1–33.

Polak, J. (1971) *Some Reflections on the Nature of Special Drawing Rights*, Washington, DC: IMF.

Poole, K.E. (1947) 'National economic policies and international monetary cooperation', *American Economic Review*, 37: 369–75.
Prébisch, R. (1969) 'Statement of Raul Prébisch' (to Joint Economic Committee, Subcommittee on International Exchange and Payments, 91st Congress, 1st Session), reprinted in G. Meier, *Problems of a World Monetary Order*, 230–3, New York: Oxford University Press.
Reder, M.W. (1982) 'Chicago economics: permanence and change', *Journal of Economic Literature*, 20: 1–38.
Rist, C. (1950) 'Gold, international currency', reprinted in C. Rist, *The Triumph of Gold* (1961), 90–101, New York: Philosophical Library.
—— (1952a) 'Progress in monetary conceptions', reprinted in C. Rist, *The Triumph of Gold* (1961), 183–7, New York: Philosophical Library.
—— (1952b) 'The failure of the International Monetary Fund', reprinted in C. Rist, *The Triumph of Gold* (1961), 188–93, New York: Philosophical Library.
—— (1954) 'Forecasts on the convertibility of currencies', reprinted in C. Rist, *The Triumph of Gold* (1961), 220–6, New York: Philosophical Library.
—— (1961) *The Triumph of Gold*, New York: Philosophical Library.
Robbins, L. (1951) *The Balance of Payments*, University of London: Athlone Press.
Robertson, D. (1943) 'The post-war monetary plans', *Economic Journal*, 53: 352–60.
Robinson, J. (1943) 'International currency proposals', *Economic Journal*, 53: 161–75.
Roosa, R.V. (1978) 'Foreword', in R. Triffin, *Gold and the Dollar Crisis Yesterday and Tomorrow*, Essays in International Finance No. 132, Princeton, NJ: International Finance Section, Princeton University.
Röpke, W. (1942a) *International Economic Disintegration*, London: William Hodge.
—— (1942b) *The Social Crisis of Our Time*, London: William Hodge.
—— (1952) *The Economics of Full Employment*, New York: Putnam.
—— (1960) *International Order and Economic Integration*, 2nd edition, Dordrecht: D. Reidel Publishing Company.
—— (1961) 'World without a world monetary system', reprinted in W. Röpke, *Against the Tide* (1969), 221–34, Chicago: Henry Regnery.
—— (1963) *Economics of the Free Society*, Chicago: Henry Regnery.
Rosenof, T. (1997) *Economics in the Long Run. New Deal theorists and their legacies*, Chapel Hill: University of North Carolina Press.
Rueff, J. (1961a) 'Gold exchange standard a danger to the West', reprinted in H. Grubel (ed.) *World Monetary Reform* (1963), 320–8, Stanford, Calif: Stanford University Press.
—— (1961b) 'The West is risking a credit collapse', *Fortune*, 126–7, 262–8.
—— (1961c) 'The money problem of the West', reprinted in J. Rueff, *The Age of Inflation* (1962), 113–28, Chicago: Henry Regenry.
—— (1966) 'Triffin and I', reprinted in J. Rueff, *The Monetary Sin of the West* (1972), 106–14, New York: Macmillan.
—— (1967a) 'Increase the price of gold', reprinted in L. Officer and T. Willett (eds) *The International Monetary System* (1969), 179–85, Englewood Cliffs, NY: Prentice Hall.
—— (1967b) *Balance of Payments*, New York: Macmillan.
—— (1969) 'What is to be, will be', reprinted in J. Rueff, *The Monetary Sin of the West* (1972), 158–78, New York: Macmillan.
—— (1970) 'Precarious dominance of the dollar', reprinted in J. Rueff, *The Monetary Sin of the West* (1972), 179–98, New York: Macmillan.
Rueff, J. and Hirsch, F. (1965) *The Role of Rule of Gold: an argument*, Essays in International Finance No. 47, Princeton, NJ: International Finance Section, Princeton University.

Ruggie, J. (1983) 'International regimes, transactions and change', *International Organization*, 36: 379–405.

Salant, W. (1956) 'Comment', in W. Salant (ed.) *Policies to Combat Depression*, 404–11, Princeton, NJ: Princeton University Press.

—— (1976) 'Alvin Hansen and the fiscal policy seminar', *Quarterly Journal of Economics*, 90: 14–31.

Salerno, J.T. (1985) 'Gold and the international monetary system: the contribution of Michael A. Heilperin', in L.H. Rockwell and L.B. Yeager (eds) *The Gold Standard: an Austrian perspective*, 81–112, Lexington, Mass.: D.C. Heath.

Sally, R. (1998) *Classical Liberalism and International Economic Order*, London: Routledge.

Samuelson, P.A. (1976a) 'Alvin Hansen as a creative economic theorist', *Quarterly Journal of Economics*, 90: 24–31.

—— (1976b) 'In memoriam. Alvin H. Hansen', *American Economic Review*, 66: 986–7.

Scammell, W.M. (1975) *International Monetary Policy, Bretton Woods and After*, London: Macmillan.

—— (1987) *The Stability of the International Monetary System*, London: Macmillan.

Schumpeter, J.A. (1954) *History of Economic Analysis*, London: Allen & Unwin.

Schwartz, A. (1986) 'Alternative monetary regimes: the gold standard', in C.D. Campbell and W.R. Dougan (eds) *Alternative Monetary Regimes*, 44–72, Baltimore, Md.: Johns Hopkins University Press.

Selgin, G. (1999) 'Ludwig von Mises and the case for gold', *Cato Journal*, 19: 259–77.

Selgin, G. and White, L. (1994) 'How would the invisible hand handle money?', *Journal of Economic Literature*, 32: 1718–49.

Simons, H.C. (1934) 'A positive program for laissez-faire', reprinted in H.C. Simons, *Economic Policy for a Free Society* (1948), 40–77, Chicago: University of Chicago Press.

—— (1936) 'Rules versus authorities in monetary policy', *Journal of Political Economy*, 54: 1–30.

—— (1942) 'Hansen on fiscal policy', reprinted in H.C. Simons, *Economic Policy for a Free Society* (1948), 184–219, Chicago: University of Chicago Press.

—— (1943) 'Postwar economic policy: some traditional liberal proposals', reprinted in H.C. Simons, *Economic Policy for a Free Society* (1948), 240–59, Chicago: University of Chicago Press.

—— (1944a) 'Money, tariffs and peace', reprinted in H.C. Simons, *Economic Policy for a Free Society* (1948), 260–76, Chicago: University of Chicago Press.

—— (1944b) 'Economic stability and antitrust policy', reprinted in H.C. Simons, *Economic Policy for a Free Society* (1948), 107–20, Chicago: University of Chicago Press.

—— (1944c) 'The U.S. holds the cards', *Fortune*, September: 157–9, 196, 199–200.

—— (1945a) 'Introduction: a political credo', reprinted in H.C. Simons, *Economic Policy for a Free Society* (1948), 1–39, Chicago: University of Chicago Press.

—— (1945b) 'Discussion', *American Economic Review*, 35: 294–6.

Solomon, R.S. (1977) *The International Monetary System 1945–76: an insider's view*, New York: Harper and Row.

—— (1999) *Money on the Move: the revolution in international finance since 1980*, Princeton, NJ: Princeton University Press.

Spitzer, E.G. (1969) 'Factors in stabilization programs', in J.K. Horsefield (ed.) *The International Monetary Fund 1945–1965*, Vol. III: *Analysis*, 494–510, Washington, DC: International Monetary Fund.

Stein, H. (1969) *The Fiscal Revolution in America*, Chicago: University of Chicago Press.

—— (1987) 'Simons, Henry Calvert', in J. Eatwell, M. Milgate and J. Chipman (eds) *The New Palgrave: a dictionary of economics*, Vol. IV, 333–5, London: Macmillan.

Stigler, G. (1962) 'Comment', *Journal of Political Economy*, 70: 70–1.

Tavlas, G.S. (1991) *On the International Use of Currencies: the case of the Deutsche mark*, Essays in International Finance No. 181, Princeton, NJ: International Finance Section, Princeton University.

—— (1997) 'Chicago, Harvard, and the doctrinal foundations of monetary economics', *Journal of Political Economy*, 105: 153–77.

Tew, B. (1988) *The Evolution of the International Monetary System: 1945–88*, London: Hutchinson.

Tobin, J. (1976) 'Hansen on public policy', *Quarterly Journal of Economics*, 90: 32–7.

Tower, E. and Willett, T.D. (1976) *The Theory of Optimum Currency Areas and Exchange-Rate Flexibility*, Special Papers in International Economics No. 11, Princeton, NJ: International Finance Section, Princeton University.

Triffin, R. (1947a) 'National central banking and the international economy', in L. Metzler, R. Triffin and G. Harberler, *International Monetary Policies*, 46–81, Washington, DC: Board of Governors, Federal Reserve System.

—— (1947b) 'International versus domestic money', reprinted in R. Triffin, *The World Money Maze* (1966), 177–9, New Haven, Conn.: Yale University Press.

—— (1949) 'Suggested adaptation in Fund policy', reprinted in R. Triffin, *The World Money Maze* (1966), 182–90, New Haven, Conn.: Yale University Press.

—— (1954) 'The exhumation of convertibility *à la* key currencies and the oncoming dollar glut 1953–60', reprinted in R. Triffin, *The World Money Maze* (1966), 201–29, New Haven, Conn.: Yale University Press.

—— (1956) 'International currency and reserve plans', in W. Salant (ed.) *Policies to Combat Depression*, 377–404, Princeton, NJ: Princeton University Press.

—— (1957) *Europe and the Money Muddle*, New Haven, Conn.: Yale University Press.

—— (1960) *Gold and the Dollar Crisis*, New Haven, Conn.: Yale University Press.

—— (1961a) 'After the gold exchange standard', reprinted in H. Grubel (ed.) *World Monetary Reform* (1963), 421–39, Stanford, Calif.: Stanford University Press.

—— (1961b) 'Briefing the man in the street', reprinted in R. Triffin, *The World Money Maze* (1966), 240–8, New Haven, Conn.: Yale University Press.

—— (1963) 'The alternation of dollar and sterling crises: 1960–65', reprinted in R. Triffin, *The World Money Maze* (1966), 102–32, New Haven, Conn.: Yale University Press.

—— (1964a) *The Evolution of the International Monetary System: historical reappraisal and future perspectives*, Princeton Studies in International Finance No. 12, Princeton, NJ: International Finance Section, Princeton University.

—— (1964b) 'Groping for a consensus', reprinted in R. Triffin, *The World Money Maze* (1966), 39–45, New Haven, Conn.: Yale University Press.

—— (1965a) 'General De Gaulle's monetary "forces de frappe" and the sterling crisis', reprinted in R. Triffin, *The World Money Maze* (1966), 340–5, New Haven, Conn.: Yale University Press.

—— (1965b) 'Updating the Triffin plan', reprinted in R. Triffin, *The World Money Maze* (1966), 346–73, New Haven, Conn.: Yale University Press.

—— (1966a) *The World Money Maze*, New Haven, Conn.: Yale University Press.

—— (1966b) 'The balance-of-payments seesaw', in W. Fellner (ed.) *Maintaining and Restoring Balance in International Payments*, 85–108, Princeton, NJ: Princeton University Press.

—— (1969a) 'Discussion', in R. Triffin, *The International Adjustment Mechanism*, 53–63, Boston, Mass.: Federal Reserve Bank of Boston.

—— (1969b) 'The thrust of history in international monetary reform', *Foreign Affairs*, 3: 477–92.

—— (1969c) 'Neither gold nor the dollar', in L. Officer and D. Willett (eds) *The International Monetary System*, 3–11, Englewood Cliffs, NY: Prentice-Hall.

—— (1971) 'Issues and options', in R. Hinshaw (ed.) *The Economics of International Adjustment*, 18–21, Baltimore, Md.: Johns Hopkins Press.

—— (1972) 'International monetary collapse and reconstruction April 1972', *Journal of International Economics*, 2: 375–400.

—— (1978) *Gold and the Dollar Crisis Yesterday and Tomorrow*, Essays in International Finance No. 132, Princeton, NJ: International Finance Section, Princeton University.

United States Department of State (1948) *Proceedings and Documents of the United Nations' Monetary and Financial Conference*, Washington, DC: Department of State.

Viner, J. (1943) 'Two plans for international monetary stabilization', reprinted in *International Economics* (1951), 192–215, Glencoe, NY: Free Press.

—— (1944) 'The Bretton Woods Agreements', reprinted in *International Economics* (1951), 232–46, Glencoe, NY: Free Press.

—— (1946) 'International finance in the postwar world', reprinted in *International Economics* (1951), 323–36, Glencoe, NY: Free Press.

—— (1947a) 'International economic cooperation', reprinted in *International Economics* (1951), 282–99, Glencoe, NY: Free Press.

—— (1947b) 'America's lending policy', reprinted in *International Economics* (1951), 337–44, Glencoe, NY: Free Press.

—— (1950) 'Economic foundations of international organization', reprinted in *International Economics* (1951), 367–81, Glencoe, NY: Free Press.

Vines, D. (2003) 'John Maynard Keynes 1937–1946: the creation of international macroeconomics', *Economic Journal*, 113: F338–F361.

Whittlesey, C.R. (1952) 'Frank Dunstone Graham 1890–1949', *Economic Journal*, 62: 440–5.

Williams, J.H. (1932a) 'The crisis of the gold standard', reprinted in J.H. Williams, *Postwar Monetary Plans and Other Essays* (1949), 271–85, Oxford: Blackwell.

—— (1932b) 'Monetary stability and the gold standard', reprinted in J.H. Williams, *Postwar Monetary Plans and Other Essays* (1949), 286–99, Oxford: Blackwell.

—— (1936) 'International monetary organization and policy', reprinted in J.H. Williams, *Postwar Monetary Plans and Other Essays* (1949), 306–30, Oxford: Blackwell.

—— (1937) 'The adequacy of existing currency mechanisms under varying circumstances', *American Economic Review*, 27: 151–68.

—— (1941) 'Deficit spending', reprinted in J.H. Williams, *Postwar Monetary Plans and Other Essays* (1949), 216–35, Oxford: Blackwell.

—— (1942) 'The implications of fiscal policy for monetary policy and the banking system', reprinted in J.H. Williams, *Postwar Monetary Plans and Other Essays* (1949), 235–54, Oxford: Blackwell.

—— (1943) 'Currency stabilization: the Keynes and White plans', reprinted in J.H. Williams, *Postwar Monetary Plans and Other Essays* (1949), 141–54, Oxford: Blackwell.

—— (1944a) 'After Bretton Woods', reprinted in J.H. Williams, *Postwar Monetary Plans and Other Essays* (1949), 103–22, Oxford: Blackwell.

—— (1944b) 'Currency stabilization: American and British attitudes', reprinted in

J.H. Williams, *Postwar Monetary Plans and Other Essays* (1949), 155–69, Oxford: Blackwell.

—— (1944c) 'Post-war monetary plans', reprinted in J.H. Williams, *Postwar Monetary Plans and Other Essays* (1949), 170–84, Oxford: Blackwell.

—— (1944d) 'The joint monetary plan', reprinted in J.H. Williams, *Postwar Monetary Plans and Other Essays* (1949), 185–204, Oxford: Blackwell.

—— (1945a) 'The Bretton Woods Agreement', reprinted in J.H. Williams, *Postwar Monetary Plans and Other Essays* (1949), 123–40, Oxford: Blackwell.

—— (1945b) 'Testimony before Senate Committee on the Bretton Woods Agreements Act', reprinted in J.H. Williams, *Postwar Monetary Plans and Other Essays* (1949), 331–66, Oxford: Blackwell.

—— (1945c) 'Free enterprise and full employment', in P.T. Homan and F. Machlup (eds) *Financing American Prosperity*, 350–93, New York: Twentieth Century Fund.

—— (1947a) 'Economic lessons of the two world wars', reprinted in J.H. Williams, *Postwar Monetary Plans and Other Essays* (1949), 43–64, Oxford: Blackwell.

—— (1947b) 'International trade with planned economies: the ITO charter', reprinted in J.H. Williams, *Postwar Monetary Plans and Other Essays* (1949), 85–102, Oxford: Blackwell.

—— (1948a) 'An appraisal of Keynesian economics', reprinted in J.H. Williams, *Postwar Monetary Plans and Other Essays* (1949), 3–23, Oxford: Blackwell.

—— (1948b) 'The task of economic recovery', reprinted in J.H. Williams, *Postwar Monetary Plans and Other Essays* (1949), 65–84, Oxford: Blackwell.

—— (1949) *Postwar Monetary Plans and Other Essays*, Oxford: Blackwell.

—— (1953) *Economic Stability in a Changing World*, New York: Oxford University Press.

—— (1954) *Trade Not Aid: a program for world stability*, Cambridge, Mass: Harvard University Press.

—— (1976) '[Alvin H. Hansen:] tribute', *Quarterly Journal of Economics*, 90: 8–9.

Williamson, J. (1973) 'Surveys in applied economics: international liquidity', *Economic Journal*, 83: 685–746.

—— (1977) *The Failure of World Monetary Reform*, Sunbury-on-Thames: Nelson.

—— (1985) 'On the system in Bretton Woods', *American Economic Review*, 72: 74–9.

Williamson, J. and Miller, M.H. (1987) *Targets and Indicators: a blueprint for the coordination of economic policy*, Washington, DC: Institute for International Economics.

Yeager, L.B. (1961) 'The Triffin plan: diagnosis, remedy, and alternatives', *Kyklos*, 14: 284–313.

—— (1966) *International Monetary Relations*, New York: Harper and Row.

Zmirak, J. (2001) *Wilhelm Röpke: Swiss localist, global economist*, Wilmington, Del.: ISI Books.

Index

Printed in the United Kingdom
by Lightning Source UK Ltd.
110237UKS00006B/91

9 780415 324120